ORNAMENTAL WATERFOWL

Hartmut Kolbe

Ornamental Waterfowl

GRESHAM BOOKS

Translated from the German
by Ilse Lindsay
Revised by Prof. Dr. Aloys Hüttermann

English edition
Published by
GRESHAM BOOKS,
Unwin Brothers Limited,
The Gresham Press,
Old Woking
Surrey. GU22 9LH

© 1977 Edition Leipzig
© 1979 Unwin Brothers Ltd.

All rights reserved. No part of
this publication may be reproduced in any form
or by any means without the permission of
the publishers.

ISBN 0 905418 49 2

First published 1979
Printed in the German Democratic Republic

Introduction

This book, ORNAMENTAL WATERFOWL, is a richly illustrated work of reference aimed at the large number of those interested in the care and breeding of waterfowl as a hobby. Moreover, it is hoped that the book will provide ornithologists in zoological gardens and bird sanctuaries with new and useful guidance and information.
In the main, the book is centred on eighty of the best-known and most popular ducks, but it also draws attention to other bird species which may be kept on ponds, in parks and landscape meadows. For the first time in literature, the zoological expert and breeder is offered a rather comprehensive guide with a wealth of information on the most important, representative members of wading birds, flamingos, rails, cranes and species of gulls.
The sections devoted to aviculture evaluate well-tried and also the most modern methods of care; details are given on suitable housing, diet and breeding. Personal experience will complete the picture. Paragraphs dealing with hybridization give the breeder information on birds with tendencies to interbreed which he has to bear in mind if he wishes to avoid undesired hybridization.
Anyone who wants to rear and breed successfully the species depicted in this work ought to have a basic knowledge of the birds' natural habitats and characteristics. If birds are to be kept, allowing them to fly freely, the migratory behaviour ought to be understood; how they are housed during the winter should depend on the climatic conditions of their natural habitat. On all these topics the book hopes to give the reader brief, but adequate information.
With a number of species, problems and difficulties regarding their maintenance and breeding are mentioned. Before a responsible enthusiast with a proper regard for the well-being of his birds makes a choice of those he wishes to keep he should first ascertain whether he can offer them the right kind of environment.
Each bird described has a paragraph devoted to its 'status'. It is the first time that a book for bird lovers and breeders sets out to give a detailed account of the species' natural population distribution and dynamics. Such knowledge should appeal to people in a position of responsibility, by enabling them to decide whether it is right to acquire birds possibly threatened with extinction in their natural habitats, or whether it might not be better to settle for a similar, less vulnerable kind.
As the illustrations are predominantly in colour, detailed description of the bird's appearance is not necessary. Distribution maps obviate long and rather tedious lists of geographical names; it is hoped that the maps will give the breeder and keeper sufficient information on the spread of a particular species.

Much of my working knowledge has been shaped by careful study of available literature. Many have helped me to obtain the books I needed and I should like to thank them all. Furthermore, numerous letters have reached me and supplied me with much valuable information which has added to my own knowledge acquired by my breeding of waterfowl. Informative letters from breeders like J. BENKE, Malkwitz, E. SEEBOLD, Rotenburg/Wümme, B. WEISSJOHANN, Cloppenburg, and J. WIENANDS, Viersen, have been most helpful. I offer my sincere thanks to them, as well as to K. KUSSMANN, Berlin (West), whose numerous photographs, advice and additional information enrich the volume. I should also like to express my gratitude to the biologist, K. JACOB, Zoological Gardens, Cottbus, and Dr. W. GRUMMT, Tierpark, Berlin, for their critical appraisal of the manuscript. My friend Prof. Dr. A. Hüttermann, Göttingen, improved by his profound knowledge both in the field of ornithology and the English language the English edition of this book; he also deserves my sincere thanks.

Lastly, I should like to thank the staff of the original German publishers, EDITION LEIPZIG, particularly their erudite editor, Dr. K. JUNGE; I am much in their debt for their kindly and fruitful collaboration.

In our present age, rearing and breeding of endangered species is of real importance and may well prevent them from becoming totally extinct. May this book promote the idea that threatened species should be kept and bred so efficiently in preserves that their numbers increase so that wildfowl no longer are caught and taken from their natural environment. Actually, the Hawaiian goose was very nearly extinct; it has bred so well in captivity that it became possible to re-introduce it to its own ecological habitat. Let us hope that the same will be possible with other rare species.

Rosslau-Meinsdorf, January 1979   HARTMUT KOLBE

Contents

Introduction 5
Long-legged Wading Birds
    Grey Heron—*Ardea cinerea* L. 11
    Little Egret—*Egretta garzetta* (L.) 13
    Squacco Heron—*Ardeola ralloides* (Scopoli) 15
    Night Heron—*Nycticorax nycticorax* (L.) 17
    White Stork—*Ciconia ciconia* (L.) 19
    Black Stork—*Ciconia nigra* (L.) 20
    Marabou Stork—*Leptoptilos crumeniferus* (Lesson) 22
    Glossy Ibis—*Plegadis falcinellus* (L.) 24
    Sacred Ibis—*Threskiornis aethiopica* (Latham) 26
    Roseate Spoonbill—*Ajaia ajaja* (L.) 27

Flamingos
    Greater Flamingo—*Phoenicopterus ruber roseus* Pallas 29
    Caribbean Flamingo—*Phoenicopterus ruber ruber* L. 31
    Chilean Flamingo—*Phoenicopterus chilensis* Molina 41
    Lesser Flamingo—*Phoeniconaias minor* Geoffr. 43

Swans, Geese and Ducks
    Cuban Whistling Duck—*Dendrocygna arborea* (L.) 46
    Red-billed Whistling Duck—*Dendrocygna autumnalis* (L.) . . 48
    Fulvous Whistling Duck—*Dendrocygna bicolor* (Vieillot) . . . 49
    Plumed Whistling Duck—*Dendrocygna eytoni* (Eyton) 51
    White-faced Whistling Duck—*Dendrocygna viduata* (L.) . . . 52
    Coscoroba Swan—*Coscoroba coscoroba* (Molina) 54
    Black-necked Swan—*Cygnus melanocoryphus* (Molina) . . . 56
    Black Swan—*Cygnus atratus* (Latham) 65
    Mute Swan—*Cygnus olor* (Gmelin) 67
    Greylag Goose—*Anser anser* (L.) 68
    Lesser White-fronted Goose—*Anser erythropus* (L.) 70
    Pink-footed Goose—*Anser brachyrhynchus* Baillon 72
    Bar-headed Goose—*Anser indicus* (Latham) 74
    Snow Goose—*Anser caerulescens* (L.) 75
    Emperor Goose—*Anser canagicus* Sewastianow 77
    Brent Goose—*Branta bernicla* (L.) 79
    Canada Goose—*Branta canadensis* (L.) 81
    Barnacle Goose—*Branta leucopsis* (Bechstein) 82

Red-breasted Goose—*Branta ruficollis* (Pallas) 84
Hawaiian Goose—*Branta sandvicensis* (Vigors) 85
Andean Goose—*Chloephaga melanoptera* (Eyton) 87
Magellan Goose—*Chloephaga picta* (Gmelin) 89
Ashy-headed Goose—*Chloephaga poliocephala* Sclater 90
Ruddy-headed Goose—*Chloephaga rubidiceps* Sclater 92
Cereopsis—*Cereopsis novaehollandiae* Latham 93
Common Shelduck—*Tadorna tadorna* (L.) 95
Radjah Shelduck—*Tadorna radjah* (Lesson) 96
Ruddy Shelduck—*Tadorna ferruginea* (Pallas) 106
Cape Shelduck—*Tadorna cana* (Gmelin) 108
New Zealand Shelduck—*Tadorna variegata* (Gmelin) 109
Australian Shelduck—*Tadorna tadornoides* (Jardine & Selby) . . 111
Egyptian Goose—*Alopochen aegyptiacus* (L.) 112
European Wigeon—*Anas penelope* L. 114
American Wigeon—*Anas americana* Gmelin 116
Chiloe Wigeon—*Anas sibilatrix* Poeppig 117
Falcated Duck—*Anas falcata* Georgi 118
Baikal Teal—*Anas formosa* Georgi 120
Mallard—*Anas platyrhynchos* L. 122
Grey Duck—*Anas superciliosa* Gmelin 124
Spotbill—*Anas poecilorhyncha* Forster 125
Philippine Duck—*Anas luzonica* Frazer 127
Chestnut Teal—*Anas castanea* (Eyton) 128
Green-winged Teal—*Anas crecca* L. 129
Chilean Teal—*Anas flavirostris* Vieillot 131
Pintail—*Anas acuta* L. 133
Bahama Pintail—*Anas bahamensis* L. 134
Red-billed Pintail—*Anas erythrorhyncha* Gmelin 136
Versicolor Teal—*Anas versicolor* Vieillot 145
Hottentot Teal—*Anas punctata* Burchell 147
Cape Teal—*Anas capensis* Gmelin 148
Marbled Teal—*Anas angustirostris* Ménétries 150
Garganey—*Anas querquedula* L. 151
Blue-winged Teal—*Anas disc`rs* L. 153
Cinnamon Teal—*Anas cyanoptera* Vieillot 155
Common Shoveler—*Anas clypeata* L. 156
European Eider—*Somateria mollissima* (L.) 158
Rosybill—*Netta peposaca* (Vieillot) 160
Red-crested Pochard—*Netta rufina* (Pallas) 161
European Pochard—*Aythya ferina* L. 163
Canvasback—*Aythya valisneria* (Wilson) 165
Common White-eye—*Aythya nyroca* (Güldenstädt) 166
Tufted Duck—*Aythya fuligula* (L.) 168
Ring-necked Duck—*Aythya collaris* (Donovan) 170
Lesser Scaup—*Aythya affinis* (Eyton) 172
African Pygmy Goose—*Nettapus auritus* (Boddaert) 173
Maned Goose—*Chenonetta jubata* (Latham) 174
Mandarin Duck—*Aix galericulata* (L.) 176
North American Wood Duck—*Aix sponsa* (L.) 186
Brazilian Teal—*Amazonetta brasiliensis* (Gmelin) 187
Ringed Teal—*Calonetta leucophrys* (Vieillot) 189
Velvet Scoter—*Melanitta fusca* (L.) 190

Long-tailed Duck — *Clangula hyemalis* (L.)	192
Goldeneye — *Bucephala clangula* (L.)	194
Hooded Merganser — *Mergus cucullatus* L.	196
Red-breasted Merganser — *Mergus serrator* L.	197
North American Ruddy Duck — *Oxyura jamaicensis* Gmelin	199

Rails and their Relatives

Red and white Crake — *Laterallus leucopyrrhus* (Vieillot)	202
Moorhen — *Gallinula chloropus* (L.)	204
Purple Gallinule — *Porphyrio porphyrio* (L.)	206
Coot — *Fulica atra* L.	207
Sunbittern — *Eurypyga helias* (Pallas)	210

Cranes

Common Crane — *Grus grus* (L.)	213
Hooded Crane — *Grus monacha* Temminck	215
Sandhill Crane — *Grus canadensis* (L.)	216
Sarus Crane — *Grus antigone* (L.)	230
Wattled Crane — *Bugeranus carunculatus* (Gmelin)	231
Demoiselle Crane — *Anthropoides virgo* (L.)	233
Stanley Crane — *Anthropoides paradisea* (Lichtenstein)	235
Crowned Crane — *Balearica pavonina* L.	237
West African Crowned Crane — *Balearica pavonina pavonina* (L.)	237
East African Crowned Crane — *Balearica pavonina regulorum* (Bennett)	238

Waders and Gulls

Oyster-Catcher — *Haematopus ostralegus* L.	241
Lapwing — *Vanellus vanellus* (L.)	243
Crowned Plover — *Stephanibyx coronatus* (Boddaert)	245
Ruff — *Philomachus pugnax* (L.)	246
Avocet — *Recurvirostra avosetta* L.	248
Black-headed Gull — *Larus ridibundus* L.	250
Common Gull — *Larus canus* L.	252

Bibliography	255
Index	257
Sources of Illustrations	259

Long-legged Wading Birds

The order of ciconiformes is a diverse group of long-legged, long-necked wading birds — inhabitants of marshes, lakes, and swamps. They are a group of approximately 100 species. Apart from those featured in the book, several other well-known species belong to the order: bitterns, Shoebills – *Balaeniceps rex*, and Hammerheads – *Scopus umbretta*. The latter are conspicuous for their huge nests. Caring for them presents no great problem; however, a number of points are worth noting. The birds feed on living animals, predominantly fish. Modern formulated animal foods offer a good substitute, but fresh meat or fish should never be completely omitted from their diet. Birds which feed on fish have a very active metabolism. Droppings are white and very acidic and destroy plant life, or most of it. As herons and ibises are sociable birds they should be kept in groups and this is something that cannot be ignored by anybody caring for vegetation; it will be damaged fairly quickly.

Should herons or storks by chance get into the possession of a bird enthusiast, he can keep them easily over a number of years. They will give him much pleasure and reward him with their intriguing behaviour.

Grey Heron
Ardea cinerea L.

Comparative Size: Almost the size of a stork.
Plumage: Mature birds see plate 3; upper parts mostly light ash-grey; belly white; elongated crest plumes and neck streaked black. F. normally has shorter ornamental plumes and is somewhat darker overall than the male. Juv. predominantly grey-brown, darker than the adult M. with no elongated plumes.

Natural Habit

Status: Widely distributed and only endangered in certain areas because of too much hunting or changes in environment (land drainage). Many populations have adapted to feeding on mice and other small animals instead of fish.
Habitat: Different types of waters of the lowlands and hilly landscapes as long as the former have shallow, swampy banks with a rich aquatic fauna. Breeding grounds are near lakes and river beds with a good supply of fish. Outside the breeding season the birds can be met in the neighbourhood of narrow meadow ditches and in fields, hunting for mice.
Breeding Biology: Nests are built in colonies in the tops of very high trees; in

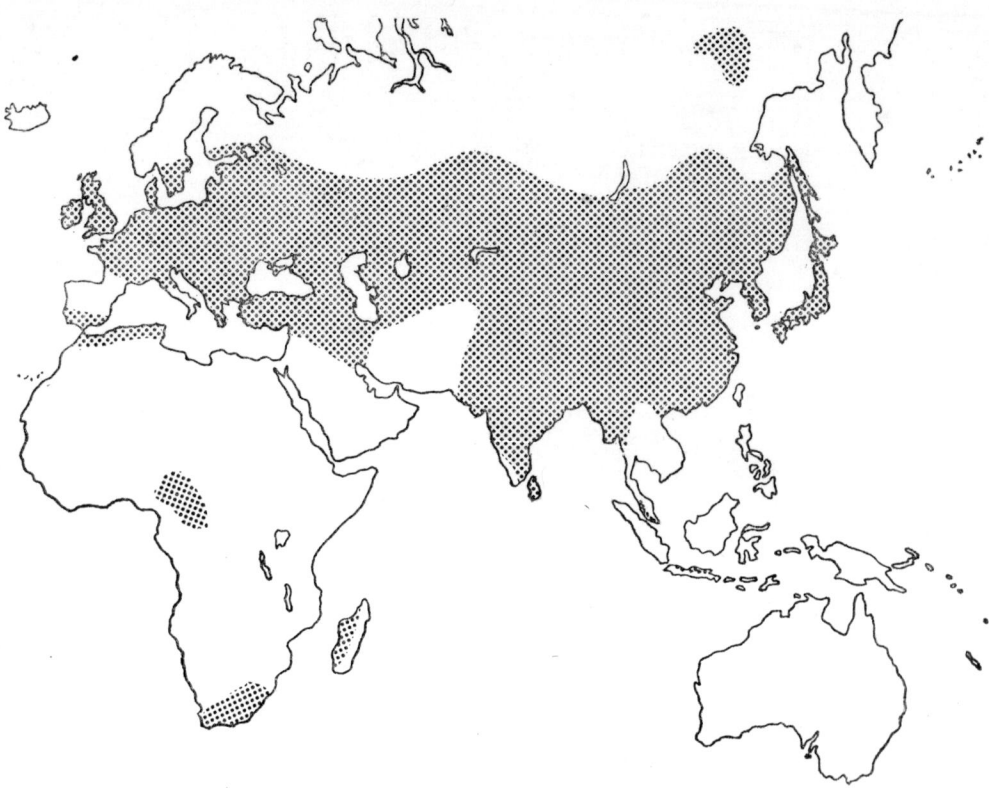

bushes of the marsh or in reeds. They are made of sticks, reeds and small twigs. Display, pair formation and copulation take place on the nesting site. A full clutch will consist of 4–5 mat, light blue-green eggs. Incubation takes 25–28 days. 4–5 weeks old herons first climb the branches surrounding the nest and, when they are 8–9 weeks old, they are able to fly.

Migration: Nearly all heron populations leave the breeding grounds in autumn. The British breeding birds roam the country; the European birds either migrate to East or South Africa; many winter in the Mediterranean zone, and quite a few in central and western Europe.

Yearly Cycle: Herons return to their breeding grounds from end-February onwards and to the actual nesting sites shortly afterwards; old nests are re-occupied and repaired if necessary. Otherwise new nests are built. Eggs are laid after March (to May). When young herons are fledged they start juvenile roaming and between August and November they migrate to their wintering quarters.

Climate: Breeding and wintering grounds stretch southwards as far as the tropics. However, as far as climate is concerned, grey herons are very robust and often leave northern areas only when frost and snow rob them of food.

AVICULTURE

If grey herons are injured, or weakened by winter conditions, or fairly newly fledged, they are relatively easily caught by well-meaning enthusiasts. If one takes good care of them, the only problem might be the supply of food. HEINROTH (1926/27) reported: "Our young herons surprised us by their affectionate and extremely friendly behaviour. They were delighted as soon as they saw us, crowded near us with a terrific amount of noise and were most reluctant to let us leave them." Even mature birds adjust quickly, but never become quite as intimate. There may be some danger of getting hurt by a heron's bill if the bird has been obtained when mature; young herons should be quite harmless. However, it is always wise to take care.

Housing: Can be kept free in large gardens, zoological gardens, parks or large aviaries if pinioned (a pond or lake should be provided). If a number of birds live in a confined space one should not forget that herons have an active metabolism and therefore produce a great deal of white droppings.

Food: Fish (preferably fresh-water fish with a low fat content), lean meat, mice and shrimps. Daily ration needed: 330 to 500 grammes.

Breeding: Grey herons breed every year in the large heron aviaries of zoological gardens and bird preserves. They build their nests with sticks in the tops of the highest trees, incubate their brood and rear the young. They can experience difficulties in recognising their mate. Even birds of the same sex seem to go through the motions of pairing, display, nest building and breeding. For that reason, if the size of the aviary permits it, one should always keep more than one pair. Heron chicks are quite easily reared without parents. When they are only a few hours old they will take meat out of one's hands once it touches the culmen. They advertise their appetite by loud calls of 'keck-keck-keck'. Later on they feed out of a trough.

Hybridization: Very much inclined to interbreed with purple herons and it is therefore not advisable to keep both species together; hybrids are fully able to breed.

Little Egret

Egretta garzetta (L.)

Comparative Size: Considerably smaller than the white stork or grey heron.

Plumage: Adult birds in breeding plumage see plate 1; M. and F. both pure white; bill and legs black; feet yellow. Non-breeding plumage lacks loose-webbed ornamental plumes and the long aigrettes hanging from the crown. Juvenile birds rather like adult birds in resting plumage; bill is brownish. The very similar American Snowy Egret, *Egretta thula* (see plate 4), has all crest plumes elongated as ornamental plumes.

Natural Habit

Status: Very much hunted for ornamental plumes, particularly at the turn of the century when populations were badly reduced. Nowadays legally protected and populations have been largely regenerated.

Habitat: Marshes with bushes and groups of trees which contain large areas of shallow water with not too dense marsh vegetation; otherwise rice fields, mangrove or flooded pastures.

Breeding Biology: Little egrets normally build their nest colonies in bushes in the marshes, far less often in high trees or reed. Rather carelessly constructed nests are made of brushwood and twigs. Clutch of 3–5 pale, blue-green eggs is incubated by M. and F. for only 21–22 days; both parents then feed the young birds which soon spend their time climbing

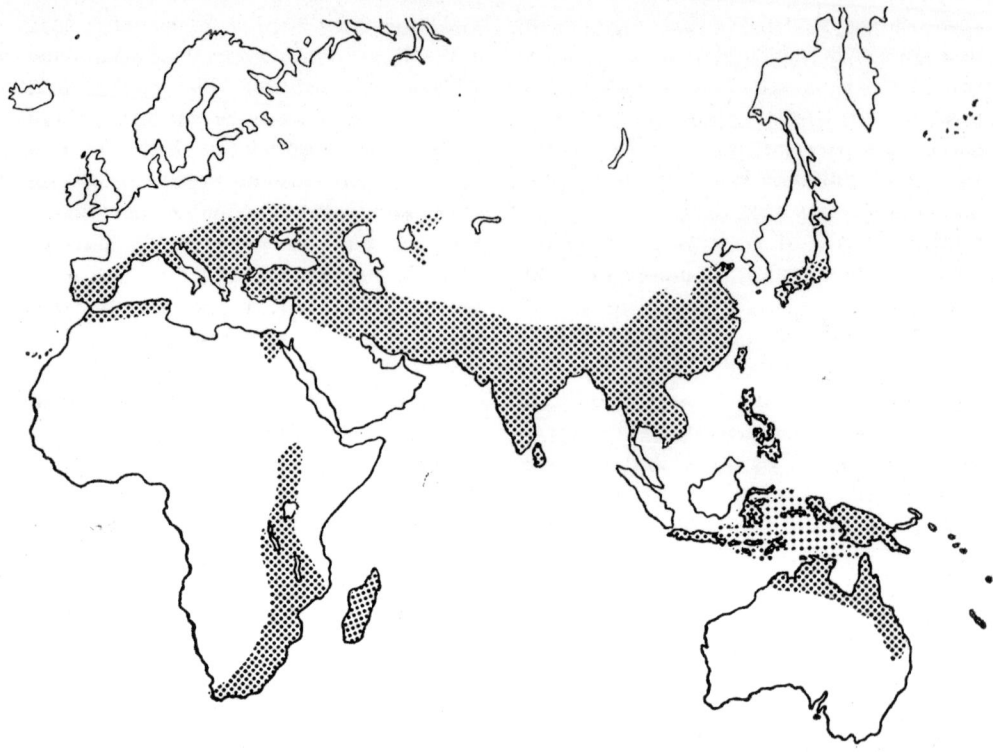

the twigs near the nests. When little egrets are a month old they are able to fly and leave the colony.

Migration: Migratory bird wintering in Africa or southern Asia. Some southern European brood colonies stay within the area for the whole of the year as active residents (e. g. Camargue) or they undertake migratory flights which might take them as far as central or western Europe.

Yearly Cycle: European breeding birds return between March and May; start laying from end-April onwards, but it can be delayed until June. Migratory flights occur during the summer; autumnal migration can begin end-August, normally takes place in September and finishes by November.

Climate: Most of the breeding grounds are in tropical and subtropical zones, but also in the temperate latitudes of areas with warm local climates such as the Camargue, the Hungarian plain and the Danube delta.

AVICULTURE

In North America the snowy egret takes the place of the little egret. The birds are very alike. These small herons weigh only 500 grammes and their glowing white plumage and great activity make them quite enchanting.

Housing: Little egrets are very clever climbers and are thus able to get over most fences. Therefore they are kept in parks and zoological gardens—together with other heron species—in large aviaries. Their natural habitat of a wooded river zone can be compensated for by providing them with a pool, up to 30 cm deep and with shallow edges, a lawn and trees. BENKE (personal communication) keeps two little egrets on the shores of his duck-breeding lake; they are wing-clipped. They do not wander off (although they would be able to do so if they wished); they spend the day in certain familiar areas on the shore, and the night in the thin branches of a willow. In a cold climate they should not be exposed to frost in the winter. They need to have good opportunities for bathing; otherwise their plumage gets very dirty with the fish on which they feed.

Food: Natural diet consists of water insects, water snails, amphibians and small fishes. In captivity, small herons are fed on minced fish, shrimps, a good formulated food (such as is used for the rearing of pheasants) and on additional minerals and vitamins. As a special delicacy they can be given the occasional piece of fish or small, whole fishes—less then 15 cm in size.

Breeding: Breeding results of little egrets have long been known to be good; snowy egrets are less successful. Little egrets are amongst the most sociable of herons and apparently tend to breed only where they can live in company with other pairs. If kept in groups of 5–10 pairs there is a real chance of a brood. They build nests close together in high trees of aviaries, quarrel about nesting places and material in the manner of all colony breeders and, in spite of the apparent disorder, manage to rear their young. How many herons can be kept in an aviary depends largely on the degree of mess made by droppings and food remnants. Solitary pairs rarely have the necessary breeding impulse.

Hybridization: The little egret interbreeds with the snowy egret; their descendants are fertile (GRUMMT personal communication); hybridization rarely takes place in colonies of little egrets, night herons and squacco herons.

Squacco Heron

Ardeola ralloides (Scopoli)

Comparative Size: Slightly smaller than the little egret.

Plumage: Adults see plate 5; M. und F. white, body plumage has tones of ochre yellow; elongated crown plumes brownish, but shorter in resting plumage. Bill lead-grey or yellow-green like the legs. Juveniles dark grey-brown on upper side with light barring.

The very similarly coloured Cattle Egret, *Ardeola ibis*, differs from the squacco heron by having a yellow-orange bill and legs.

NATURAL HABIT

Status: Above average stock curtailment in certain areas because of land drainage of former feeding and breeding grounds. Main breeding colonies are in Africa; European total population relatively small.

Habitat: Large marshes and river deltas containing bushes and groups of trees. Also swampy river banks, rice fields, brackish and salt-water lagoons.

Breeding Biology: They like making their nests in trees of medium height in mixed brood colonies in company with little egrets and night herons. Both parent birds together build nests with coarse sticks. Eggs have a particularly rough shell and are blue-green (normal clutch 4–6); parents incubate them for 22–24 days. It does not take young squacco herons long before they start climbing the branches of the nesting trees. When they leave the nest forever on the 32nd day they are barely able to fly properly.

Migration: Predominantly migrates to Africa for the winter, less to southern Europe. Migratory flights in mid-summer (particularly juveniles) quite often take them North to France, Great Britain and Denmark.

Yearly Cycle: In southern Europe squacco herons return to their breeding grounds towards the end of April where they immediately become very active with pairing, display and nest building. They leave these in August and September.

Climate: Breeding grounds and wintering quarters are almost exclusively in warm climatic zones. Therefore, northern breeding grounds are occupied later in the year and left earlier. They are a species which likes warm climates.

AVICULTURE

Squacco herons, and particularly cattle egrets are often sold by the animal trade and can be found in most zoological gardens and bird preserves. They are easy to keep, robust and peace-loving. In a well-arranged aviary with good vegetation containing a fair-sized group, the white colouring of the herons stands out clearly against the green of the trees and the lawn; the spectator will be able to enjoy watching the intriguing and busy behaviour of these active birds in all kinds of situations.

Housing: Substantially the same as for little egrets. It is important to adjust the optimal number of herons that should be kept in an aviary. A large group develops far more quickly and it is more diverse (also in its sexual behaviour) than a single pair, which may become rather sluggish. On the other hand, in an over-populated aviary trees and ground vegetation rot quickly because of the acidic droppings. If the ground does not drain moisture sufficiently well, rain soon causes a morass of earth, droppings and left-over food—a most unpleasant sight and also a source of infections. It is advisable to settle for one or two species only and to give up any idea of keeping many different kinds. Im some parks and preserves successful attempts have been made to keep cattle egrets living and flying free.

Food: See little egrets; fish should be cut into very small pieces. Cattle egrets particularly spend hours hunting for flies; careful stalking and a speedy thrust of the bill gives prey little chance of escape. The flies which the birds catch supplement quite adequately the diet they need while they are rearing their young (according to KUSSMANN pers. comm.).

Breeding: If a sufficiently large group (5–10 pairs approximately) is kept in a proper environment, little egrets and cattle egrets start breeding activities quite quickly. If they are given enough nest-building material (sticks and thin twigs), herons make firm nests with enough space for the nestlings. Nest building, display and pairing keep a small colony busy for several months. Just how successful the breeding results can be in an average group of 10 pairs of cattle egrets may be seen in the Berlin Tierpark. From 1961 to 1969, a total of 150 young birds were reared. In some cases, breeding activities took place from January until October.

During the period of rearing the young should be given especially finely minced food.

Hybridization: No marked tendencies, not even among closely related species.

Night Heron

Nycticorax nycticorax (L.)

Comparative Size: Approximately the same as the little egret.
Plumage: Adults in breeding plumage see plate 2; M. and F. black back with steel-grey chin, wings and tail grey, belly white, irides red. Juvenile plumage dark grey-brown marked with many white long blotches. Irides yellow-green.

Natural Habit

Status: A very prolific species. Distributed all over the southern half of Europe up to the turn of the century; later driven back to South and South-East Europe where they are still fairly abundant.
Habitat: In wooded and bushy plains, swamps and water-rich wooded pastureland and river banks. Feeding grounds are in flooded meadows, rice fields and on muddy river banks. Resting and roosting places may be quite a distance away from water.
Breeding Biology: Night herons are colony breeders which build nests fairly low in swampy bushes. Old pairs often re-occupy their previous nests and repair them. Younger birds fight for existing nests or build new ones. Full clutch 4–5 blue-green eggs which are incubated for 21 days. The young leave the nest when they are 3–4 weeks old; at 6 weeks they are able to fly and they are independent when they are 7–8 weeks old. Sexual maturity is normally reached in the second year.
Migration: Night herons winter in Africa; however, non-breeders and those who have finished breeding, often undertake

long, roaming flights and have been observed occasionally in central and western Europe.

Yearly Cycle: End-March/early April they usually arrive in their European breeding grounds, and many pairs have produced a full clutch by the end of April. It is considered likely that two broods are not too uncommon, particularly as the autumn migration does not begin until September.

Climate: Predominantly inhabitants of the Mediterranean zone and the tropics. Although night herons obviously prefer warm climatic conditions they are quite able to withstand short periods of cold if they have to do so.

AVICULTURE

Night herons are also sociable birds, but to a lesser degree. They are far more individualistic than, for instance, little egrets. It is quite feasible to keep single night heron pairs in company with other heron species. Once they have the impulse to mate, breeding is more than likely. On the other hand, their own specific characteristics—particularly in display—only become prominent when there are several pairs of night herons in one preserve. They are robust, peaceable and far less sensitive to cold than the white heron species.

Housing: See little egrets and squacco herons. HEINROTH (1926/27) wrote: "Night herons have the distinction that they always keep their plumage spick and span, even if they are kept in less than satisfactory conditions. They are quietly behaved birds, not given to impetuous attempts at escape and they conduct themselves well in quite small cages. In addition, they belong to the group of birds producing down-powder, used to dress their feathers; as a result their plumage never looks bedraggled, even if they have no opportunity either to take a bath or get cleansed by rain."

Food: Like little egrets and grey herons; fish may be up to 30 cm long.

Breeding: Night heron broods occur with the same frequency as in the species described previously. In contrast to the grey herons which build nests in tops of the highest trees, night herons make their nests of sticks approximately halfway up in a tree. Display and mating take place in the nest they are building. In the Berlin zoological gardens, egg laying started as early as mid-February in some years. There it was observed that one-year old birds, not yet fully coloured, were rearing young.

HEINROTH, the keen observer of bird behaviour, gave a report on a developing, young night heron: "Initially the chick was quite helpless; from the fifth day onwards it got more lively, picked at the food it was offered and uttered begging calls. In the second week it showed obvious affection for its foster parents; on the 18th day it left its basket for the first time and started climbing around in the room. First flight attempts were observed on the 39th day. When the young heron was given to the zoo at the age of two months, it was aggressive towards strangers. When we visited it, it was always amiable and showered us with affection. It came to us the moment it saw us and—gently nibbling—touched our faces with its bill".

Hybridization: Negligible.

White Stork

Ciconia ciconia (L.)

Size: Total length approximately 1 m. Wing-span 2 m. Weight 3–4.5 kg.

Plumage: Adults see plate 8; all plumage black and white; bill and legs red. In immature birds dark parts rather brown-black, bill and legs red-brown; the latter black during the nestling period.

NATURAL HABIT

Status: Numbers are declining in many countries—in central Europe by approximately 50 per cent over the last few decades—despite protective measures and man's sincere affection for the birds as part of the environment. It is true the birds are being hunted in some countries on their migration, and electricity lines and pollution will injure them, but such adverse factors account only in part for the decline.

Habitat: Fields and agricultural lands with tree growth; in central and western Europe in water-rich plains and wide river valleys. Wintering quarters often in dry grasslands.

Breeding Biology: Males return first to breeding ground, occupy former nests and attract females passing overhead by frequent clattering with their bills. If an adult female returns early, pairing, nest building and laying follow soon afterwards. If a young and strange female joins the nest, pairs may change partners; if the adult female should return later, the well-known stork fights may ensue. The reason for them appears to be a shortage of nesting sites. The nest is massive, made of sticks and erected either on roof tops or in high trees; the inside is lined with various materials (grass, rags, paper) and a clutch of 3–5 chalk-white eggs are laid in it. Incubation takes 31–33 days, and it is done by both parent birds; later on both feed the nestlings and also supply them with water. Nestlings are independent at 10 weeks and they reach sexual maturity in the 4th or 5th year.

Migration: Storks migrate to East and South Africa in two narrow zones, either via Spain or via S. E. Europe.

Yearly Cycle: European breeding birds return to their nests in March and April and have laid a full clutch 3–4 weeks later. Young storks form loosely-knit troops in mid-summer and join the adult birds for the autumn migration (August/September).

Climate: Most storks remain in the zones of Africa of the Mediterranean all the year round; birds of the temperate zones return to home breeding grounds relatively late and leave them rather early.

AVICULTURE

Very few bird species enjoy the same popularity as the white storks. Each spring their arrival is welcomed and, from then onwards, the storks' family life is watched with great interest until they leave their home breeding grounds again. Every year, during this period, storks get into possession of animal-lovers. Their sympathy may be aroused because a storm causes a nestling to fall out of the nest, a young stork may have an accident during a first flight attempt, or an experienced bird may get entangled in an electricity line. Most of these birds are given help gladly and successfully. Young storks of any age can be reared quite easily and may be set free at a later stage. If an adult bird breaks his wings they rarely heal sufficiently well for the bird to undertake the long autumn migration. The heavy wing primaries make the wing hang downwards so that the bones mend in the wrong position. Such storks then have to be looked after and cared for.

Housing: Storks need a great deal of space in which they can move around; it may be an unfenced garden or a large poultry yard. Unless they are on a lawn and have opportunities for bathing their white plumage gets dirtied very easily. Storks consider eggs and chicks as delicious tidbits so that it is advisable to take care. In zoological gardens, white storks—in company with cranes, geese and flamingos—look very decorative on the large meadows reserved for wading birds.

In winter one should take care that they are not exposed to real frost.

Food: Fish, meat, shrimps, insects, worms; dead mice, chicks and sparrows; also cooked potatoes mixed with a prepared food or a mixture of grain and fish food.

Breeding: White storks are reared in numerous zoos and preserves. Adult birds are usually wing-clipped; however, as they like to breed fairly high above ground, nests should be prepared for them at a height of approximately 1.5 m. If slanting branches are fixed up for them, the birds can climb upwards towards their nests. New nests are sprayed with lime-water to simulate splashes from droppings; thus activating the birds' breeding impulse. In captivity, storks normally start laying in March, sometimes even earlier. Incubation and rearing are completed almost without losses. It is quite possible to rear young storks without parents to take care of them. A basket lined with twigs and grass is a good substitute for a nest. A one-day old chick will start nibbling the nest lining and pick up food deposited there with the side of the mandibles.[1] From the second week onwards food may be given in a trough. All pieces of food should be moistened and from the 10th day the young birds should be given water to drink. Young storks do not like direct sun-light; in its natural habitat an adult stork will always stay in the nest to provide shade for the nestlings.

[1] Adult storks vomit the load on the ground of the nest. Therefore hungry food-expecting young storks do not beg with erect bills, but direct them to the nest ground.

Black Stork

Ciconia nigra (L.)

Comparative Size: As white stork.
Plumage: Adults see plate 7; black with a purple metallic sheen, belly white. Bill and legs glowing red at breeding time; afterwards red-brown. Immature birds brown without lustre; lighter head and neck in particular; bill and legs grey-green, colour changes beginning in February.

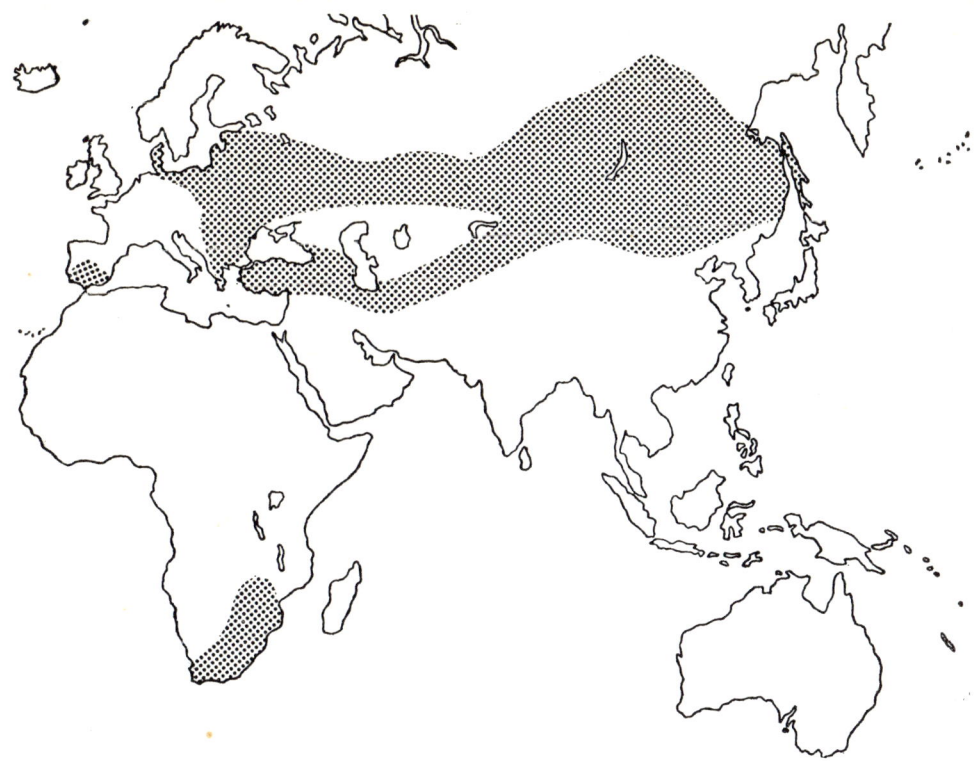

Natural Habit

Status: They dislike human habitations and, with increasing land cultivation in Europe, the birds lost many breeding grounds in central and western Europe. Populations may be regarded as stable in eastern Europe and Asia. Nowadays breeding populations are increasing in central Europe owing to influx of birds from the East.

Habitat: In large dense natural forests of water-rich plains and river basins interspersed with ponds, ditches and meadows. In South-East Europe also in mountain forests; in central Asia nests of breeding birds may be found occasionally on roofs or single trees.

Breeding Biology: Nests are made in the crowns of large, old trees with dense foliage in coniferous or deciduous woods. They are occupied year after year and, in certain circumstances, they are far away from any water. Clutch of 3–5 white eggs is incubated by both parent birds for 30 days. Nestlings are fed with food moistened with water and regurgitated from the parent's gullet. Young storks leave the nest for the first time when they are 9–10 weeks old but continue to return to the nest with the parents for the night.

Migration: Winter quarters are in Africa, predominantly north of the equator and in India. Generally, the birds avoid the Mediterranean.

Yearly Cycle: Arrive in the spring only a few days later than the white stork; however, laying rarely starts before May. Because of their retiring habits, black storks are practically never seen in the spring; one may be able to catch sight of them in June while they are hunting for food for their young and more regularly in July and August accompanied by the young storks. Autumn migration until October.

Climate: Most breeding grounds are in cool and temperate zones—in fact, many breeding sites in these areas are situated in really cool micro-climates.

Aviculture

In many ways the black stork is the direct opposite to its white relative. It avoids the proximity of man and builds its nest in hidden places in the depth of large, dense woods. It is threatened with extinction on the European continent, yet its total population is more stable than that of the white stork although the latter is far more frequent here. It is difficult to make contact with the shy black storks. On the other hand, animal dealers can obtain them from south-eastern Europe and Asia so that they are not a rarity in preserves.

Housing: As white stork, with clipped wings on wading-bird lawns or without clipped wings in very large aviaries. In contrast to herons and ibises, storks which are adjusted to their surroundings hardly ever attempt to climb; as a rule, fences of a height of 70–100 cm are sufficient as an obstacle. For the winter the black stork should be given a space which is free from frost with dry ground-covering. If black storks are in a confined area there may be quarrelsome fights often ending with the death of one of the adversaries. This particular feature must be taken into account, particularly in their winter accommodation.

Food: As white stork, but the amount of fish as part of diet may be increased.

Breeding: Black storks have been reared repeatedly in the wading-bird compounds of zoos and in well-arranged bird preserves. Preparation of nests—see white stork. Pairing and display of the black stork are relatively inconspicuous; they do not make the typical clattering noises with the bill thrown backwards. In the Berlin Tierpark, black storks began laying eggs mid-March, more often in April. During the last few years they have nested in the wintering boxes which are only a few square metres large. There they have also incubated and reared their young. As black storks start incubating from the moment the first egg is laid, the nestlings hatch in intervals of two days. If they have no parents, black stork chicks can be reared in the same way as those of the white stork.

Hybridization: Very insignificant. In the Basle zoological garden a white stork male and black stork female interbred and produced two chicks. The elder died on the 53rd day; it looked similar to a white stork nestling.

Marabou Stork

Leptoptilos crumeniferus (Lesson)

Comparative Size: Larger and more massive than white stork.

Plumage: Adults see plate 10; back, wings and tail slate-grey with greenish sheen; underparts white. Head bare, neck and crop has growth of sparse white down. In old birds crop develops into a large air-filled pouch which hangs down the neck. Juvenile birds' head and neck have more down and some single feathers.

Natural Habit

Status: Can be met everywhere in open landscapes of Africa where large game or cattle herds, or refuse from human settlements supply them with a good source of food. Population not threatened; in Uganda alone 4,000 to 5,000 birds have their habitat; many of them live exclusively off refuse from fish factories, slaughter houses and refuse dumps. Marabou storks are hardly ever hunted as they dispose of carrion.

Habitat: Large waters with shallow banks in open savannas as well as adjoining steppes.

Breeding Biology: Nests are built in colonies either in tops of high trees, on rocky ledges or else on roof tops in villages; also in colonies of pelicans. The M. fetches the nest material (twigs) which the F. makes into a nest. Full clutch 2–3 white eggs; period of incubation approximately 30 days. Nestlings are initially fed on frogs, fish and insects (grasshoppers), later on, with carrion. The marabou stork spends 16–18 weeks as a nestling.

Migration: Predominantly a stationary bird, but it may undertake roaming flights if food supplies which depend partly on rainfall are insufficient. At present 2,000 marabou storks inhabit the Ruwenzori National Park of Uganda.

Yearly Cycle: They start their breeding cycle during the rainy period: pairing, nest-building, laying and incubating. Rearing of the young follows during the dry period while aquatic fauna gets condensed in drying out pools and when the supply of carrion is particularly plentiful. Breeding period in Uganda is between December and March.

Climate: All species of marabous inhabit humid and arid tropical zones.

AVICULTURE

Nowadays a number of tropical storks are exhibited in zoological gardens and similar institutions; the marabou stork is used here as representing them all. In varying numbers there are others such as wood ibis[1] and openbills[2] of Africa and India, jaribu[3] of Central and South America, Abdim's stork[4] and saddlebill[5] of Africa.

In preserves, the large, massive marabous behave in a really lethargic manner; they may stand for hours in their typical resting position (see plate 10) with their neck pulled in (the pouch serves as an upholstered support for the heavy bill) and one leg drawn upwards at an angle. It is difficult for the observer to imagine the birds in their native habitat of Africa hunting in the steppes for small mammals and in the water for fish.

Housing: The metabolism is so active that the very acidic droppings quickly destroy vegetation in a small preserve. Marabou storks are therefore usually kept in large antilope reserves, or they are housed separately in places with thick gravel covering. For the cold time of the year they need a well-warmed room. They can get very bad-tempered towards other inhabitants of a preserve and have been known to kill them with stabs of their bill. Birds up to the size of a pigeon may be killed at their feeding troughs and are eaten on the spot.

[1] *Ibis ibis*
[2] *Anastomus lamelligerus*
[3] *Jaribu mycteria*
[4] *Ciconia abdimii*
[5] *Ephippiorhynchus senegalensis*

Food: Meat, bowels, fish and additional minerals and vitamins. Favourite tidbits are eggs, small mammals and small birds (mice, chicks, sparrows). Marabous plunder any nests they can reach within a preserve.

Breeding: Tropical storks are often kept in a very unsuitable manner because they look spectacular in a zoological garden; few parks have special preserves for them. Therefore, their breeding results are rather haphazard. At times they lay, but the eggs are not fertilized (KUSSMANN, pers. comm.). The International Zoological Yearbook quotes a total of 26 broods of 6 different tropical stork species for the period from 1960–1972, but these were produced throughout in zoological gardens within the tropics and sub-tropics.

SCHNEIDER (1952) wrote about the marabou: nest building activities and attempts to copulate are relatively marked; egg laying, however, rarely takes place. In the zoological gardens at Dresden a marabou pair was breeding at the turn of the century, but the F. and her chicks were killed by the M.

Hybridization: Occasional interbreeding within the wood ibis and marabou groups; very few hybrids survive.

Glossy Ibis
Plegadis falcinellus (L.)

NATURAL HABIT

Comparative Size: Approximately the same as the little egret.

Plumage: Adults see plate 9; M. and F. dark red-brown throughout; upper side with green metallic sheen; resting plumage darker and less glossy. Juveniles dark black-brown, head and neck lighter; throat partly almost white.

Status: Bird which breeds in many places, e. g. Roumania's Danube delta where 5,000 breeding pairs were recorded in the 1960s. Considerable variations in numbers are known of many colonies owing to the ibises' restlessness and roaming habits. A small Central American colony was presumably started by a group of European birds which flew across the Atlantic, settled, and now nests there where it shares the habitat with the old-established American species.

Habitat: Extensive swampy plains, river deltas, rice plantations, but also salt and brackish water lagoons with poor vegetation, outside the breeding season shallow seaboards.

Breeding Biology: Ibises often breed in company within the colonies of herons and spoonbills—in thickets and reed-banks of marshes; in certain areas also in high trees. Clutch is 3–4 shining white eggs; it is predominantly the male who does the incubating which takes 21 days. Reed-bank nests are very close together and half-fledged young gather in large flocks to be fed communally.

Migration: European nesting birds winter in the Near East and in Africa; before the autumnal migration they undertake long roaming flights without any particular aim (e. g. to Iceland, Ireland, Madeira).

Yearly Cycle: Ibises arrive in their southern European breeding grounds in April and May; they leave these in August and September. Between July and September they roam about within the area of their distribution, often far beyond it. They are keen flyers.

Climate: Distributed in many varying warm zones; only a few brood colonies can be found in climatically favourable areas of the temperate latitudes.

AVICULTURE

Ibises are the most graceful and active as well as the smallest members of the order of Ciconiformes. In preserves it is usual practice to keep the glossy ibis together with the White Ibis, *Eudocimus albus* (L.), and the Scarlet Ibis, *Eudocimus ruber* (L.) (see plate 22). They are reared successfully and all three species are sociable birds. They should always live in groups or together with herons. Ibises are hardy; in the zoo at Magdeburg several ibises which had been bought in 1958 were still doing well in 1975.

Housing: Either not pinioned in very large aviaries with some willow-bushes, or wing-clipped on landscaped lake-shores with sparse growth. Wintering in moderately warm accommodation. Sufficient water for bathing has to be available right through the year, otherwise the plumage gets dirty rather easily.

Food: A formulated food is mixed with minced fish, meat, carrots as well as shrimps and seaweed meal. Meal-worms, water-flies and some grain are also popular. Food may be given in a moistened crumbly consistency or as a semi-fluid pap.

Breeding: The three above-mentioned ibis species have been reared repeatedly in zoos and bird preserves. The Berlin Zoo tried breeding them as early as 1876 and in 1881 had good results with glossy and scarlet ibises.

The Zoo at Magdeburg[1] has been keeping 10 mature birds since 1958 in a medium-sized aviary; since 1960, between 3 and 4 pairs have been breeding every year in the crowns of the willow trees; more than 25 young birds have been reared. As ibises build only small, flat nests, small wicker baskets are fixed to the branches underneath the nests, or a net is placed beneath the nesting tree; in either case eggs or young birds which fall out of the nest are caught and can be put back into it. Both parent birds build the nest, incubate and rear the young. Laying begins in April, but is more usual in May and June. Main time of hatching is between June and August, more rarely in September. On the whole, young ibises are reared without many problems; the main reasons for casualties are accidents, particularly falling out of the nest.

Hybridization: Manifestly high between glossy, scarlet and white ibises.

[1] personal comm. by M. SCHRÖPEL, Magdeburg

Sacred Ibis

Threskiornis aethiopica (Latham)

Comparative Size: Adults see plate 11; naked head and neck are black. Plumage white; only tips of wings glowing black-green and loose-webbed, ornamental plumes black-blue with purple sheen. Sexes not properly distinguishable from each other. Juveniles' head and neck grown with black and white feathers; ornamental plumes washed-out white in colour.

NATURAL HABIT

Status: Characteristic bird of the interior and coastal areas of Africa where it occurs widely; very common in East Africa.

Habitat: Areas with eutrophic shallow waters and muddy river banks rich in vegetation and small fauna. Brood colonies are found in papyrus, on bushes and trees. During the rainy season the birds like frequenting wet meadows and flooded zones.

Breeding Biology: Ibises' nests are usually very close to each other; they are large, built by the M. and F. and lined with grass and reed-heads. The 2–4 rough-shelled, blue-green eggs have red-brown spots and are incubated for 21 days. The first plumage of young ibises consists of black down; they are able to fly when they are 5–6 weeks old.

Migration: On the whole permanent residents but often roaming within certain areas. When it appeared in southern Egypt the old Egyptian dynasties regarded the sacred ibis as the harbinger of tidings of the approaching fertile alluvium Nile deposits. The bird was sacred as the embodiment of Thoth, the God of wisdom and scribe of the gods; it was duly honoured.

Yearly Cycle: In East Africa the breeding season lies between February and June, in West Africa between May and August and in South Africa between September and December; depending on the regional, climatic conditions.

Climate: Tropical to sub-tropical throughout; divergent annual rainy periods in all regions.

AVICULTURE

In former years sacred ibises were restricted to large zoological gardens; the idea was to exhibit as many species as possible — usually together with herons — in big aviaries. Ideas have changed in modern aviculture; members of one particular species are now kept in larger groups and zoologists concentrate on their breeding and rearing. This has proved to be quite successful in many zoological gardens, bird preserves and private parks. The excellent breeding results of the Bald Ibis or Waldrapp, *Geronticus eremita* (initiated by the Basle Zoo in 1957) may prevent this species, which is threatened with extinction in its natural habitat, from dying out altogether.

Housing: In large to medium-sized aviaries; breeding results are quite possible in 40–50 m² large aviaries. Nowadays ibises are often kept pinioned on lake shores and on wading-bird meadows where breeding results have also been satisfactory. Wintering in rooms with an even temperature with opportunities for bathing.

Food: See glossy ibis; larger ibis species, including the sacred ibis, like small pieces of fish or meat as an addition to their diet. If herring is given to them, the plumage gets dirty very quickly.

Breeding: Although less prolific than the bald ibis, broods of the sacred ibis have been successful (first attempts in the Zoo at Berlin as early as 1876) as have been those of the Black Ibis, *Pseudibis papillosa*, and the Straw-necked Ibis, *Carphibis spinicollis*; for further ibis brood results see under glossy ibis. Even in preserves, most ibises build large nests of twigs, sometimes as nest colonies with several nest hollows. Egg-laying takes place in our spring and summer months (includins second clutches). Incubation and rearing are done by both parent birds, but in bad weather periods brooding and chicks may suffer a set-back. In the Hagenbeck Zoological Gardens at Hamburg a sacred ibis was independent and able to fly when it was 7 weeks old.

Hybridization: Interbreeding is known to take place amongst a number of ibis species, but—at least partly—the reason may well be that a mate of the same species is not available

Roseate Spoonbill

Ajaia ajaja (L.)

Comparative Size: Considerably smaller than white stork.

Plumage: Adults see plate 6; both sexes have the same colour; body plumage white with pink blush; wings light pink in colour, upper wing-coverts glowing carmine-red. The pink tint may grow much paler in the birds which inhabit preserves; head and throat are naked. Juvenile birds white; wing-coverts intermingled with brown feathers; head predominantly feathered.

Natural Habit

Status: In many areas either displaced or threatened with extinction owing to building and land cultivation. Protective actions which were started in 1940 were successful but birds are now endangered again because of land drainage and over-use of strong chemical and toxic insecticides to fight mosquitos. There are still large populations in existence in distant areas and, at present, the birds are spreading in Texas, Florida and Louisiana.

Habitat: Large brackish and fresh-water lagoons with low bushes, swampy plains, reed thickets, shallow river banks and mangrove woods along the coasts. Nests are placed in bushes, in reeds, or on islands near the coast.

Breeding Biology: After a very pronounced mating display and pairing, nests are made of brushwood and sticks; they are large and it is the M. which fetches the nesting material to be made into the nest by the F. Actual mating always takes place in the nest. Clutch size 2–4 rough-shelled eggs, white with brown spots. M. and F. take turns in incubating for 23–24 days, after which time the eggs are hatched. Nestlings leave the nest with 5–6 weeks while they are still climbing; they reach full flight ability when they are approximately 7–8 weeks old and sexual maturity in the third year.

Migration: The South and Central American populations are either permanent residents of infrequent migrants. Those that nest in the southern states of the

USA migrate to the South; some small groups winter in South Texas and South Florida.

Yearly Cycle: Central and North American populations return to their breeding grounds in February and March, breed from April to June and leave again in September and October.

Climate: Roseate spoonbills are purely tropical birds; they reach the sub-tropics only on the northern and southern boundary of their distribution.

AVICULTURE

In appearance, coloration and manner, roseate and eurasian spoonbills are attractive heronlike birds. They are kept predominantly in bird preserves and zoological gardens. There is no doubt that both species would add considerable charm to under-populated duck enclosures, but as they are endangered in their natural habitat catching and selling them in any numbers would be forbidden.

Housing: All spoonbill species are sensitive to cold and, if they are not adequately housed, their plumage soon gets dirty and wet. During the summer months, zoos and bird preserves keep spoonbills together with herons and ibises in large aviaries with a bathing pool of up to 60 cm deep. There they will thrive and may start breeding. In the winter, however, they are housed in relatively small, heated rooms where their plumage gets dirty from droppings and food remnants, particularly if the birds are fed on oily fish (herring). Concrete and very soiled flooring (the latter due to over-crowding) may also prove to be harmful and lead to inflammation of the feet. The very large, modern tropical aviaries are much better for the birds; just a small group of roseate or other spoonbills should be kept with other bird species.

Food: Mainly animal food consisting of a mixture of minced fish and meat, shrimps and a nourishing formulated food. Additionally small fish or pieces of meat may be given. If the birds are to maintain their pink coloration, they need extra carotene with their food.

Breeding: All spoonbill species are difficult to breed, much more so than, for instance, white ibises and herons. Pairing took place a number of times, nest material was collected and occasionally a nest was built; in HEINROTH's times at the Berlin Zoo, three females laid eggs a number of times; however, there is no recorded result of a successful rearing of a brood.

HEINROTH (1931) reared 5 spoonbills from wild birds' eggs; he fed them on a mixture of soaked, crushed pieces of shrimps, minced fish and meat as well as a prepared food. The adult birds particularly liked fish heads.

Hybridization: At the beginning of the century several hybrids—the results of interbreeding between the Eastern Asiatic Spoonbill, *Platalea minor*, and the Oriental Ibis, *Threskiornis melanocephala*—grew to maturity; when these hybrids were mated with ibises they were fertile.

Flamingos

Flamingos are highly specialised water birds, completely adapted to feeding on small aquatic animals and algae. Organic matter on the surface of the mud is sucked up passing water through the lamellae of the filter-type bill, allowing the filtered water to run out again. Greater, Caribbean and Chilean flamingos are able to take food up to the size of small molluscs, snails, water insects and seed of aquatic plants in such a way. On the other hand, lesser, Andean and James' flamingos feed exclusively on microscopically small blue-green algae and protozoa.

If flamingos are to be kept in preserves food needs to be adapted to the birds' feeding habits. For the first 3 species this has been managed quite effectively for the last 100 years, but caring for the other species has only been possible for a few decades. Nowadays large zoos and great bird preserves show all five species (the greater flamingo is only a sub-species of the Caribbean flamingo); Chilean, greater and Caribbean flamingos can be met in private grounds, and they are the three species which breed successfully in captivity.

Greater Flamingo

Phoenicopterus ruber roseus Pallas

Comparative Size: Slightly smaller than Carribean flamingo.

Plumage: Adults see plate 24; pink tint fading, always most intensively coloured after moult; flight feathers black, otherwise wings scarlet red; parts of bill are light and legs are pale pink; no proper sexual dimorphism in coloration, size and voice. Juveniles dirty-white with brown wings.

Natural Habit

Status: Within the area of distribution approximately 20 breeding grounds are known to exist; their individual populations fluctuate widely. The total population is estimated to consist of just under 800,000 birds; in one colony in N. W. India approximately 500,000 mature birds were present in 1945.

Habitat: Large lagoons on the coast, also extensive, very shallow lakes in steppes (normally with a saline content). Since the water level of the lakes fluctuates new mud banks are constantly formed; these are covered with a thin layer of saltwater vegetation.

Breeding Biology: The parent birds build nest mounds, a truncate cone of mud, set very closely to each other, either in shallow water or along the banks; the mounds are approximately 30 cm high.

Clutch is only one very rough-shelled initially white egg, which is incubated in the shallow nest depression for 27–32 days. Soon after hatching the chick leaves the nest and walks around within the colony. Flamingos feed their young for

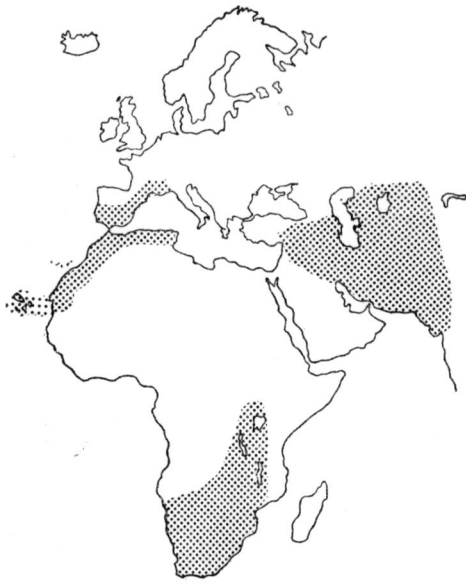

more than one month on a red nutritious liquid they secrete from their oesophagus, in fact for the period it takes the chick to develop the filtering device of the bill which enables it to feed itself. Greater flamingos are able to fly when they are approximately 70 days old, and it is assumed that in their natural habitat they do not breed for the first 5 or 6 years of their life.

Migration: Depending on climatic conditions they are either residents, infrequent migrants or migratory birds. On the other hand, lack of rainfall—which may mean drying up of the lagoons—can lead to invasion-like migrations.

Yearly Cycle: Irregular in the tropical zones, in others according to seasons. In the Camargue (southern France) nesting birds arrive at the end of February and lay between April and June. They migrate from July to October; a few spend the winter there. But for a number of years flamingos may not visit the Camargue (nor several other breeding grounds at all).

Climate: Breeding colonies are throughout in areas with hot, sunny summer months. However, some flamingos have been observed wintering on central European waters (probably birds which had escaped from preserves) so it may be assumed that they possess a certain hardiness in less clement climates.

AVICULTURE

Since the mid-19th century flamingos have been shown in many zoos; in particular they inhabit large and well-arranged animal parks and bird preserves. Bird enthusiasts only found out after 1950 that it is possible to care for the birds in a private park.

In a natural environment, flamingos live in huge flocks, a fact which cannot be ignored by those who want to breed them successfully in captivity. Three birds is the absolute minimum size of a group; 5–8 birds will be a proper group with behaviour typical of their species, and with 10 or more birds good breeding results can be expected. Flamingos have a very high life expectancy; in zoos some have lived to the age of more than 40 years.

Housing: Duck lovers may keep flamingos in small flocks at their duck ponds; a lake should have a stretch of several metres of shallow water and it should not have concrete flooring. It is more sensible to arrange a 'flamingo lagoon'. Around the edges of the lake, earth should be dug up to approximately 40 cm below normal water level; the edge itself should be concrete, becoming gradually more shallow, and the space between the edge and the water—up to 10 cm below water level—should be filled up with clay, loam and mud from a pond. The ground thus established is the flamingos' favourite place where they can build nest mounds with the mud mixture. Greater flamingos are not particularly sensitive to cold but, if injury to their legs and lamellae of their bills is to be avoided they should be housed free of frost during the winter.

Food: A nutritious, protein-rich prepared food should be mixed to a paste and given to the birds in buckets or deep feeding troughs. They are also fed on rice and wheat—either soaked or boiled—and soaked bread and shrimps. In preserves with large populations, the birds do not find enough natural food (algae and water flies); it is important, therefore, to give them additional carotene so that they retain the red tint of the plumage.

Breeding: Until very recently the actual breeding results were in sad contrast to the number of birds kept in zoos; they were very poor indeed. It was not until 1963 that the Berlin Zoo managed the first breeding result in Germany—103 years after first introducing flamingos. The reasons for the low rate of productivity—or rather the conditions necessary for successful breeding of flamingos—are now largely known; it is essential to have a sufficient number of birds, the correct depth of water, suitable mud for nest-building, properly balanced food and—last but not least—a warm, dry summer. The colony in Berlin in 1963 consisted of 32 greater flamingos and slightly fewer Chilean flamingos; the first laying took place mid-May—in later years between end-April and end-July. Parent birds take turns in incubating and also jointly look after the chicks. Unfortunately the proportion of unfertilized eggs is fairly high. The wing-clipped mature birds have problems in keeping their balance whilst they are copulating. If the colony life is not disturbed too much by outside influences, the young grow up splendidly under parental care; they still beg to be fed when they are 3–4 months old. It is possible to rear chicks without parents, but is very troublesome. Under the conditions of a zoological garden, females may start laying in their second year.

Hybridization: See Caribbean flamingo.

Caribbean Flamingo

Phoenicopterus ruber ruber (L.)

Comparative Size: Largest flamingo species.

Plumage: Adults see plate 24; all plumage and wing-coverts glowing red, flight feathers black. Legs light-coloured; tarsus joints and feet scarlet-red. Juveniles dirty-white with brown wings.

Natural Habit

Status: In 1972 the total population was 50,000 to 60,000 birds; among them were 15,000 breeding pairs which nested in 8–10 large colonies. Strong protective laws have been passed, but their effectiveness varies from country to country. The birds may be disturbed by several factors, amongst them tourism, construction of extensive salt works in the breeding lagoons as well as construction of several airports.

Habitat: As greater flamingo, although the majority of breeding grounds are near the ocean, i. e. in the vicinity of large coastal lagoons.

Breeding Biology: See greater flamingo.

Migration: An isolated population of resident Caribbean flamingos inhabits the Galapagos Islands; the ones from the Caribbean area—sometimes as far as Surinam—are occasional migratory birds.

Yearly Cycle: Manifestly influenced by the northern seasons.

Climate: Tropical heat with minimal seasonal changes throughout although amount of rainfall during the summer months varies considerably.

AVICULTURE

Although the total world population is endangered, Caribbean flamingos are nevertheless offered for sale by the animal trade every year, and groups of the glowing red birds are inhabitants of many preserves. The Berlin Zoo has had the birds on show since 1882. Greater and Caribbean flamingos are members of the same species. Geographical separation excludes the possibility of interbreeding; in captivity they should also be kept separately.

Housing: They should spend the winter indoors in well-warmed rooms where it is important that they have a large shallow water basin so that the horny scales of their legs do not dry out and split.

Food: Like greater flamingos Caribbean flamingos need large quantities of carotene in their food to form the red coloration of the plumage. The colour substance exists only in certain vegetables such as carrots and peppers. It reaches the basal part of the feather shaft through food and the blood vessels and is deposited in the feathers as the red pigment. In the natural environment of the birds the xantophyll of the algae has the same effect.

Breeding: Again see greater flamingo, although on the whole, Caribbean flamingos offer a rather better chance of breeding success[1]. In the Berlin Zoo an egg was laid on the gravel of a lake shore in 1934, even though the birds were unable to make a nest mound. In 1936 the flock of 30 birds was offered artificial concrete nests in the shallow water. Several pairs made use of them, added mud to them to make them into nest mounds and began to lay and incubate in June. No young birds were hatched, so the eggs were obviously infertile. In the Berlin Tierpark Caribbean flamingos have been reared repeatedly since 1966; they have been kept in a mixed colony of both sub-species. Egg laying started mid-May. The smallest breeding group known to exist to date consisted of only 6 Caribbean flamingos which were housed on a lake with a concrete bottom in the Duisburg Zoo. In June 1969 a chick was hatched and also reared to maturity.

Hybridization: Presumably there are no intrinsic biological isolating mechanisms towards interbreeding between the greater flamingo and the Caribbean flamingo, but they do seem to exist between them and the Chilean flamingo and even more in respect of the other species.

Therefore, the likelihood of interbreeding in a mixed colony will be in relation with the above tendencies.

---

[1] Up to 1972 in 34 Zoological gardens and aviaries of the whole world Caribbean flamingos have been breeding, greater flamingos in 16 and Chilean flamingos in 11.

1 ↑ Little Egret
2 ↗ Night Heron
3 ↓ Grey Heron

4 ↑ Snowy Egret
5 ↗ Squacco Heron
6 ↓ Roseate Spoonbill

7 ↑ Black Stork
8 ↗ White Stork
9 ↓ Glossy Ibis

10 ↑ Marabou Stork
11 ↗ Sacred Ibis
12 ↓ Coscoroba Swan

13 ↑ Mute Swan
14 ↗ Black Swan
15 ↓ Black-necked Swan

16 ↑ Lesser Snow Goose, blue phase
17 ↓ Lesser Snow Goose, white phase

18 ↑ Brent Goose
19 ↓ Bar-headed Goose

20 ↑ Canada Goose
21 ↓ Barnacle Goose

Chilean Flamingo
Phoenicopterus chilensis Molina

Comparative Size: Considerably smaller than Caribbean flamingo.

Plumage: Adults see plate 25; plumage of the body white tinted with delicate pink, wings have red coverts and black primaries. Bill from tip to above the bend black, then yellowish up to the base; legs and tarsus joint red. Juvenile plumage white and streaked with grey feathers.

NATURAL HABIT

Status: Most common species of flamingos in South America with nearly 500,000 birds. They are effectively protected by state law in certain areas only. Mass slaughter of mature birds (for meat), half-fledged, young birds (for fat) as well as large-scale collection of the eggs (as a source of food) are apparently compensated by the production of a sufficient number of offsprings.

Habitat: Large saline lagoons with poor vegetation in the highlands of the Andes, the zone of the Argentinian grass-steppes and along the coasts, particularly in the lagoons of big river deltas. Breeding biology and other characteristics of the various flamingo species coincide to a large degree. Therefore, an extract from a travel journal of a trip to Bolivia written by the Swiss, Charles CORDIER[1] — famous for catching wild animals — follows below:

"From Lima we set off in a small lorry and looked for flamingos in all lagoons within reach. In April (1963) we found a large colony of Chilean flamingos on a lake of Yaúri-Víri with thousands of young end eggs."

He writes about the second-largest lake of Bolivia:

"This lagoon Po-opó is approximately 100 km long, between 20 and 40 km wide and may be up to 6 m deep in some places, but on the whole it is a shallow basin with a depth of only 40 cm. The salt content of the lake is very high as it has no outlet; the rivers flowing into it are fresh-water. Muddy, lonely banks — many km wide — surround the water. It would not be too much to say that this area which has a height of 3,700 m and is extremely inhospitable and barren, is literally the most ideal flamingo habitat of our earth."

And about one of the other lagoons:

"The Coipassa Lake is a stretch of saline water with an area of 20 by 30 km; it is surrounded by massive salt flats over which one can drive a lorry."

He reports on a drive across the salt flats:

"At night the temperature dropped to −14 °C. Between June and August it may go as low as −25 °C[2] and stormy winds may howl across the salt-covered land."

[1] Flamingos in Bolivien. Freunde des Kölner Zoo Jg. 11, 1968
[2] Because of the high salinity, the water remains free of ice.

About the persecution of the flamingos by the native Indians, CORDIER reports as follows:

> "Twenty families live in the village of Quetana. Each family collects approximately 800 flamingo eggs (usually James') per annum from the Colorado Lagoon—a total of 16,000 eggs every year. Last year 10,000 eggs were taken from the Curúta Lagoon. As soon as the flamingos have laid their eggs, which is normally between the months of November and April, the natives collect them, wherever possible. The chicks which still manage to survive are herded together—still in their nestling down plumage—and are driven on land, often as far as 100 km, to a place where there is fire wood. There they are killed and their oil is extracted. Moulting, mature birds are driven on land and slaughtered or they are caught with snares in the night."

> "One may well aniticipate that this kind of systematic persecution will make the flamingos die out. It is to be hoped that, with increasing civilisation, the youth of the Morato and Chipaya Indians who now attend school, will find something better to do with their life than stalking flamingos under conditions of cold of −18°C."

AVICULTURE

Nowadays, the international animal trade offers for sale mainly Chilean flamingos which means that the species is more frequently kept in preserves in Europe than is the European greater flamingo. Chilean flamingos are rather hardy and their wintering is not difficult; birds in preserves often live to an age of 30 years. They are good-natured (even towards small ducks), but they cannot compete with large flocks of their larger relatives in certain situations. Therefore both species should be kept in separate lagoons which also prevents undesirable hybridization.

Housing: Artificial lakes with shallow banks as have been described for housing greater flamingos. In modern preserves the birds are enclosed by scenery pleasant to the eye—such as flower beds, paths and low walls. They spend the winters indoors in light aviaries, free from frost; there should be a water basin for them, approximately 30 cm deep, and feeding troughs should be in the immediate vicinity of it. Although Chilean flamingos are used to conditions of cold from their natural mountain habitat, ice (particularly sharp icy ridges) can damage the skin of their legs very easily.

Food: See greater flamingo.

Breeding: In relation to the number of Chilean flamingos kept in preserves, the number which actually breed is negligible. Zoos and preserves keep large flocks on perfectly arranged lagoons, but the birds neither build nests nor do they lay eggs. The first breeding result was achieved in 1958 in the Basle Zoo (breeding attempts since 1957) and the first German breeding success was in the Berlin Zoo in 1965. At the time the group in Berlin consisted of approximately 80 greater and Chilean flamingos; 10 to 15 pairs were breeding annually in clearly separated colonies. In Berlin laying began in early June, in Basle in mid-June and in the British Wildfowl Trust between mid-May and mid-June. It was found that incubation took 29 days; both parents shared the task and also jointly took care of the chicks.

Hybridization: See Caribbean flamingo.

Lesser Flamingo

Phoeniconaias minor Geoffr.

Comparative Size: Smallest flamingo species.

Plumage: Adults see plate 23; plumage pale pink, elongate feathers on shoulders more intensively coloured; wing coverts strong pink and primaries black. Bill dark carmine-red with black tip; legs red; juvenile birds considerably paler than adults.

NATURAL HABIT

Status: It is estimated that the world population of all flamingos is 8 million birds, of which 6 million are lesser flamingos; on Lake Nakuru (Kenya) alone, up to 2 million flamingos spend the summer months. Long prevailing periods both of rain and drought affect the bird population to a large extent. In very dry years no eggs may be laid at all.

Habitat: Large salt lakes of African plains and arid S. W. Africa. The shallow lagoons form an immense amount of animal and vegetable plankton; on the other hand, because of the high salt content, they lack the usual swamp vegetation.

Breeding Biology: Groups of flamingos leave the huge flocks of non-breeding birds and wander off to quiet lakes where they may breed. In such places nest mounds are built in muddy, shallow water—often within colonies of the greater flamingos—and the single egg is incubated for 30 days. During the first weeks of its life the chick is fed on the fluid secreted by the parents and stays within the colony. While its feathers are growing, the lamellae of the bill are also developing and, afterwards, the young birds sieve their own food from the water.

Migration: Within the area of their occurrence, lesser flamingos migrate between their resting and breeding lagoons. Furthermore, they may be induced to migrate elsewhere if the water level falls sharply because of a lack of rainfall. How the birds subsist—whether they starve or have abundant food—depends on the amount of water in a lake or lagoon.

Yearly Cycle: It is regarded as certain that only some of the mature birds of the world's total flamingo populations ever breeds annually. Fluctuating water levels and resultant variations in food supply (as mentioned before) are seen as the causes. The breeding season of African flamingos is irregular.

AVICULTURE

For a long time it was difficult to provide lesser, Andean[1] and James[2] flamingos with the proper food; since in their natural habitat all three species feed on microscopically small organic matter, and in captivity their food thus has to be

[1] *Phoenicoparrus andinus*
[2] *Ph. jamesi*

equally fine. The problem has now been solved and the observer can watch all six flamingo kinds in quite a few zoological gardens. So far very few bird ethusiasts have had the courage to keep instead of the Caribbean flamingo, which is an endangered species, lesser flamingos on private estates. Lesser flamingos have the same glowing red plumage but enjoy a good status since very large flocks of the birds still inhabit the African lakes.

Housing: Like all flamingo species, on sunny shallow lakes; they have to be kept warm in the winter.

Food: During the warm seasons, lesser flamingos should be allowed to sieve some food out of the water for themselves. In a preserve, a good flamingo lake should be warm and shallow with plenty of aquatic vegetation and organic matter (it should not be biologically dead water). The birds' droppings and food remnants sink to the bottom and form the nourishment for the lowest organisms and forms of life and, in turn, these very adequately supplement the diet the birds are given. The food is presented to them in troughs and should consist of a mixture of dust-free and sieved formulated food, shrimp meal and milk powder; additional minerals, vitamins and carotene are also necessary.

Breeding: The colour plate shows a colony of lesser flamingos in the Tierpark Berlin. Several pairs make nest mounds on the lake's edges and display in courtship with plumes erected on their backs, but up to the present no egg has been laid. Nest mounds have also been built in the Zoo of San Diego (USA) and the British Wildfowl Trust; in fact, in the latter an egg was laid in 1972.

The African ornithological magazine "Bokmakierie" (1973) reported in detail the rearing of two chicks without parent birds. They were fed—amongst other things—on water with a concentrated amount of algae; the young birds thrived and it was possible to set them free at a later stage.

Hybridization: Non-existent to all appearances. On the African lakes where thousands of greater and lesser flamingos breed in mixed colonies no hybrids have been born to date.

Swans, Geese and Ducks

The order of Anseriformes consists of 145 species which are divided into 247 sub-species; with the exception of the Antarctic they inhabit all large regions on earth. They are remarkable for their extreme adaptability to all kinds of geographical-climatic conditions as may be seen by the breeding habits of several species of geese under arctic conditions and the occurrence of the Andean goose and the bar-headed goose in high mountain regions; for such habitats the birds are neither particularly adapted nor do they have any particular requirements regarding their environment. The latter is the main reason why so many species are able to re-adjust so successfully to the conditions of a preserve and remain there as breeding birds over many generations. The British Wildfowl Trust at Slimbridge has the largest collection of Anatidae in the world; up to 1975 the Trust had managed to keep 128 species (divided into 180 sub-species), and far more than 100 species (divided into about 160 sub-species) were actually breeding.

Keeping ducks and geese and caring for them can be done in a number of ways. Two to three pairs of—for instance—North American wood ducks, mandarin ducks, red-billed pintails and many other *Anas* species need only a relatively small water surface and can be kept quite easily on an artifical pond in a garden. Whistling ducks and European wigeons need larger and really deep lakes, and marine ducks and mergansers require water of very high quality. The majority of duck species becomes very tame when being fed; mergansers reared by people lose all timidity. Swans need a great deal of space and should be kept on large lakes which also gives smaller birds the chance to escape from the swans' aggressiveness. Tame swans accepting food from people are a familiar sight in parks; however, it should always be borne in mind just how aggressive the birds can be, especially during the breeding season. They may be a real danger to children. According to popular belief, geese are 'stupid', but this is not at all true; in fact their behaviour is characterised by quietness and prudence. Young geese which are reared without either parents or foster-parents get very attached to people as shown by the groups of greylag geese of Konrad LORENZ and Bengt BERG; very enthusiastic books have been written about them. The modern tropical houses offer a number of new possibilities for keeping waterfowl, and here successful breeding should be achieved of the small *Nettapus* species and the interesting Madagascar and South African white-backed ducks and the small pygmy geese in the near future.

In contrast to the other groups of waterfowl which are discussed in the book, the problems of breeding Anatidae have been largely solved. On the whole, the stock requirements of preserves are met by birds breeding there. Nine species which are threatened with extinction in their natural habitat have been reared in captivity and some birds have been re-introduced to suitable areas of their natural environment. Such efforts are well-known in respect of the Hawaiian goose, but marbled teals, New Zealand diving ducks and even North American wood ducks have also been released—2,579 birds of the latter in New England (USA) between 1922 and 1939. However, a limited import of wild waterfowl is an essential requirement if preserve birds are to be maintained in a healthy genetic condition.

In some groups, birds have a definite inclination to interbreed with members of other species. If a lake in a park is normally stocked with mallards, it is not advisable to introduce spotbills and grey ducks to it. Within a few years the lake will contain a population of hybrids which are fully fertile, and it will be difficult to find a single really beautifully coloured mallard drake. If geese are kept in large preserves together with other *geese* species they also tend to interbreed. A third, slight risk of hybridization exists amongst red-crested pochards, rosybills and diving ducks. Breeders (also some zoos and preserves) either arrange small preserves for one single breeding pair, or they keep larger flocks of different birds in several enclosures, but each containing only one of the species likely to interbreed.

Ducks and geese moult once the breeding season in finished: the whole of the plumage of the body is moulted within a few weeks; the wing feathers are shed within a few days or even hours and mature birds are unable to fly for several weeks. The plumage of the males of the northern species after the moult has the same colour as the female (eclipse plumage), but in autumn and winter it is moulted again into the splendidly coloured breeding plumage. Although southern species of ducks wear plumage of the same coloration—either mature or immature—throughout the year, they undergo two annual moults nevertheless. In adult geese and swans the colour of the plumage remains constant (mature plumage).

Cuban Whistling Duck
Dendrocygna arborea (L.)

Comparative Size: Measurements of body approximately the same as mallard drake, but longer legs and an upright position make the birds appear larger.

Plumage: Adults see plate 30; plumage of the body dark to black-brown throughout; it contains white spots and is edged in light-brown; feathers of tail and wings are monochrome blackish-brown. To determine the difference between the sexes is only possible from the birds' habits, size or behaviour. Juveniles similar in colouring to adults, but somewhat lighter and the white markings are brownish.

Natural Habit

Status: Exact situation unknown, but endangered without doubt. Within its small range of distribution, populations on many small islands are either driven back by man or exterminated.

Habitat: In typical Caribbean localities of dense swampy woods, marshes of the plains with bushes, and the mangrove woods surrounding lagoons and stretches of the coast.

Breeding Biology: Nests have been found in ground vegetation, tree holes and on the epiphytically growing bromelias. Full clutch consists of 10–14 white eggs which are incubated for 30–31 days. Nests are not lined with down; males and females take turns in incubating so that the eggs are never left uncovered. Chicks are cared for by both parents.

Migration: They are stationary residents.

Yearly Cycle: Northern world hemisphere and nearness to the equator determine the life cycle of Cuban whistlings ducks; breeding season is from February to October; afterwards—and temporarily—the birds join up in troops consisting of a number of families.

Climate: Tropical sea climate with high temperatures throughout the year and only insignificant changes between day and night as well as the seasons.

AVICULTURE

Although the unpretentious black-grey coloured Cuban whistling ducks have been kept in large zoological gardens for a long time and, in some few cases, have been bred, systematic attempts to save this endangered species from extinction have been made only during the last two decades. Nowadays, whistling ducks are kept in numerous private parks where they breed successfully; the same applies to several zoological gardens.

Housing: They need a great deal of space and should therefore have a large lake at their disposal; they should have slightly heated shelters for the winter. Where only one pair is kept, good breeding results are quite possible, but then the Cuban whistling ducks give the appearance of being 'bored'; they may spend hours resting on one leg or they may look for food in an unhurried fashion.

Food: Grain and one of the simple food brands are their staple diet in addition with duckweed, chopped lettuce and grass make up their diet.

Breeding: Recognition of the sexes was—and partially still is—the great problem and, no doubt, the reason for difficulties in breeding the birds. There are no definitive differences in coloration and behaviour; even the cloaca test, i. e. evaginating the penis, is only possible with some of the drakes. However, if pairs are kept in favourable conditions they may become quite active and breed. Eggs are laid in nesting boxes (from March onwards, more usually in May or June) at 24-hour intervals. The nest is not lined with down. Male and female are supposed to take turns in incubating, but I myself know of one pair with only the female breeding. The chicks are hardy but need and love a great deal of warmth; they are undemanding and can be reared quite easily without parents. Sexual maturity is attained by the end of the second year.

Hybridization: Very insignificant; in Houston (USA), 11 young birds were hybrids—the result of interbreeding of the Cuban whistling duck and the fulvous whistling duck in 1972; they grew to maturity.

Red-billed Whistling Duck
Dendrocygna autumnalis (L.)

Comparative Size: Smaller than Cuban whistling duck; proportions of body approximately the same as a medium-sized dabbling duck.

Plumage: Plate 29 shows adults of the northern sub-species, plate 28 of the southern sub-species; the northern red-billed whistling duck has chestnut-brown chest, shoulder and back feathers with overtones of wine-red; in the southern sub-species head and both sides of the neck are grey of greyish-brown. Birds bred in captivity may have transitions in colour tones and scales because of interbreeding. Juveniles have grey instead of red bills.

Natural Habit

Status: Total population not endangered; rare in certain localities owing to hunting, land drainage or use of insecticides. Quite common, however, in large swamps or rice plantations.

Habitat: Shallow waters of the plains which are rich in vegetation and other nourishment, particularly if they are surrounded by groups of trees and bushes.

Breeding Biology: Both mates choose the nesting site, either large holes in trees or nesting boxes or dry areas in the ground vegetation. Normal clutch size up to 16 cream-coloured eggs; they are incubated by both parents for 27–28 days. Chicks are cared for by both parents; young birds attain sexual maturity in the second year.

Migration: Breeding birds of the southern United States are migratory birds (migrations as far as South America); birds inhabiting more southerly zones either roam to areas of varying distances or remain in their breeding grounds throughout the year.

Yearly Cycle: In Texas the northern red-billed whistling ducks return in April, breed between May and July and migrate southwards in November. Southern red-billed whistling ducks nest acording to regional climatic conditions which depend largely on rain-fall; breeding seasons are very varied therefore.

Climate: All red-billed whistling duck populations remain in moist tropical and sub-tropical zones throughout the year which are characterised by only small fluctuations in temperature.

Aviculture

The red-billed whistling duck, in particular the southern sub-species, has been imported quite regularly for a long time; small groups of them enliven the duck ponds of numerous zoos and sanctuaries. In private parks breeders have kept them in greater numbers only for the last ten years.

At present, they are the most easily bred *Dendrocygna* species; however, I consider them to be less hardy and more sensitive to cold than, for instance—the Cuban or fulvous whistling ducks.

Housing: In the summer on ponds of any size, together with other ducks; red-billed whistling ducks are peaceable and thus suitable to be included in a collection of small and delicate species. They should have a shelter for cool and rainy days in spring and autumn; they have to spend the winter in areas free from frost.

Food: Like Cuban whistling duck.

Breeding: Over the last few years breeding of red-billed whistling ducks has made great progress. Excellent results of several West European breeders and the Wildfowl Trust at Slimbridge (UK) (in the latter 447 young birds grew to maturity between 1964 and 1974), have made it possible to arrange collections of pairs which were born and reared in preserves; they are far more likely to breed than the wild birds which are caught and taken from their native winter habitats.

In spring, pairs in breeding disposition search for nesting places in all sorts of different areas whilst they utter calls which are surprisingly melodious for duck-like birds. Eggs are usually laid in nesting boxes—in the Wildfowl Trust the southern sub-species of red-billed whistling ducks begin laying in the last ten days of March (elsewhere usually in April). The northern sub-species lay from May 15th onwards. Whenever possible incubation and care of the chicks should be left to the parent birds. Losses of young birds are rare, nor are they likely to occur if the eggs are put into an incubator. During the first few days of their life, chicks should sieve their food from a water trough; they like fine, floating vegetable matter, shrimp meal and duckweed. Their need for warmth is greater than that of ordinary ducklings.

Hybridization: There are obviously no barriers against interbreeding between the two sub-species; if a breeder wishes to have pure breeds, he should keep both kinds in separate enclosures.

Fulvous Whistling Duck

Dendrocygna bicolor (Vieillot)

Comparative Size: Like red-billed whistling duck; medium sized *Dendrocygna* species.

Plumage: Adults see plate 27; M. and F. have the same coloration and sexes can only be told by cloaca test. Juveniles have coloration which is similar to adults, but they are darker overall and the feathers of their back are edged with red-brown instead of yellow.

The very similar Wandering Whistling Ducks, *Dendrocygna arcuata*, have a faint but nonetheless distinct marking on the chest.

NATURAL HABIT

Status: Large populations on three continents with tendencies to spread to South Africa and the southern states of USA where they settle on artificially created surfaces of water (rice plantations, sewage-plants and dams).

Habitat: Shallow, warm lakes with a wealth of vegetation and forms of animal life, also ponds and quiet river courses of open grass and wooded landscapes. After the breeding season also on large lakes and lagoons.

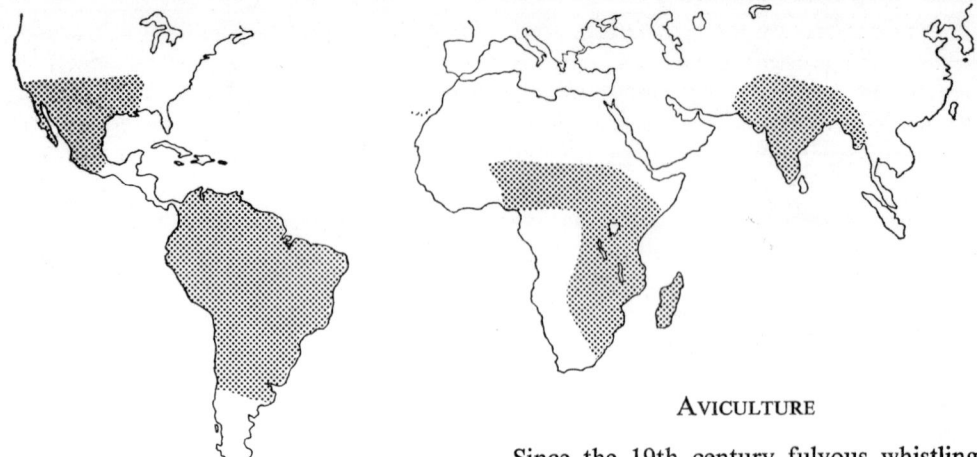

Breeding Biology: Nests are built predominantly in ground vegetation, partly in the shallow water region, in rice plantations and on the banks of dams. Both male and female build a compact nest. The female lays in it 10 to 15 light cream-coloured eggs in 24 hourly intervals; incubation takes 24 to 26 days and most of it is done by the male. Afterwards both parents guide and take care of the chicks. Juvenile birds become mature in the second year of life.

Migration: The majority of populations are birds of passage; after finishing the rearing of their young, swarms of the birds congregate on large water areas. Birds which breed in the southern states of USA migrate to Central and South America, those that breed in South Africa in part far to the North.

Yearly Cycle: In Louisiana the fulvous whistling ducks arrive relatively late in April; main time of laying is June and July, weeks later than other duck species which are residents there. Breeding seasons in tropical zones are very variable and depend on the regional weather cycles.

Climate: Fulvous whistling ducks inhabit exclusively tropical zones and a few border areas to the North and South with very hot summers.

AVICULTURE

Since the 19th century fulvous whistling ducks have been imported to Europe quite regularly and nowadays there is hardly a zoo or large bird preserve where they are missing. Kept in small groups, they add considerable liveliness to the waterfowl grounds. The interest of enthusiasts in the birds increased in the same extent as it became possible to breed the species in captivity. At present, many fulvous whistling ducks inhabit private parks where they are cared for and bred with a high rate of success. They are attractively coloured, hardy, peace-loving and very lively water birds. When fulvous whistling ducks have a quarrel with another species they do not solve it by snapping, but instead they utter loud high-pitched screams with wide open bill.

Housing: A breeder keeps the species on ponds which should not be too small and have a depth of not less than 60 to 80 cm (whistling ducks enjoy diving) and offers birds to winter in areas free of frost.

Food: See Cuban whistling duck.

Breeding: One year old birds frequently mate, search for nesting holes and stand on nest-like platforms of plants which grow under water (calamus, sedges); however, eggs are laid very seldom. In spring, sexually mature pairs carry on in a very similar manner. The male is continually searching for a suitable nesting site; the female accompanies him, all burrows are examined, and reed bushes are trodden down. In my own preserve egg laying began in mid-May, in the British Wildfowl Trust it often starts in March and April. Apparently the female alone incubates for the first six weeks, after which most of the sitting on the eggs is taken over by the drake. Nests are not lined with down; eggs remain uncovered in breeding intervals. The chicks are attractive with grey and white markings; they have an enormous need for warmth, like to bathe in warm water and, initially, only want to take food which they can filter out of the water. Later on they accept moist crumbly food, but with every full beak they run to the water. I believe it to be more suitable to allow the parent birds to rear the young themselves, rather than using technical devices. At the age of 6 weeks, the ducklings have most of their feathers and, when 8 weeks old, they are full-grown.

Hybridization: Very insignificant; some interbreeding is known to occur in the Dendrocygna genus.

Plumed Whistling Duck

Dendrocygna eytoni (Eyton)

Comparative Size: Like red-billed whistling duck; medium-sized *Dendrocygna* species.

Plumage: Adults see plate 31; M. and F. are alike in appearance; no eclipse plumage. Juveniles less intensively coloured than adults; falciform feathers are shorter and therefore less curved. Bill and feet initially grey, but the colour changes to that of the adults in the same autumn.

NATURAL HABIT

Status: Large swarms of plumed whistling ducks inhabit many areas of Australia. Their populations are not endangered. If rate of increase is poor at times in some areas because of insufficient rain-fall, favourable years provide the necessary compensation.

Habitat: Shallow waters of tropical grasslands (the Australian common name for the birds is "Grass Whistle Duck") and flooded meadows. Outside the breeding season muddy and gravelly banks of large river courses which do not dry out, as well as lakes.

Breeding Biology: Nests are found in high grass or underneath small bushes; they are sparsely lined with grass stalks. A full clutch consists of 10 to 12 white to pale cream coloured eggs. Incubation period 27 to 28 days, according to JOHNSTONE (1970) 30 days. Both male and female take turns in incubating and jointly take care of the young. FRITH (1967) believes it possible that wild birds pair permanently.

Migration: Far distance migratory flights are undertaken on the Australian continent while the birds are searching for ecologically favourable areas; these vary continually owing to differences in changes from dry to rainy periods. Such flights may take the birds South and South West far beyond their breeding areas.

Yearly Cycle: As they are fully dependent on the rainy period, plumed whistling ducks in North Australia breed between February and April. Since their nests are in meadows and far away from the water, they are the first of the waterfowl who start laying their eggs; their chicks hatch when the seed of the aquatic plants are ripening. Sinking of the water levels during the dry periods leads to formation of large swarms which gather on lakes and rivers that contain water all the year round.

Climate: Tropically hot throughout.

AVICULTURE

Because of rigid export regulations, relatively few plumed whistling ducks have found their way from Australia to either Europe or North America, and as a result they are only rarely seen in zoos and breeding preserves. However, once the imported birds have settled into their new surroundings they are perfectly hardy so that most zoos, preserves and breeders are able to keep at least single pairs. Non-breeding plumed whistling ducks are not quarrelsome; pairs that breed may be somewhat aggressive.

Housing: Large sunny grounds, preferably with a stretch of healthy grass. It might be wise to keep breeding pairs in single pair enclosures as long as these have good vegetation. The latter should consist of short lawn for grazing and high grass for nest building. During the winter months the birds need a shelter which should be at their disposal in frosty or wet-cold periods at night as well as during the day-time.

Food: Grain, mixed food, duck-weed and —as previously mentioned—good opportunities for grazing.

Breeding: One of the first and most successful breeders was the Dutchman, Peter KOOY t'Zand; a pair imported in 1957 started breeding in 1961 and turned to be very prolific. In 1964, 33 young birds out of three clutches of the one pair were growing to maturity in his preserve, a unique success, judged by available literature. The female builds a nest in dry grass at a distance from the lake. Beginning of laying from May onwards; in the Wildfowl Trust, Slimbridge, from June onwards. KOOY (personal communication) managed to rear the chicks almost without losses; he fed them on normal food for rearing ducks and duckweed and after a short time also gave small grain and millet.

Hybridization: Not pronounced; interbreeding with the fulvous whistling duck is known to occur; it is assumed that this only happens if a mate of the same species is lacking.

White-faced Whistling Duck

Dendrocygna viduata (L.)

Comparative Size: Medium-sized whistling duck.

Plumage: Adults see plate 26; distribution of black-white markings on face and throat as well as width of black stripe on underside vary, but are not characteristics linked either to sex or location. Juveniles are easily recognisable by the typical plumage of the young bird (paler and lighter colouring throughout, feather edges paler).

NATURAL HABIT

Status: Abundant in most suitable habitats; frequently the typical duck. In 1972 observers from an aeroplane counted 64,000 white-faced whistling ducks in the deltas of the Niger and the Senegal.

Habitat: Warm, shallow, nutritious waters of the plains and swamps in wooded and open landscapes; lagoons near the coasts; also banks of inland lakes and rivers.

Breeding Biology: Pairs have a close bond with each other; they leave the flocks of non-breeding birds and find their own territory. Nests are predominantly found in the reeds, only rarely in tree holes. They are not lined with down. Full clutch consists of 8–12 pale cream-coloured eggs and it is assumed that the male does most of the incubating which lasts 28 to 30 days. Both parents take care of the young ducklings.

Migration: Mass gatherings of swarms of these whistling ducks in the West African river deltas and other areas show that they possess a strong migratory urge. It is a known fact that even breeding populations may become wandering.

Yearly Cycle: In very many birds of the tropics the urge to breed is triggered by the onset of the rainy periods; the white-faced whistling ducks belong to this category. Thus although in single areas breeding seasons are relatively constant, in the whole area of distribution, the breeding season of the ducks extends over every month of the year. Moult and resting period follows upon the breeding season and, during this time, single pairs and family units often gather into considerable flocks.

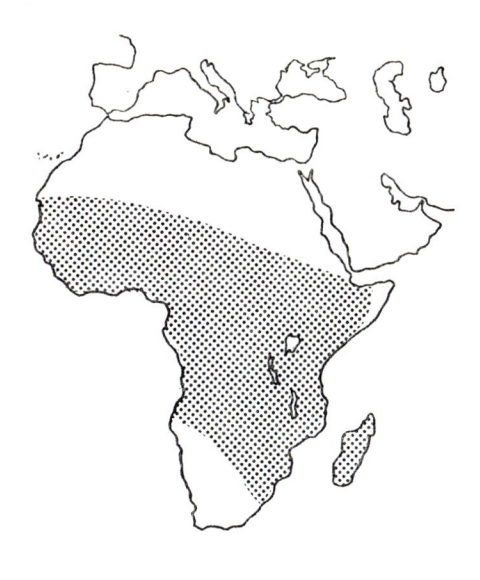

Climate: Occurs only in the tropics.

AVICULTURE

White-faced whistling ducks are among the most beautifully coloured *Dendrocygna* species. They are imported in large numbers and offered for sale by the animal trade. Undemanding in their nourishment requirements and—apart from their sensitivity to cold—unproblematical regarding keeping and care, they populate the lakes of zoos in large numbers. Attempts at breeding the species were successful to some degree; however the number of pairs with the necessary breeding impulse is still relatively low.

Housing: In zoos and preserves where they are on show they should be kept in groups as they are very sociable birds. A breeder normally keeps pairs of white-faced whistling ducks on communal ponds, or in large enclosures for single pairs which have to have good vegetation. They have to be wintered in houses free of frost. The birds should always be given the opportunity to bathe properly and to dive and, in case they show the urge, to have access to a free range.

Food: See other whistling duck species.

Breeding: As so many of the birds have been imported and sold at low cost, no-one tried systematically to breed them in captivity until fairly recently. Breeding in captivity was initiated by the British Wildfowl Trust in 1950 and other West European breeders followed the example with success after 1960.

Imported birds need a long time to become acclimatized, and only rarely show any desire to breed. There is a far better chance for breeding with birds reared in captivity. They are sexually mature in their second year of life, although they may be observed copulating much earlier. White-faced whistling ducks build their nests in high grass by preference, also like tall reeds and placing their nests on islands. Eggs are laid daily; nests are not lined with down. Laying rarely begins before mid-May; if eggs are removed, replacement by further laying is quite possible. Rearing of the chicks is apparently not without problems. Initially the ducklings need a very great deal of warmth and they also need guidance on how to take food (an ordinary duckling may be used to instruct them, for instance). They should be given a nourishing floating food, e. g. ant cocoons and water fleas placed on top of duckweed. After approximately one week food will be taken from a bowl. Whenever possible, a breeder should leave the care of the young ducklings to the parent birds.

Hybridziation: No marked tendencies, which also applies to other members of the genus *Dendrocygna*.

Coscoroba Swan
Coscoroba coscoroba (Molina)

Comparative Size: Smallest swan species, similar in size to a large domestic goose.

Plumage: Adults see plate 12; M. and F. with black tips on their primaries; bill red; irides pale orange-yellow or cream in M., dark brown in F; feet flesh-coloured. Juveniles white plumage containing some brown parts; bill grey, later pale red.

NATURAL HABIT

Status: Quite common in water-rich plains and, at present, breeding in a number of habitats. However, effective legal protection is lacking; the birds are large and easy to shoot so that they are becoming rare or even absent in areas densely populated by man.

Habitat: Large shallow lakes and lagoons in open landscapes of Patagonia and the Pampas. It appears that no literature exists so far on the different ecological needs of the Coscoroba swan compared with the black-necked swan.

Breeding Biology: The breeding season starts with pair formation, display and territory defence. A large cone-shaped nest is built in the vegetation of the shallow water. Full clutch consists of 6–9 grey-white eggs which are incubated by the female alone in 35 days. The cygnets are accompanied by both parents while they are being reared; during this period Coscoroba swans like to graze on meadows near embankments—much more so than other swans, and rather in the manner of geese.

Migration: All southern populations escape the winter's cold by flying North (as far as southern Brazil and Bolivia); many spend the winter on the lakes of the Buenos Aires province and Bolivia; the others are either infrequent migrants or stationary birds.

Yearly Cycle: In Argentina it is an accordance with the southern seasons, i.e. beginning of breeding season in September, most clutches laid in October, rearing of the young during the summer months—December to February. Afterwards migration to northern areas.

Climate: Beneath the rain shadow of the Andes range dry tussock grass steppes dominate plains and hills from the Falkland Isles to Gran Chaco. Whereas on the Falkland Isles night frosts may occur during the breeding season and the average temperature is 10°C, breeding grounds in the northern areas have predominantly sub-tropical summers and mild winters.

AVICULTURE

In 1870 Coscoroba swans were imported into Europe for the first time and, since then, they have appeared in nearly all large collections of zoological gardens. However, in private preserves and smaller zoos they are not nearly as common as the far more hardy *Cygnus* species discussed in the following chapters. The dainty rather than stately Coscoroba swans are not aggressive, they may become a little bit quarrelsome only during the breeding seasons. Like geese they enjoy grazing and resting on short-cut lawn. Acclimatized birds in captivity differ from other swans very little in their behaviour.

Housing: Fairly large pond areas with good quality water surrounded by meadows or lawns. For the winter they should have shelters which they may leave during the day time if they wish.

Food: See black-necked swan.

Breeding: A first successful brood was achieved on the estates of the Duke of Bedford at Woburn Abbey (UK) in 1914, the second in the Philadelphia Zoo (USA) in 1950. Since then, private breeders and zoos have intensified their attempts at breeding the species and several young birds have been reared. Nonetheless the Coscoroba swan is still regarded as a waterfowl which is difficult to breed and rear. Presumably the successes of the Philadelphia Zoo are rather unique, GRISWOLD (1973) reported on them as follows: A sibling pair bred in 1950 reared 83 young birds up to 1972 in a pen measuring 10 m × 17 m; eggs were laid between February and April (in San Antonio Zoo between January and August); full clutch consists of four to six eggs, a maximum of eight eggs. The female alone incubates them for 34 to 36 days. Eggs are put into an incubator a few days before they are ready for hatching and the cygnets are reared without parents; normally the latter were laying a second clutch.

Hybridization: Up to the present no reports have come in of hybrids.

Black-necked Swan
Cygnus melanocoryphus (Molina)

Comparative Size: Smaller than the mute swan; body very slender.
Plumage: Adults and cygnets see plate 15; M. and F. have sky-blue bill with a red knob surmounting it and pale flesh-coloured legs. F. is smaller, has a less pronounced knob, and a shorter neck, and can be spotted quite easily. Juveniles have a brown/black neck in the first year and grey feathers on the body; knob does not develop until the second year of their life.

NATURAL HABIT

Status: Far-ranging population counts are not available; however it seems to be significant that the province of Buenos Aires which is the most agricultural as well as the most populated area is also the main breeding ground of the black-necked swans (WELLER 1969).

Habitat: Large open lakes and lagoons of the hard-grass steppes which are very common in South America and where wide river zones are grown with reeds, tall rushes and floating and underwater vegetation. Surrounding scenery is covered by tussock and other hard grasses.

Breeding Biology: Breeding behaviour of black-necked swans does not differ very much from that of other swans. Clutches consist of three to six yellowish eggs which are incubated by the female in 36 days. Both parents care for the cygnets. Juveniles reach sexual maturity in the third year as a general rule.

Migration: Stationary resident birds in most places where they may gather into local winter flocks. They may migrate away from some southern regions or from areas of drought.

Yearly Cycle: Black-necked swans breed predominantly in the southern spring months of September to December; however, regional rainy seasons may result in breeding periods during other months.

Climate: See Coscoroba swan.

AVICULTURE

The majority of black-necked swans in Europe and North America are birds bred in captivity and thus adapted to local climate and yearly cycle; although they are rather hardy they are sensitive to cold. Of all *Cygnus* species they are the ones most sought after and much care and diligence is expended to increase their numbers and to help them to thrive. Black-necked swans are peaceable towards ducks and geese; although the gander defends the nest territory and the cygnets, he never gets as hostile as the mute swan, let alone the whooper swan.

Housing: They need a fair amount of space. The quality of water does not need to be of a particularly high standard, but a lake should be large enough to give the birds adequate opportunity for

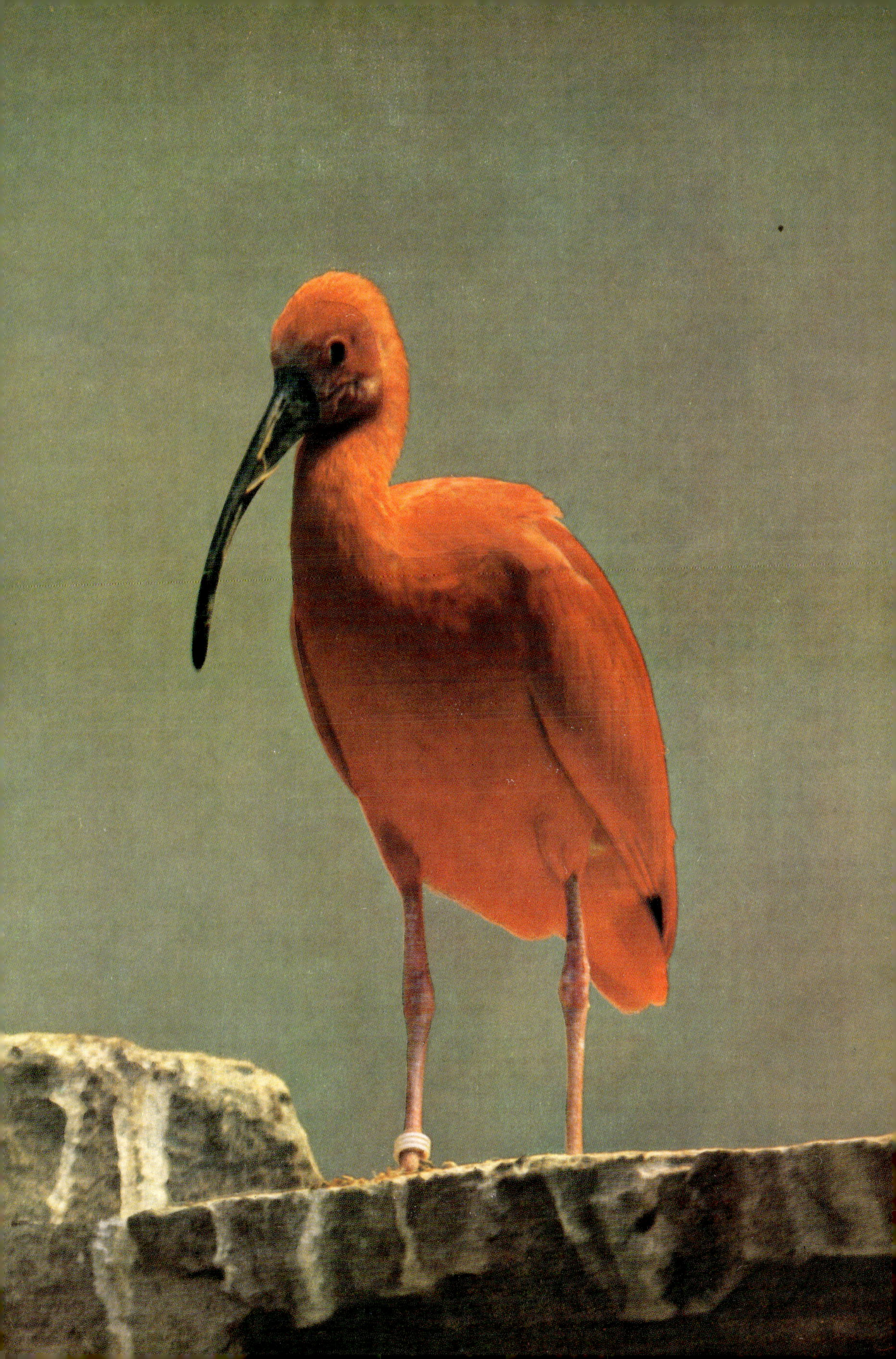

22 ← Scarlet Ibis
23 ↑ Lesser Flamingo
24 ↓ Caribbean and Greater Flamingo

25 ↑   Chilean Flamingo
26 ↓   White-faced Whistling Duck

27 ↑ Fulvous Whistling Duck
28 ↓ Southern Red-billed Whistling Duck

29 ↑   Northern Red-billed Whistling Duck
30 ↗   Cuban Whistling Duck
31 ↓   Plumed Whistling Duck and young

32 ↑ Greylag Goose and young
33 ↓ Lesser White-fronted Goose

34 ↑ Emperor Goose, several years old
35 ↗ Pink-footed Goose
36 ↓ Emperor Goose, one year old

37 ↑   Hawaiian Goose
38 ↓   Red-breasted Goose

bathing and at the same time enable other users of the lake to get out of the birds' way in case of possible attacks. In unfavourable climate the birds should spend the winters in shelters. They are not as suited to being kept on ponds in urban parks as are black or mute swans.

Food: Grain with mixed duck food; if possible fresh plants all the year round (duckweed, lettuce, winter greens and scraped carrots).

Breeding: Nowadays it is quite possible to have black-necked swans breeding if one provides them with the proper conditions. Birds reared in captivity normally reach sexual maturity towards the end of their second year of life but the clutches of these pairs are rarely fertile. In the winter the swans should have a nest foundation prepared for them, either on an island or on the shore of a lake; it should consist of straw, twigs and reeds. Egg-laying may start as early as February even if temperatures are near freezing point. Second broods are by no means rare. Rearing the cygnets is best left to the parents but turkey hens may be used as foster mothers. The grey-brown juveniles moult into their adult plumage in the autumn of the same year; adult coloration of bill and the development of the knob at its base take place in the following spring.

Hybridization: In 1972 an Italian magazine reported a case of a black-necked swan hybridizing with a mute swan.

Black Swan

Cygnus atratus (Latham)

Comparative Size: Smaller than mute swan.

Plumage: M. and F. adults see plate 14; dark feather parts are velvety black, bill and irids glowing red. M. usually larger than F. with a thicker neck (feathers are more ruffled); juvenile plumage dark grey with light-coloured feather edges and hardly ruffled.

NATURAL HABIT

Status: Not an endangered species; in recent times their habitats has spread out in Queensland and populations have increased in Tasmania and New Zealand (in the latter they were imported by man).

Habitat: Inland lakes surrounded by reed-grass, coastal waters, and quiet bays of large river systems. Outside the breeding season also lagoons poor in vegetation, and large lakes.

Breeding Biology: Nests are either built separately in the reeds surrounding a lake, or they are built in colonies on grassy islands of large shallow inland lakes. Full clutches consist of five to six (four to ten) rather long, grey-green eggs. Incubation takes 39–41 days (according to JOHNSTONE (1970) 36 days), and male and female take turns in incubating. Cygnets need almost six months to become fully developed and they are not sexually mature until they are three to four years old.

Migration: Predominantly infrequent migrants; outside the breeding period (end of the dry season) great flocks often gather on large areas of water.

Yearly Cycle: In tropical Queensland laying period is between February and June, rearing of the young up to October; in temperate Tasmania eggs are laid from July to September, and rearing of the young and adult moulting takes place up to February.

Climate: In Australia, black swans occur mainly in tropical and sub-tropical savannas—areas which have periodic rainfall and high temperatures; in Tasmania and New Zealand, on the other hand, warm temperate climates provide the conditions under which the black swans live.

AVICULTURE

The black swan is smaller and less aggressive than the mute swan; however, it is lust as robust, undemanding and long jived. Black swans and mute swans are likewise kept in zoos, bird preserves and on ponds in parks where they are bred and reared to maturity. Some free flying populations evolved on some western European lakes, particularly in Great Britain, but their life expectancy was short, unless food was provided all through the year.

Housing: On lakes of all sizes. It should be noted, however, that all swans need a great deal of space during the breeding season. If mute swans inhabit the same lake as the black swans, the latter usually succumb as they are by far the weaker of the two. Real peace is only possible where breeding territories do not touch or where only one pair inhabits the lake. A similar maxim applies to breeding preserves; if a lake or pond is too small, the swans put the ducks under pressure and poor breeding results would be the consequence. Black swans should spend the winter on water free of ice; where necessary a truss of straw should be built for them on shore.

Food: See mute or black-necked swan.

Breeding: Most pairs should be able to breed successfully provided they really have attained sexual maturity. Young swans pair in the second year of their life and build a nest, but egg laying does not follow. Clutches of three year old birds are normally not fertile and nests are deserted after a few days' incubation. Only birds of at least four years have a real chance of success in breeding. In common with many Australian species, black swans have a slight tendency towards breeding in the winter; either they start laying very early in the spring, or else they do not begin before the autumn. Second broods are by no means rare. It is advisable to prepare a foundation for the nest in a suitable spot (e. g. on an island); it may be made of straw or reeds and most pairs accept it gladly. The incubating is done mainly by the female, but the male takes turns to give her a chance to feed. The male's main function is in guarding the nest site and not only does he attack the ducks which may share a preserve, but he also attacks people if they come too near the nest. The cygnets stay in the nest for up to 36 hours after they have hatched, after which period the female guides them to the water. The young swans develop quickly and as the neck grows in length fairly soon, it does not take long before they can feed themselves and appear together with the adults at the feeding site. Where second broods occur the juveniles of the first brood are no longer tolerated by the family.

Hybridization: Hybridizing is known to have taken place with the greylag goose, the Canada goose as well as the whistling swan and mute swan.

Mute Swan

Cygnus olor (Gmelin)

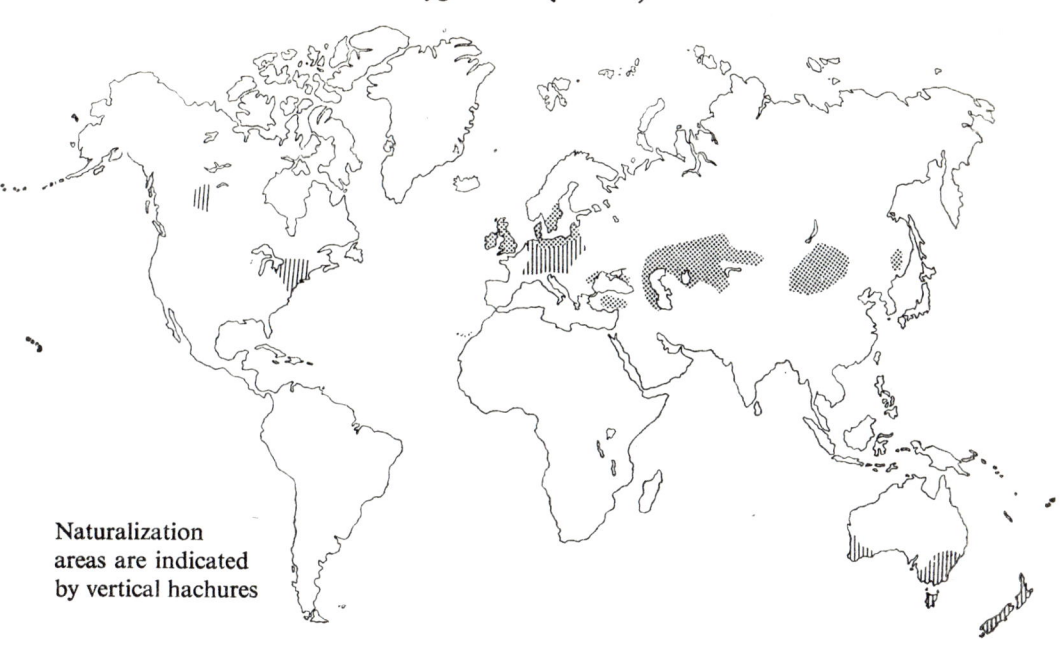

Naturalization areas are indicated by vertical hachures

Size: Approximately the same as the trumpeter and whooper swan; it is the third largest water bird; normal weight 10 to 13 kg.

Plumage: Adult F. with cygnets see plate 13; M. and F. white throughout, bill orange-red, knob at base of bill and legs black; M. has thicker neck and knob more developed than F. Cygnets' plumage dark greyish-brown, later on white interspersed with brown feathers. In parks albinos may be seen; their bills are light red and their feet are flesh-coloured (down and first plumage white in this case).

NATURAL HABIT

Status: Semi-domesticated mute swans are increasing in western and central Europe, and in certain areas their numbers have had to be curtailed. The total populations of the wild swans, however, are relatively small, but they remain constant and, at present, the species cannot be said to be threatened with extinction.

Habitat: Large inland lakes surrounded by broad banks of rushes, and coastal waters (deltas and fiords) with rich underwater vegetation within easy reach. Half-wild pairs nest on small inland lakes and rivers.

Breeding Biology: Juveniles frequently pair in the second year of their life, they are sexually mature from the third or fourth year onwards; they pair for life. Courtship display of the males reaches its climax whilst the nest site and territory are being selected. Nests are either placed among reeds, or on islands or dams. The clutch of five to seven (up to 10) grey-green eggs is incubated by the female in 35–37 days. Both parents look after the cygnets and they live as a close-knit family.

Migration: In Europe they are either stationary residents or infrequent migrants; the western part of the Baltic Sea offers the largest winter quarters. The Asiatic populations migrate to the mouths of those rivers which flow into the Black

and Caspian sea and also to the central Asiatic lakes.
Yearly Cycle: As soon as the ice thaws on the waters of their breeding grounds the swans return to them. Eggs are laid from mid-April and the young are reared in June and July. The female moults her wings from the moment she accompanies the newly hatched cygnets; males moult their wings approximately six weeks later.
Climate: Breeding grounds are predominantly in temperate latitudes; in Asia they are in the regions with summer-hot continental climates.
Wintering mute swans remain on water even under severe conditions of frost, until the water is completely covered by ice.

AVICULTURE

Mute swans have been kept and bred on lakes of parks and castles since the times of classical Greece. In European countries they experienced a rapid spread in the 19th and 20th century. Much has been done to ensure breeding success, and many people find great pleasure in feeding the swans. Much the same is now taking place in North America where the mute swan has replaced the Whooper and Whistling Swans, *Cygnus cygnus* and *Cygnus columbianus*, neither of which is very suitable for breeding and rearing. Mute swans are also settling in New Zealand.
Housing: Large ponds in parks, towns and villages as well as water areas of zoos and bird preserves; on the latter they may be kept with other hardy species. Should fencing be necessary, this has to be only approximately 50 to 70 cm high. Regular feeding will restrain the birds from wishing to escape.
Food: A coarse-grained mixture of boiled potatoes, bread and simple food for domestic fowl, corn and vegetables.
Breeding: The majority of mute swan pairs become broody each year. If their lake or pond is not overpopulated, brood and rearing are usually successful under the sole supervision of the parent birds. A nest is prepared—where possible on an island—and building materials include straw, twigs and reeds. Eggs are rarely laid before mid-April, even in the case of park swans. If a brood is unsuccessful a second clutch is quite likely. While the cygnets are accompanied by the parents, sufficient food should be provided for them on smaller ponds; on larger lakes of parks families come to their feeding places less often. The males drive away the young swans from the nest site during the winter, or—in any case—during the spring. Swans able to fly retreat to nearby lakes and ponds; pinioned birds have to be removed and taken elsewhere.
Hybridization: This is known to occur with several *Anser* species, with the Canada goose as well as with all *Cygnus* species; however, such tendencies towards hybridization are not particularly marked.

Greylag Goose
Anser anser (L.)

Size: One of the largest of the grey geese; weight 2.3 to 3.5 kg; length of body 75 to 90 cm.
Plumage: Parent birds with goslings see plate 32; pale silver-grey fore-wings and an orange or flesh-coloured bill are typical for the species. Older birds often have dark brown markings on the belly; juveniles altogether more speckled grey-brown.

NATURAL HABIT

Status: Large total populations; in countries with modern hunting laws an increase in populations is noticeable. Breed sporadically only west of the river Elbe.

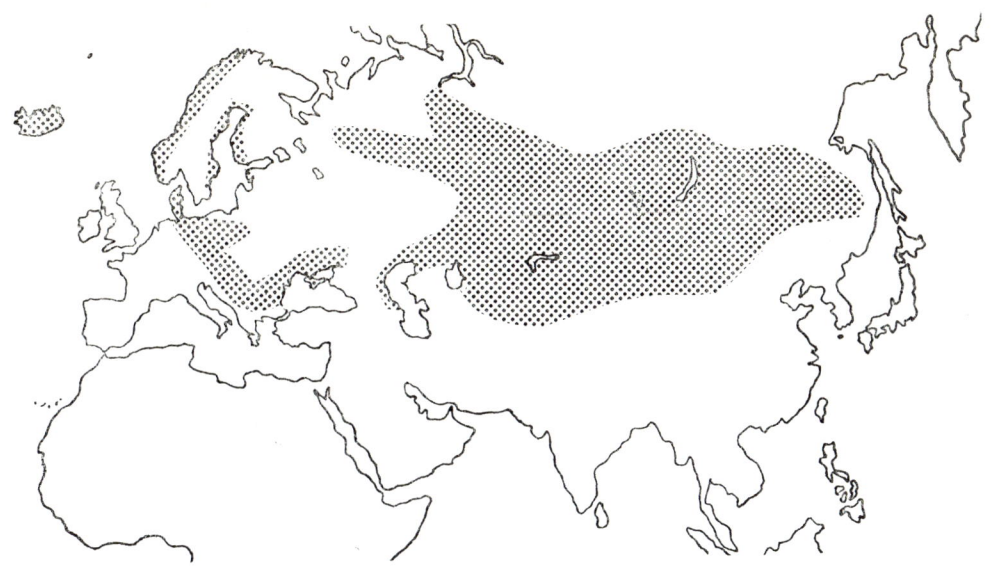

Habitat: During the breeding season large quiet lakes with broad rush banks surrounding them; otherwise islands with adjoining pasture lands; grass-grown rocky islets; shallow lakes of steppes. During the winter season, agricultural and pasture lands in the vicinity of large lakes and plains.

Breeding Biology: Juveniles pair after one year and attain sexual maturity in the second year of their life. Nests are placed in inaccessible areas of reeds, on islands and—where conditions permit it—they are built as colonies. A full clutch consists of six to nine matt white eggs; incubation takes 28–29 days. Families reside in meadows adjoining nest sites or river zones.

Migration: Predominantly birds of passage; most of the birds breeding in Europe winter in Great Britain and southwards as far as Spain; a few spend winters in North Africa and central Europe.

Yearly Cycle: Central European greylag geese arrive in their breeding grounds from February onwards and lay their eggs between mid-March and end-April. After a complete moult the adult birds again achieve full flight ability in August, coinciding with the time the juveniles have learnt to fly properly. Autumn migration is in September and October.

Climate: Breeding in temperate to cool regions of Europe, Asia and North America, also in hot zones of deserts and steppes.

AVICULTURE

Greylag geese were known and bred 2000 years ago; they are the ancestors of the domestic goose. Until quite recently peasants and fishermen collected greylag eggs and goslings—which unfortunately is illegally done even today—and reared them with their domestic fowl for eventual slaughter. Initially only zoological gardens kept greylags as ornamental waterfowl; nowadays many bird enthusiasts also take a keen interest in them. These geese are so robust that they are very suitable for being kept on large urban lakes and ponds where they look very picturesque; once they have become properly acclimatized it is possible to keep them without clipping their wings.

Housing: Ponds or lakes with adjoining meadows. If birds are kept without pinioned wings they should have a large

69

plot of land with short vegetation at their disposal (perhaps at the outskirts of town); with the lake on which they nest and their pasture close to each other. Breeders must also supply them with plenty of space for free movement, or allow them to roam together with domestic fowl.

Food: Their basic foods are the grasses and herbs they find on the meadows; additionally they are given corn or a simple food-mixture.

Breeding: Greylag geese are monogamous; when young birds pair they do so for life. If adult birds are caught and taken from their mates or if they are sold they rarely pair for a second time. However, breeding results are usually good providing there is in the flock a sufficient number or young birds ready to pair. Such pairs will produce offsprings each year, even if there is a deterioration of the conditions under which they are kept. Greylag geese are not at all particular in their selection of a nest site; they are steady breeders and faithfully accompany their goslings. It is of the utmost importance that the breeder protects his geese from predators (including hedgehogs), or adult geese, goslings and eggs alike will suffer. Development of the young geese is as follows: during the first three weeks their body growth is marked; afterwards their feathers begin to grow, and at six to seven weeks they are normally fully feathered. Once this has happened they undertake practice flights at an ever increasing rate and, when young greylag geese are 11 weeks old their wings are fully grown and developed.

Hybridization: Equally pronounced in male and female. They are known to hybridize with most *Anser* and *Branta* species as well as with mute swans, Egyptian geese and Muscovy ducks.

Lesser White-fronted Goose
Anser erythropus (L.)

Comparative Size: Considerably smaller than greylag goose and European whitefront.

Plumage: Adults see plate 33; black barring on the belly varies but increases slightly with age. The bird differs from the larger European white-front in that the white forehead extends further up the head and the ring around the eye is bright yellow. Juveniles are paler, and white forehead and belly barring are missing.

Natural Habit

Status: Total populations are obviously not endangered and are remaining constant. Lesser white-fronted geese spend winters in large numbers in the area between the Hungarian plains and the Caspian Sea.

Habitat: On grassy stretches near tundra lakes grown with low bushes; on swampy high plains, and steep slopes from the most northern Taiga zone to the southern bushy tundra areas. On the whole the birds prefer altitudes (mountain goose) in contrast to the white-fronted goose which breeds in the plains.

Breeding Biology: Lesser white-fronted geese breed in single pairs, not in colonies. A nest mound is scraped underneath a bush, in the heather or next to large stones. Later it is lined with grasses and down. A full clutch consists of from four to eight rough-shelled white eggs. Incubation takes 25–28 days. Parents and goslings stay near the water and—in case of danger—hide under pygmy bushes. Juveniles are able to fly when they are five weeks old and attain sexual maturity in the second year of their life.

Migration: Bird of passage; spends winters in large flocks in the vicinity of extensive water areas in the continental steppes and prefers grass landscapes to agricultural land.

Yearly Cycle: Lesser white-fronted geese return to their breeding grounds in early May (Lapland) and June (Siberia). Eggs are normally laid in June; incubation, rearing of the young and moult of adults take place up until August; in September the birds migrate to their winter quarters.

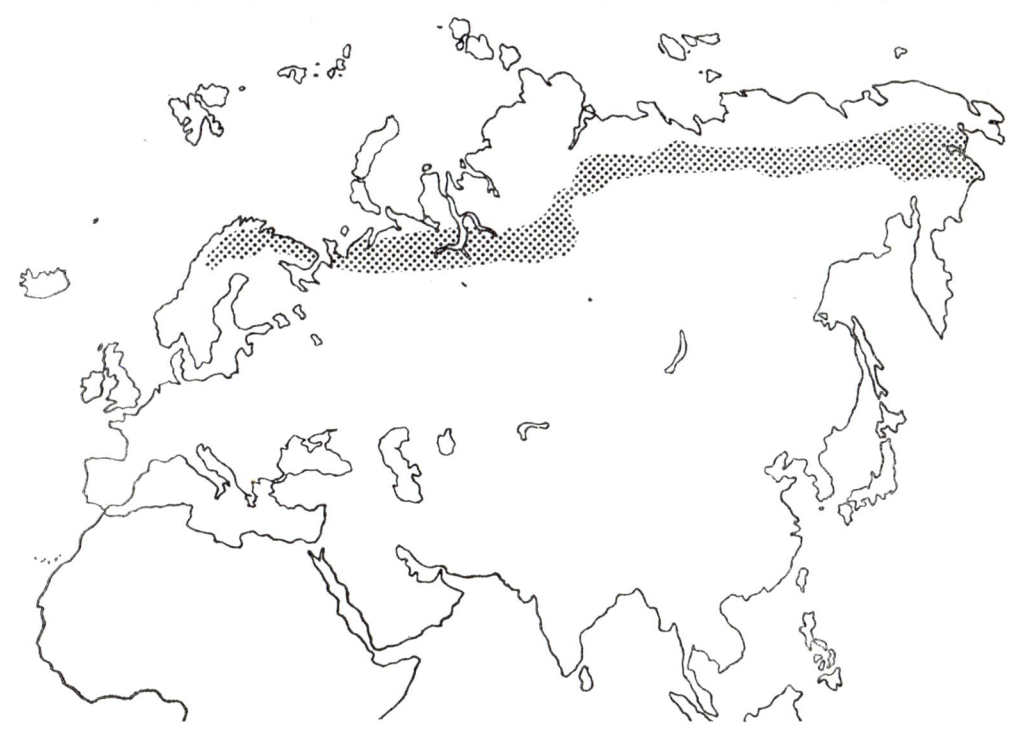

Climate: In the breeding grounds the period of good vegetation lasts four months; then follows a winter lasting eight months. Although average temperatures are only 15°C in July, a wealth of plant life nevertheless develops during the long days of summer.

AVICULTURE

Lesser white-fronted geese can often be seen in private parks and in zoological gardens. The majority of birds kept in West European preserves have been reared in captivity which makes further breeding relatively easy. On the other hand the larger white-fronted geese are nearly all caught wild and thus have only a low rate of reproduction as they lack the breeding stimulus. A not very experienced breeder might do well to consider keeping the lesser white-fronted geese; they are undemanding and peaceable, their plumage always remains smooth and their quiet dignified behaviour makes them attractive birds to look after.

Housing: Either in pairs or in small groups where good grass is available; as they are not quarrelsome they can be kept together with small ducks. Although the geese prefer large lakes with good quality water, smaller ponds neither interfere with their well-being nor with their breeding impulse.

Food: Their basic food should be the grasses they find for themselves; additionally they should be given some wheat and a simple food-mixture.

Breeding: The lesser white-fronted geese of preserves are always monogamous and, among adult birds, a change of mates is difficult and may take a long time. It is therefore practical to build up a group of young birds for breeding purposes. If pairs form within the group, breeding results should soon follow. Eggs are laid between the end of April and June; they are laid in quiet spots of the preserve—in high grass, under bushes, on islands of a pond, or even in boxes. The female breeds inconspicuously and reliably and, once the eggs have been hatched, she accompanies the goslings together with the gander. Losses or damage to eggs and goslings are rare. The thick down plumage of the goslings makes it easier for them to bear cool weather rather than hot summer days; in periods of prolonged rain they should be driven into a dry place—at least during the night. When they are approximately six months old the coloration of their plumage changes into that of the mature bird; the white forehead and dark barring on the belly are obtained after moulting, the ring around the eye turns yellow.

Hybridization: Unmated birds have a strong tendency to interbreed with all *Anser* and the smaller *Branta* species.

Pink-footed Goose
Anser brachyrhynchus Baillon

Comparative Size: Approximately the same as greylag goose and white-fronted goose.

Plumage: Adults see plate 35; M. and F. have the same coloration. The bird differs from the bean goose by having a short bill with a pink band near the bill tip and by having pink (as opposed to orange) legs. Juveniles are similar to adults, but the band on the bill is a pale pink and the plumage of the body is washed-out brown.

Natural Habit

Status: Although breeding and winter quarters are very confined, the species is not endangered; in fact, since 1960 a marked increase has been noticeable.

Habitat: On Greenland and Spitzbergen they favour rocky, cleft grass plateaux of the mountain ranges; in Iceland swampy meadows and moors which are rich in vegetation and fill the very wide valleys at the bottom of the glaciers. In the winter the pink-footed geese graze on fields, meadows, and marshes.

Breeding Biology: Nests are built in loosely-knit colonies, on narrow, rocky ledges or in tundra meadows, areas which can be easily watched over. A clutch of five to eight yellow-white eggs is incubated by the female in 28 days. The gander guards the nest territory; later on, both parents accompany the yellow/olive-green goslings.

Migration: Birds nesting in Greenland and Iceland winter in Great Britain; those that breed in Spitzbergen migrate via Denmark along the North Sea coast to Holland.

Yearly Cycle: Arrival in breeding grounds first half of May (Iceland) to June (Greenland); egg laying begins a few days after arrival. Wing moult of mature birds takes place at the same time as the young are fledged; this is in August. In September they depart for their winter quarters where they arrive in October.

Climate: Pink-footed geese arrive in their breeding grounds as the snow is thawing; night frosts during the breeding season are by no means rare and even occur while the young are being reared during the Arctic summer.

AVICULTURE

The pink-footed goose is closely related to the various types of bean geese. Originally bird preserves and zoos only managed to obtain birds while they were staying in their winter quarters and accordingly different sub-species could be seen in different places: the East Asiatic Thick-billed Bean Goose, *Anser fabalis serrirostris*, in Japan; the Western and Russian Bean Goose, *Anser f. fabalis* and *Anser f. rossicus*, in central and eastern Europe; and—particularly in Great Britain—the pink-footed goose.

Housing: All these geese are very suitable for keeping in spacious preserves with large areas of grass. The birds are long-lived, undemanding and good natured towards all species of ducks.

Food: See lesser white-fronted goose.

Breeding: As a general rule, wild birds in captivity need a very long time to become acclimatized and to start breeding. In November 1970, I was given an adult female with a damaged wing. As early as the following summer the goose started making a nest mould, carried nesting material and—when I came near her—pushed her body close to the ground, behaviour which is typical of breeding pink-footed geese. In January 1973 I was given a gander which had lived in the Berlin Tierpark for 12 years. In April the two birds were observed at courtship display and the female's belly looked as though she was ready for laying. However, towards the end of May the breeding stimulus decreased. In 1974 the geese were observed to be copulating and the first proper nest was built in 1975. But not a single egg had been laid up to 1976.

Nowadays the pink-footed goose is kept very successfully in western Europe, particularly in Great Britain. Most of these birds have been bred in captivity and are therefore imbued with a far greater breeding stimulus then captured wild geese. *The Institut für Verhaltensforschung* (Institute of Ethology), Seewiesen, Oberbayern, found out May 1st as the mean average for the beginning of the breeding season.

Hybridization: Apparently very pronounced with all *Anser* species; in Seewiesen 50 per cent of all broods of the pink-footed goose are from mates of a different species.

Bar-headed Goose
Anser indicus (Latham)

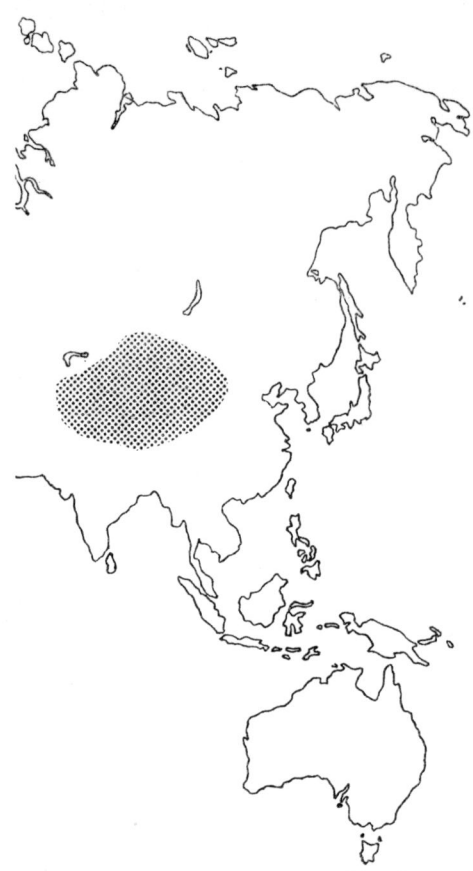

Comparative Size: Similar to white-fronted and greylag goose.

Plumage: Parent birds and goslings see plate 19; overall coloration pale silver-grey, dark parts of the neck black-brown; bill and legs yellow to orange-red. Juveniles indistinct brown-grey, lines on the neck are missing; bill and legs yellow-green.

NATURAL HABIT

Status: The breeding grounds of the bar-headed goose are situated in such inaccessible places of high mountain zones where only few human settlements can be found and civilization has so far not endangered them. Although some migrating birds may be shot over the Indian sub-continent, no stock curtailment has been noticeable as yet.

Habitat: River courses, lakes, moors and swampy plains in the zones of continental mountain steppes and high plateaux, the latter 4,000 to 5,000 m high; they spend the winters in lower altitudes on pastures and agricultural lands.

Breeding Biology: When the first rivers thaw and become free of ice pairs of bar-headed geese arrive in their breeding grounds. Nests are built in loose-knit colonies either on rocky ledges along the river courses, or in trees in old nests of birds of prey, or—most of all—on grassy islands on the lakes of the steppes. A full clutch consists of four to five pale cream eggs; incubation takes 28–30 days. Goslings are guided to the water (or they may jump off the rocky slopes), and there they are looked after by both parents.

Migration: Some bar-headed geese wander down to lower lying valleys of Tibet, but the majority flies across the Himalayas and winters in the mountains further to the south; a few fly to the Indian plains. Migrating bar-headed geese have been sighted (honking!) in the Himalayas at heights of 8,500 and 9,000 m.

Yearly Cycle: The well-known German Tibet explorer, E. SCHÄFER reported on the breeding populations of East Tibet: "Returning birds arrive in mid-April and begin laying at the beginning of May. Those that do not breed moult in June, whereas the adults which accompany their young moult in July. In September they all return to their winter quarters."

Climate: The climate on the high plateaux resembles that of the northern tundras. After the cold of the winter, mild spring weather begins in April followed by warm summer months; winds are always cool.

AVICULTURE

Bar-headed geese are not often kept by breeders. On the other hand, they can be seen in most zoos, quite often with their young during the summer months. On the whole, the requirements of the animal trade were met by cheap birds imported from their winter quarters (hence the name Indian bar-headed goose) and there seemed to be a general lack of interest to increase captive bird populations by breeding them. However, as these geese are not at all problematical and a chance of breeding them successfully is well above average, they are worth recommending to beginners and those breeders whose facilities are not suited to successful breeding of the Brent goose and red-breasted goose. In Western Europe, several groups of bar-headed geese are kept without having had their wings pinioned; in Sweden (Kalmarsund) they have been introduced by Bengt BERG and there they now breed freely.

Housing: Breeders keep the geese—together with others—on lawns and in parks; like the greylag goose they are suitable birds for urban parks, to which they add considerable colour. However, they do need a large and well sheltered area of water. It is possible to let them spend winters out in the open.

Food: See other *Anser* species.

Breeding: Bar-headed geese, like the greylag and snow goose, are easy to breed. The majority of birds sold nowadays may be assumed to have been bred in captivity. They attain sexual maturity in the second or third year of their life. Nests are made on the ground under cover of vegetation, on islands and—quite frequently—in small huts. In the rough weather conditions of Erzgebirge (GDR) and the damp British sea climate of the Wildfowl Trust eggs are laid between April 15th and 25th; roughly at the same time the Berlin Tierpark's bar-headed geese lay their eggs. Although second clutches may be expected, the breeder should leave the female to do the incubating and the pair to look after the young.

Hybridization: Very marked within the *Anser* species; bar-headed geese also interbreed with the *Branta* and *Tadorna* species. However, in such hybrid relationships the birds are either without a mate of their own species or single birds.

Snow Goose
Anser caerulescens (L.)

Comparative Size: Approximately the same as white-fronted and greylag goose.

Plumage: White phase lesser snow goose see plate 17; blue phase lesser snow goose see plate 16; both variants occur within the same areas of distribution. White phase: only the primary wing feathers are black.

Juvenile plumage initially light brown; intermingled with white feathers at an increasing rate later on. Blue phase: upper part of body greyish blue, head and neck always white, chest and belly white in some birds; juveniles very dark throughout. In both phases adult birds have an orange coloured bill with broad rows of black lamellae along the sides of the mandibles.

NATURAL HABIT

Status: The geese breed in approximately 20 very large colonies; it is thought that the largest is on Wrangel Island (N. E. Siberia) with circa 130,000 breeding pairs. In 1965 it was estimated that the total population of the geese amounted to 1 to 1.5 million birds.

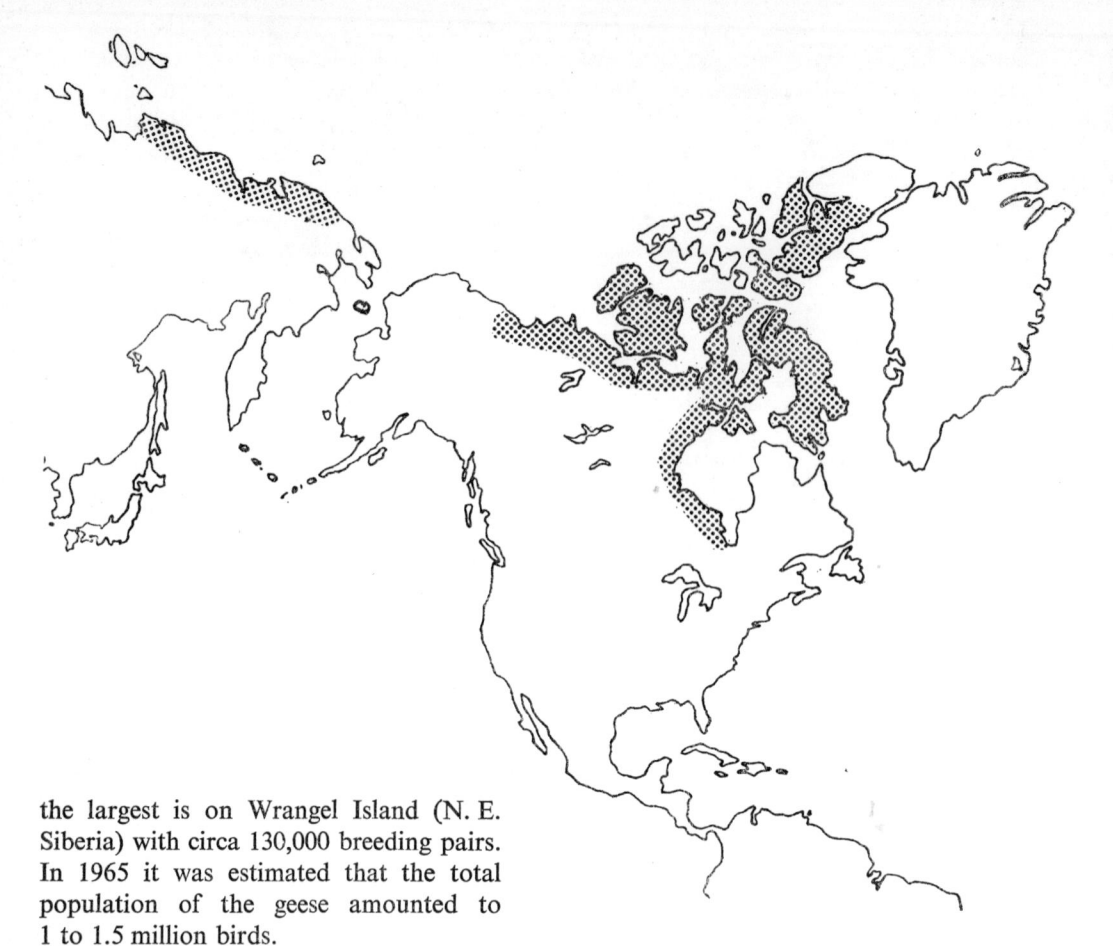

Habitat: Locations of brood colonies are on dry elevations and islands of river plains near the coast and in wide, wind-sheltered inland valleys in the region of the Arctic tundra. Here a wealth of vegetation develops during the three summer months, particularly as the previous year's goose droppings have made the soil very fertile. The geese spend the winters on cultivated agricultural lands near large water areas.

Breeding Biology: Snow geese arrive in their breeding grounds—paired and with eggs fully ready for laying in the oviduct of the female. Nests are in loose colonies which may be stretched over many square kilometres. A full clutch consists of four to six white eggs; incubation takes 23 days. Once breeding is completed the moulting adults gather in large flocks with their goslings and migrate to the moist tundra valleys. Juveniles are able to fly when they are seven weeks old.

Migration: Canadian and Siberian lesser snow geese migrate in huge flocks as far as the southern states of the USA, especially to Louisiana, Texas and California.

Yearly Cycle: The geese arrive on Wrangel Island during the last days of May; 10–12 days later all the females have begun laying, even those whose arrival has been somewhat delayed. The adults moult in July while the young are maturing. From early August onwards the lesser snow geese migrate to their wintering quarters where they stay from October to March.

Climate: All breeding grounds lie in the zones of arctic cold temperatures where the summer period has a duration of at most three months at an average temperature of 5–10 °C. On the other hand, at that time the 24 hour polar day allows the ground to thaw, at least on the surface, so that a rich, fast growing, short-lived vegetation develops.

Aviculture

Presumably snow geese were not imported into Europe before the turn of the century. Ther Berlin Zoo had a number of North American waterfowl in its collection as early as 1888, among them trumpeter swans, Canada geese and also Hawaiian geese but snow geese were missing. Some juveniles—hybrids of a blue phase and a white phase lesser snow goose—were reared there in 1898, but purely white phase broods were not achieved until 1924. Nowadays, many zoos and bird preserves rear and breed them successfully; however the smaller sub-species—the blue and white phase lesser snow goose—is more frequent than the greater Atlantic snow goose.

Housing: Because they are peaceable, hardy and able to withstand the rigours of winter, snow geese may be kept together with other waterfowl in small ornamental preserves as well as on large lakes in parks. In Great Britain particularly, several groups are kept without having had their wings clipped; however, it has to be noted that quite often some of these wander off or migrate.

Food: They are very undemanding but should have a good opportunity for grazing.

Breeding: The majority of snow geese inhabiting European preserves are bred in captivity. When juvenile pairs are put together they become broody—almost without exception—in the second or third year. Successful brood results follow as a rule. Pairing a mature bird reared in captivity with a wild captured bird can apparently be done more easily with snow geese than with other species of geese. They lay their eggs either in nest boxes or in solitary nests on the ground. A prepared cavity, 15 cm deep and 80 × 80 cm in area, filled with grass and grass roots, may well induce the birds to use it as a nest. The material makes it easy for the female to turn it into a nest and she can use the soft grass to cover her eggs during the laying period. Eggs are normally laid between mid-April and early May. Incubation and rearing are quite easy with or without parent birds; however, where local conditions allow it, both should be left to the parents.

Hybridization: Very pronounced, particularly with *Anser* and *Branta* species. A breeder should keep unpaired snow geese apart from other species.

Emperor Goose

Anser canagicus Sewastianow

Comparative Size: Approximately the same as greylag and white-fronted goose.

Plumage: Adults see plate 34; one-year old M. and F. see plate 36; upper part of the body and wing coverts pale blue-grey with narrow black and white seams at the tips of the feathers; in juveniles grey-brown with feather tips brownish and cream-yellow. With many of the birds (even juveniles) bill of the M. relatively long and predominantly colour of red flesh; that of the F. shorter and predominantly black.

Natural Habit

Status: Total population is small because of restricted breeding ranges; breeding grounds are mainly along the coasts. Moreover, there are signs at present that a further decline in numbers cannot be ruled out.

Habitat: Closely linked to oceanic coasts throughout the year. Feeding and nest territories are in areas beyond the tidal line on shallow coasts where driftwood and other material deposited by the sea exists in plenty and salt marshes and coastal tundras with small ponds and good vegetation provide nourishment.

Breeding Biology: Because of the short arctic summer, pairing takes place either in the winter quarters or on the migratory flight to breeding grounds. In the latter fights may take place in defence of a nest territory; the ganders are very aggressive by nature. Nests are normally made either amongst the driftwood beyond the tidal line or in the tundra. A full clutch consists of four to eight eggs which are incubated for 24–25 days. The goslings are reared either at the ocean's edge or on the banks of the tundra ponds.

Migration: Emperor geese winter on the coasts of the Aleutian and Komandorskie Islands, the Kamchatka Peninsula and the Kuril Islands. Some of them, particularly non-breeders, undertake moulting flights in a northerly direction (e. g. St. Lawrence Island).

Yearly Cycle: Arrival in breeding grounds end-May/early June; laying begins a few days later; incubation normally starts mid-June and the young are reared while adults moult in July and August. Migration to wintering grounds in September.

Climate: Arctic tundra climate; in places without shelter, cold polar winds blow and temperatures can drop to freezing point even at the time when the goslings are hatching.

Aviculture

Emperor geese were imported for the first time rather later than other geese (1908) and only in small numbers. Up to the 1950s they were almost entirely on show in large zoos only and were bred very rarely. Keeping them and feeding them was regarded as difficult, probably because captured birds were difficult to acclimatize and easily succumbed to disease. Present-day emperor geese in Europe and the States are predominantly birds reared and bred in captivity; their life expectancy is in line with that of other northern species of geese.

Housing: Preserves with large ranges of healthy short turf containing a lake with clear cold water. Actually nowadays it is possible to breed some birds in relatively small enclosures with an artificial water basin.

Food: Basic food should be the same as for other species of geese. Additionally, animal protein should be given (shrimps and ground meat or fishmeal). In my preserve, emperor geese gladly accept small pieces of fish, which is thrown into the water for marine ducks and mergansers.

Breeding: Just a few years after first importing the geese into Europe, BLAAUW (Netherlands) and the DUKE OF BEDFORD (UK) managed broods for the first time. But only few birds survived the Second World War. JONES of Leckford (UK) received some imported emperor geese just after the war and in 1952 they laid eggs for the first time. Nowadays this species is bred very successfully.

The breeding process hardly differs from that of other *Anser* species. Nests are made either in boxes, in short grass on the ground or—a favourite spot—on islands. In the Wildfowl Trust, Slimbridge, egg laying begins in the last ten days of April; in JONES' preserve at the beginning of May; in the Tierpark, Berlin, in the first half of May; and in Peakirk Park (UK) at the end of May and early in June. It is advisable to leave incubation and accompanying the goslings to the parents themselves. The goslings grow very fast, but they are sensitive to heat and strong sunlight.

Hybridization: They tend to interbreed with several *Anser* species but are also known to have interbred with the Brent and Magellan goose. To avoid hybrids as much as possible, new arrivals of emperor geese should be kept apart from other species—particularly single birds without mates—until they have chosen a mate amongst their own kind.

Brent Goose
Branta bernicla (L.)

NATURAL HABIT

Comparative Size: Considerably smaller than greylag or white-fronted goose.

Plumage: Adult birds and goslings see plate 18; head, chest and back always slate-grey, belly side to flanks lighter or brownish—according to sub-species; the small white patches on the neck which form a ring also vary according to sub-species; upper feathers of juveniles fringed with light brown and the white ring around the neck is lacking.

Status: Rapid decline in numbers since about the turn of the century because the Eelgrass *Zostera*—their main food in the winter—was destroyed by a fungus disease in the Atlantic and Pacific feeding grounds (including adjoining seas). Total number of dark-bellied Brents at the end of the 1960s was estimated as 23,000 to 25,000.

Habitat: River plains near the coasts, and

deltas with numbers of small islands, also fresh-water lakes and river courses of the arctic tundra which lacks trees and bushes. Outside the breeding season mainly found on the estuaries of the sea coasts.

Breeding Biology: Nests are built either singly or in small colonies, in the tundra vegetation, on dry ground but near water. Initially the nest is lined with lichen and moss and later with plenty of down. The three to six eggs are greenish or bluish-white. Incubation takes 24–26 days. For rearing their young and moulting their wings the mature geese wander off to larger lakes or river courses where several families join up and communally look after their goslings. Young geese attain sexual maturity in the second or third year of their life.

Migration: The northern European and western Asiatic Brent geese migrate in narrow lines to the southern North Sea and the French coast; many spend the winters on coastal stretches of eastern Asia and on the coasts of the USA.

Yearly Cycle: They return to their breeding grounds and begin egg laying a few days after the main thaw of the snow on June; migration to the south is from mid-August to September. Brent geese stay in their west European winter grounds from October to March, at times until May.

Climate: Compares with lesser snow goose and emperor goose.

AVICULTURE

Because of their very specific (natural) food requirements for eelgrass, green algae and sea molluscs, rearing in captivity of captured and imported Brent geese presented difficulties for a long time; their average life expectancy was probably no more than approximately five years. Even after a very long period of acclimatization and pairing few birds showed any stimulus for breeding. A first successful brood was achieved in Boston (UK) in 1953 with birds which had inhabited the preserve since 1939. The chances of obtaining breeding results are far better with birds reared in captivity.

Housing: Large enclosures with a short and healthy amount of turf and a lake which contains cold, clear water. A few trees are essential to provide shade when needed.

Food: Corn, formulated food and additional animal foods such as shrimps and a meal consisting of organic matter and blood.

If fish is fed in some enclosures (e. g. to mergansers, shelducks and eider ducks) the Brents enjoy snatching at some pieces which may be thrown to them.

Breeding: As previously mentioned, breeding the Brent goose in captivity was successful for the first time in 1953. Up to the end of the 1960s, results were unsatisfactory; only the Black Brent, *Branta bernicla orientalis*, was relatively easy to breed. Nowadays, a number of enthusiasts—particularly in Great Britain—keep birds bred in captivity; they inhabit small enclosures where they breed and rear their goslings. Such birds are far less frail and easier to keep than the former, captured and imported geese. In the British Wildfowl Trust eggs are laid between May 5th and June 1st. Captured wild pairs make their nests in the grass of a quiet spot in the preserve, but those reared in captivity also use boxes and large baskets for nest building and egg laying. Rearing of the goslings does not present any particular problem; however, they should not be exposed to too much warmth.

Hybridization: Some tendency to interbreed with *Anser* and *Branta* species; long before the first Brent geese were bred, goslings of mixed parentage existed.

Canada Goose
Branta canadensis (L.)

Comparative Size: Giant and Atlantic Canada geese are approximately swan-sized; the lesser Canada goose is roughly the size of a greylag, and the Hutchinsons Canada goose is similar in size to the Brent goose.

Plumage: See plate 20; coloration of plumage is similar in all sub-species; variations do occur in light and dark tones and also between brown and slate-grey tones in the plumage. Feathers of juveniles have broad white tips.

NATURAL HABIT

Status: The size of total populations varies greatly amongst the various races, and it is linked closely to the size of habitats of each and the specific, ecological demands that are made. Human intervention may have considerable local effect. The Atlantic Canada goose has a population of 3,000 in Great Britain and 4,500 in Scandinavia; they owe their existence in these areas to people who introduced them there.

Habitat: The smaller kinds breed on lakes and river courses of the tundras. The larger Canada geese inhabit inland lakes (particularly in the prairie areas) in the manner of our greylags, also river courses and boggy plains. They spend the winters on pasture and agricultural lands.

Breeding Biology: Canada geese are monogamous and pairs normally last for life; as a nesting site the female chooses either a small island in a lake or river, or the swamp vegetation on the banks of a river, or a dry place in the tundra near some water. The birds may nest by themselves or in colonies. A full clutch contains five to six (up to 11) cream-coloured eggs; incubation period of the Hutchinsons Canada goose is 24–25 days, of the Atlantic Canada goose 28–30 days. Young birds are able to fly when they are seven to nine weeks old; they are sexually mature from the 3rd year onwards (sometimes earlier).

Migration: North American nesting birds migrate to USA states near the coasts southwards as far as the Gulf of Mexico; most of the British birds are stationary residents, and the Scandinavian geese spend the winters anywhere from the Baltic coast of the GDR to the Netherlands.

Yearly Cycle: Tundra inhabiting species compare with emperor and Brent goose. In breeding grounds of the prairies the geese stay from April to September, in those of Europe from March to September.

Eggs are laid between March and June.

Climate: Hutchinsons Canada geese breed under the conditions of the short, arctic summer; European and all other American populations live in temperate or in cool boreal climate.

AVICULTURE

The large Canada geese inhabit a similar ecological niche in North America as the greylags in Europe and Asia; the smaller tundra species' habits are more in line with other marine geese. It is therefore easy to see why the Atlantic Canada goose has settled and been reared in Europe for a long time (since about 1678). The small Hutchinsons Canada goose is quite easy to breed in captivity nowadays, but its numbers in bird preserves are insignificant.

Housing: Large Canada geese are especially suitable for being kept on large lakes in parks where there are adjoining meadows. They also add colour to such a setting. Young birds may be kept on the waters on which they have been reared without having their wings pinioned; they show little inclination for migration. Hutchinsons Canada geese are also undemanding in their requirements and quite hardy, but if a breeder wishes to be successful with them he has to put at their disposal a spacious enclosure with good turf and a fairly large pond.

Food: The same as other geese.

Breeding: For the large geese, nests should be prepared as for swans; on large park lakes they breed in company with greylags either on reeds or muskrat mounds. Hutchinsons Canada geese prefer boxes, especially on islands. All Canada geese are very quarrelsome during the breeding season; they defend their nest territory, e. g. the island on which they may be breeding, and their behaviour may become vicious. In the British Wildfowl Trust the Atlantic, Moffitts and giant Canada geese start laying from early March; Hutchinsons Canada geese rarely lay before May.

In the Trust five to six different races of Canada geese breed every year and 10–12 sub-species have been cared for there. The breeder will be able only in a few cases to make certain to which exact race his birds belong; for instance, it is difficult to tell the difference between Moffitts and Atlantic Canada geese.

Hybridization: Very pronounced tendencies to hybridize with *Anser* and *Branta* species; it has also been reported that the Canada goose has interbred with the black, trumpeter, whooper and mute swans, the Muscovy duck and the Egyptian goose.

Barnacle Goose
Branta leucopsis (Bechstein)

Comparative Size: A little smaller than white-fronted or greylag goose.

Plumage: Adult birds see plate 21; parts of the back and wing coverts light grey with brown overtones, the rest of the bird, including legs, bill and irides black and white. Slight differences occur in markings and coloration. Juveniles overall more brownish in colour.

NATURAL HABIT

Status: It has been possible to make a fairly exact count of the birds' numbers in their winter quarters; in 1959/60 the total world population totalled between 30,000 and 37,000 barnacle geese. Protective measures have been taken (in many countries there is a total ban on hunting them) and their numbers have risen at a continuing rate.

Habitat: They breed near the coast in bare, rocky landscapes; nests are built on rocky terraces, cliffs and ledges, often high above the water. They find their food in the rich vegetation of the gravel banks in river plains and fiords. They winter in flooded meadows, in estuarine mud flats, and on grassland near the coast.

Breeding Biology: Barnacle geese pair and return to their arctic breeding grounds in small troops. Nests are built in small colonies on narrow ledges, cliffs or steep rocky walls up to 100 m above the water so that they are inaccessible to the polar fox. A full clutch consists of four to six pale yellowish eggs; incubation takes 24–26 days. It is generally taken that at least some of the goslings are carried down to the water in the parents' bill; most of them jump down by themselves, however. The young geese are able to fly when they are seven weeks old.

Migration: Barnacle geese nesting in Greenland and Spitzbergen migrate in narrow lines to the north-west of Great Britain and Ireland; the birds breeding in west Siberia migrate to the Netherlands via Schleswig Holstein.

Yearly Cycle: Arrival in breeding grounds from mid-May onwards; laying starts from end-May onwards. By the beginning of September the last of the barnacle geese have left their breeding grounds. They remain in their North Sea winter quarters from October to February.

Climate: See pink-footed goose.

AVICULTURE

Apart from the Canada goose, the barnacle goose is the marine goose which is most frequently kept and reared in zoos and by private breeders. The very attractively marked birds are much less demanding than the Brent and red-breasted goose and—even during their breeding season—they are completely peaceable. British breeders say that the maximum age a barnacle goose has reached (unpinioned) is 32 years (in one other case 23).

Housing: Communal preserves with good opportunities for grazing on pastureland. On large lakes, barnacle geese may be kept without having their wings clipped, but it is recommended that only the birds which have been reared there and thus are too well established to fly off should be allowed full freedom and not be pinioned.

Food: Mixed corn and a commercial food mixture; if the area for grazing is insufficient they should always have additional vegetables or carrots.

Breeding: Although it is known that, in some cases, the birds have needed between eight and ten years to become acclimatized, the barnacle goose has nevertheless been bred successfully for a long time (in the London Zoo since 1850); in the British Wildfowl Trust more than 300 young birds have grown to maturity between 1952 and 1972. But the barnacle is another species of goose where results are likely to be best with birds bred in captivity and paired within the first two or three years of their life. Eggs are laid between the beginning of April and mid-June (on the whole, in the second half of April). It is best to leave incubation and rearing of the goslings to the parents; losses of goslings are rare. For young and mature birds the main source of nourishment is grass so that in communal preserves with an adequate amount of pasture, no additional food has to be given.

Hybridization: Very marked tendency: unmated barnacle geese should be kept separate from other species of geese until they are firmly paired.

Red-breasted Goose
Branta ruficollis (Pallas)

Comparative Size: Considerably smaller than white-fronted goose.

Plumage: Adult M. see plate 38. Males, several years old, often with neck feathers elongated into a kind of mane; somewhat larger than females. In juvenile plumage all black feathers, particularly on the underside, edged with broad light seams; chest brown.

NATURAL HABIT

Status: Total population is estimated at 50,000 birds. For that reason the red-breasted goose—although not yet threatened with extinction—belongs to one of the most endangered and therefore most protected species.

Habitat: Breeds on steep, loamy slopes of river valleys, grown with grass and scrub and eroded with many fissures; also on rocky slopes as well as on small islands of the inhospitable wooded and bush-grown tundra. Rearing of the goslings on wind-sheltered pastures, never far from a pool.

Breeding Biology: The arctic fox is the red-breasted goose's worst enemy. To protect themselves from this danger the geese build nests in small colonies, either on steep slopes or in the immediate vicinity of nesting sites of the Peregrine falcon, or within colonies of sea gulls. A clutch consists of three to six yellow to light-green eggs; incubation takes 23–25 days. The gander guards the nest at a slight distance. The Peregrine falcons are indeed careful watchers, and their behaviour warns the breeding red-breasted geese of threatening danger.

Migration: Red-breasted geese migrate in narrow lines through Kasakhstan to the saline steppes on the south-east of the Caspian Sea. Approximately 40,000 red-breasted geese spend the winter in the area. Their occurrence during the winter in central Europe, Hungary and—especially—south of the Danube delta in Roumania (in December 1968), 25,000 of the geese were sighted here, in other winters 3,000 to 6,000), leads to the assumption that their migratory direction may have changed.

Yearly Cycle: Arrival in breeding grounds at the beginning of June; eggs are laid immediately afterwards and then incubated. The young are reared until August and the moult of the adults takes place at the same time. They start to migrate in September and arrive in their winter quarters in October/November.

Climate: Arctic tundra climate with low temperatures in summer (average in June circa 10°C), occasional frosts and very cold winds. In their winter quarters the birds often have to contend with severe frost and heavy snow-fall.

AVICULTURE

They were imported into Europe rather late and always in small numbers so that the beautiful red-breasted geese were quite rare and could be seen only in some large zoos and few private preserves. About 1960 the Soviet Union sent several large export consignments of the geese to western Europe and from there they also reached North America. Because of the low numbers of the total populations of the red-breasted goose, the birds are now strictly protected in the Soviet Union and no further birds are exported. Those that live in Europe and the USA have to maintain their numbers by breeding in captivity.

Housing: In large enclosures with healthy turf. Red-breasted geese like ponds with clear cold water, but are willing to settle for less favourable conditions. Once pairs have formed and reared young, they can be put into a smaller area where their stimulus to breed does not suffer. Red-breasted geese are not at all quarrelsome, they are hardy in the winter and, as a general rule, they are long-lived (15–20 years is by no means uncommon).

Food: Provided snow does not cover the ground, red-breasted geese should always have adequate opportunities for grazing; additionally they are given a mixture consisting of corn and mixed food. They do not need any extra protein supplements.

Breeding: First record of breeding results was in England in 1926, with birds which had lived in preserves for 13 years. Since 1960, breeding results have been reported from—amongst others—the Wildfowl Trust, Slimbridge, the Animal Park at Walsrode, and some private enthusiasts. Nowadays, this goose is bred quite regularly in western Europe and the relation of captured birds towards birds bred in captivity continually shifts in favour of the latter; again, it should be borne in mind that breeding results are far more likely to be achieved with birds reared in preserves than with captured and imported wild birds.

In preserves eggs are normally laid in June, by preference on a short-cut lawn, more rarely underneath bushes, in huts or on islands. Incubation is done by the females, but as the clutches and parent birds may be endangered by predators, occasionally it may be advisable to incubate the eggs by turkey hens or in incubators. Whenever possible, the goslings should be looked after by the parents themselves.

Hybridization: Once red-breasted geese have paired they are unlikely to copulate with strange species. Single birds or those which have not yet found a permanent mate like to attach themselves to other species of geese and may pair with them.

Hawaiian Goose

Branta sandvicensis (Vigors)

Comparative Size: Roughly the same as the red-breasted goose, but longer legged and therefore appears larger.

Plumage: Plate 37 depicts an immature bird in the second year of life; in adults sides of neck lighter and more deeply furrowed. Feathers of back and flanks have clear pale borders.

Natural Habit

Status: Owing to a very small area of distribution the total population has always been limited; however, early in the 19th century there were circa 25,000 Hawaiian geese. By 1950 there were less than 20 birds left. Later, rigid protective measures in the vulcanic mountains of Hawaii had good effect. The present stock of the geese consists of several hundred in their natural environment to which roughly 500 inhabitants of zoos have to be added as well as several pairs kept by West European and American breeders.

Habitat: On sparsely grown stretches of old lava flows on the higher strata and slopes of volcanos, approximately 2,000 m high. Alpine grasses, berry and alpine rose bushes make up the poor vegetation. Watering places usually quite distant.

Breeding Biology: Nests are placed between slabs of lava; they are mounds dug into the earth, and at the beginning of incubation they are lined with down. A clutch consists of three to seven (more usually 5) cream-coloured eggs. Incubation takes 29–30 days. The goslings mature slowly; only when they are 12–14 weeks old do they have feathers and are able to fly.

Migration: The time they are not breeding Hawaiian geese spend in the lower lying regions of the same island.

Yearly Cycle: Hawaiian geese are definite winter breeders; their clutches of eggs have been found between November and February. Because the tropical nights are so long the Hawaiian geese mature and develop slowly compared with the northern species of geese. The whole period of breeding, including moult of the adults, takes six to seven months in the case of the Hawaiian geese; the Brent and red-breasted geese need only three to four months.

Climate: The Hawaii Islands are in a zone of sub-tropical sea climate with yearly average temperatures (in areas which lie below the habitat of the geese) of 23°C; rainfall is high troughout the year.

Aviculture

The Ne-ne (this is the Polynesian name for the Hawaiian goose) has given a good deal of concern to many conservationists, zoological experts, and breeders throughout the world since the 1950s. Joint efforts to save the species—particularly by the British Wildfowl Trust where approximately 500 Ne-nes have grown to maturity since 1952—have stabilized the population to such an extent that since the autumn of 1973 some birds could even be sold. This has made them once again accessible to breeders.

Housing: Preserves with large areas of grass; a pond is not a necessity; where climate is not favourable the geese have to be provided with a shelter. Hawaiian geese are highly aggressive during the breeding season and—at the time—should be put into solitary enclosures.

Food: Apart from vegetables which they should be given throughout the year, they need a prepared food full of vitamins and protein, but low in calories—particularly at the time of laying; birds used for breeding should not be allowed to develop too much of a layer of fat. Goslings are especially fond of water cress.

Breeding: First breeding results in captivity were actually achieved with the Hawaiian goose as early as the 19th century (amongst others in the zoos of London and Berlin). Interest in this rare goose has been revived and, in 1952, the Wildfowl Trust initiated a new breeding programme with two females and one male (caught wild); as their rate of productivity decreased two further ganders were imported from Hawaii in 1964. Within the last few years several breeding stocks have evolved in North America and West Europe, rather in isolation from each other.

It is now possible to make up breeding pairs which are not genetically related in the hope that soon the bird preserves will be filled with a sufficient number of healthy birds. Most pairs have a well developed impulse towards reproduction. In the Wildfowl Trust the Ne-nes are offered as nesting places huts made of straw, or osiers; in colder climates a nest should be prepared in a winter house. Laying may start from January onwards, but most eggs are laid in February. One or two further clutches may be expected if the eggs are removed before the beginning of incubation. In a small preserve which is easy to check, incubation and rearing of the goslings may be left to the parent birds; otherwise foster parents (e. g. hens) may well be used. Sexual maturity is quite likely after two years.

Hybridization: Not at all marked; GRAY (1959) quotes only one case of interbreeding between the Ne-ne and the swan goose (Chinese goose).

Andean Goose
Chloephaga melanoptera (Eyton)

Comparative Size: More massive but more compact than *Anser* species and other sheldgeese.

Plumage: M. and F. see plate 40; no seasonal dimorphism; primaries black, otherwise wings bronze-coloured with metallic purple sheen, scapular feathers dark brown. The juvenile F. is considerably smaller than the juvenile M., their body plumage is a faded grey-brown and wings have only a slight sheen.

NATURAL HABIT

Status: There is no record of the actual size of population; however, owing to the inhospitable climate of the habitat of the Andean goose in altitudes only sparsely settled by man, their population may be regarded as stable.

Habitat: High valleys and plateaux of the Cordilleras, 3,000 to 5,000 m high, where grass meadows on the heights and slopes are extensive; they also inhabit the boggy plains of lower altitudes grown with reeds and sedge.

Breeding Biology: Breeding pairs need very large areas indeed, often far away from any water. By preference, nests are made in the dry sections of the grasslands, where possible under the shelter of large stones or high grasses. A full clutch consists of six to ten cream-coloured eggs which are incubated by the female in approximately 30 days. Goslings are reared by both parents near an area containing water.

Migration: The southern populations escape the cold seasons by going north, but the majority of Andean geese simply migrates to valleys of a lower altitude or remains in the breeding grounds all through the year.

Yearly Cycle: The reproductive cycle of the southern populations is very much in line with the seasons prevalent there; breeding from October to January, rearing of the young and moult of adults up to March, autumn migration approximately starting in May. In areas near the equator the breeding season presumably extends over most months of the year.

Climate: Alpine cold climate with low rainfall throughout the year. In subtropical latitudes temperatures fluctuate more between day and night than from season to season; during the night the temperature may go down to freezing point.

AVICULTURE

The Andean goose was on show for the first time in London Zoo in 1881; since then they have inhabited many zoological gardens in large numbers and—more recently—they have been kept by wildfowl enthusiasts successfully.

Andean geese appeal to people because of their coloration, their shape and their manner, and it does not take long before they become tame. However, like all sheldgeese they are extremely quarrelsome and can be vicious. Moreover, birds imported from their natural environment—the Andes—are very sensitive to our summer's heat and some infectious diseases (tuberculosis and aspergillosis amongst others). Once they have become adapted or if they have been bred in captivity, they are hardy, robust and easy to feed.

Housing: Breeding or single birds may be kept in spacious, communal enclosures together with other large geese. A better way, however (and also a pre-condition for successful breeding results) is to put them into shady, separate enclosures with good turf and a small lake. A draught-free, dry shelter should be at the birds' disposal, particularly during rainy periods or on cold wet days.

Food: They are definitely grazing birds, and Andean geese find their nourishment mainly from grasses and other green stuff. They should also be given some corn (e. g. maize), scraped carrots or a simple prepared food.

Breeding: First breeding result was achieved in London Zoo in 1915. In the following decades there were a number of reports of successful broods but, to a large degree, these appeared to be a matter of chance rather than planning.

Meaningful attempts to breed the Andean goose in captivity have recently been started by a number of preserves, particularly the British Wildfowl Trust at Slimbridge (breeding results since 1963); private enthusiasts were not far behind and obtained good breeding results of the species within a short space of time. In 1974 WIENANDS (written communication) bred from a clutch of 14 eggs and a second clutch of seven eggs all 21 goslings, and reared them to maturity; indeed this is proof that the Andean goose can be very easily bred in captivity. The manner in which the Andean goose breeds differs hardly at all from that of the Magellan goose. Eggs are laid in small huts which—for practical reasons—should be placed in the birds' protective shelters. In the Wildfowl Trust laying begins normally in April, more rarely in May.

Hybridization: Not at all marked; DELACOUR (1954) quotes pair of hybrids: Andean × Magellan goose.

Magellan Goose
Chloephaga picta (Gmelin)

Comparative Size: Approximately as white-fronted goose and greylag.

Plumage: M. and F. see plate 41; no eclipse plumage, but two colour variants: males horizontally dark-barred either on the whole of the underside (including the neck) or only on the flanks; juveniles similar in type of colouration to adult M. and F. but juvenile males always dark-barred on the underside.

NATURAL HABIT

Status: It seems to be a fair assumption that Magellan geese breed in the South American grassy plains in about the same numbers as it was reported some decades ago.

Habitat: Extensive grassy steppes and semi-deserts, expecially those of moist river plains and near inland lakes, with soft grasses and herbs; also similar habitats along the coasts. Winter domicile: agricultural and pasture land in the region of the Pampas.

Breeding Biology: Breeding grounds are either some distance away from inland lakes or they may be near the coast. Nests are placed in the shelter of bunches of high tussock grasses, underneath low bushes, or they may just be on the ground of the open landscape. The Magellan goose is not a colony breeder; however, the density of nests may be relatively high. A full clutch consists of eight to fifteen smooth-shelled brownish eggs. The female alone incubates which takes 30–32 days. Both parents rear the goslings on tracts of grass in the vicinity of water.

Migration: Bird of passage; it escapes the winter by flying North to the Pampas of the Buenos Aires province and here the birds live in large, though loosely knit flocks.

Yearly Cycle: On the Falkland Isles the breeding season begins from early October, in Patagonia in November and December. During the time the goslings mature, the older birds undergo their moult. Formation of large flocks and autumn migration from February, in Patagonia in March.

Climate: To the West of the Andes the climate is a cool sea climate, poor in rainfall; Patagonia has the dry climate of the steppes with temperatures from October to January averaging roughly 15°C; on the Falkland Isles the temperature is only approximately 7°C. The birds find similar climatic conditions in their wintering quarters.

AVICULTURE

Of all sheldgeese it is the Magellan goose which is most often kept in preserves. The birds are colourful and splendid to look at. There is no problem in determining their sexes as males and females differ in coloration. No doubt they would enjoy even greater popularity and affection if they were less quarrelsome. They are undemanding and quite easy to keep; their food requirements are simple; they are hardy, tenacious and quite good breeders.

Housing: The breeder should house them in separate enclosures with healthy turf and a small lake. Only in places where large predatory animals occur should they be given a shelter; the birds are not affected by frost. In zoological gardens, Magellan geese are kept together with swans and larger geese. In enclosures of this kind quarrels with other species are far less frequent because the birds concerned only rarely become broody and are therefore far less inclined to be aggressive. However, if Magellan geese do breed on a communal lake, they immediately become a serious danger to all other birds on it.

Food: Corn; in preserves without good lawn they should be given, as an addition, carrots, short grass, lettuce or cabbage leaves.

Breeding: Once birds have reached maturity and have paired, breeding success will soon follow. Young birds become sexually mature in the 2nd or 3rd year of life. On nesting sites the Magellan geese should be offered large sheltered nesting sites or small huts (the latter preferably in a shelter). Eggs are laid at intervals of 48 hours between March and May, on the whole in mid-April. If the clutches and goslings are safe from predators incubation and rearing should be left to the parent birds themselves. If the female does not incubate, a second clutch can be expected. The young goslings take a little longer until they get feathers than the northern species of geese. Magellan geese are able to fly when they are nine to ten weeks old, but they are eleven to twelve weeks old before they have all their feathers. Change of coloration to that of a mature bird starts in the first autumn but may not take place until the beginning of the third year of life.

Hybridization: Interbreeding is known to have taken place with other *Chloephaga* species as well as with barnacle, emperor, Egyptian and maned geese.

Ashy-headed Goose
Chloephaga poliocephala Sclater

Comparative Size: Only a little smaller than white-fronted and Magellan goose.

Plumage: Adult female with goslings see plate 43; sexes not very clearly definable by coloration alone; M. normally has clearer colour with distinctive brown markings on the chest and grey markings on the neck. Voices differ quite unmistakably—F. has a harsh cackle, M. a soft whistle. Juveniles are very similar to adults, but their colouring is flatter and head and neck have a brown hue.

Natural Habit

Status: Presumed to be similar to that of the ruddy-headed goose, discussed in the next chapter.

Habitat: Grass tracts of the wide gently rolling valleys at the foot of the Andes and on the plateaux of Tierra del Fuego, preferably in the vicinity of running waters or near lagoons. Scott (1953) found many ashy-headed and ruddy-headed geese around farms, but the Magellan geese he found in neighbouring pasture areas.

Breeding Biology: Pairs keep strict guard over their breeding territory although this is not very large. Nests are placed between bunches of grasses or underneath bushes. A full clutch consists of six to eight smooth-shelled brownish eggs; incubation takes circa 30 days. Families like to graze near the water, but do not actually spend much time on the water. While the mature birds moult their wings, they retain their ability to fly nonetheless.

Migration: Bird of passage; it spends winters on the cultivated lands of the Buenos Aires province within the extensive Pampas zone.

Yearly Cylce: Like Magellan and ruddy-headed goose; there are some slight differences, but it appears that they have not been investigated.

Climate: See Magellan and ruddy-headed goose.

AVICULTURE

Ashy-headed geese reached the London Zoo for the first time in 1833 and the Berlin Zoo in 1874. First breeding result was in London in 1852. Since the turn of the century there has been a marked increase in their numbers, owing to BLAAUW of Amsterdam and others. Nowadays, ashy-headed geese are imported on a regular basis from South America; they adapt easily so that they can be seen in all zoos and bird preserves; even breeders keep them among their stock. Like all other sheldgeese they are robust and hardy in winter conditions and make few demands on housing and food, but they are just as quarrelsome and vicious in their behaviour towards the other waterfowl.

Housing: It is suitable to keep them in separate enclosures with good grass, a small pond and—if possible—a shelter; in zoos they may be kept on very large communal lakes.

Food: Entirely vegetarian; fresh green food preferably throughout the year; in winter they should be given (additionally) carrots, cabbage leaves and corn.

Breeding: At the present time successful breeding by the ashy-headed goose in captivity is rarely reported. The reason for this does not lie so much in the difficulty of breeding, but in the comparative lack of interest people have for the geese, which are attractively coloured but are also extremely quarrelsome. In fact, if the birds are paired properly and inhabit preserves in which they can find enough quiet, breeding results are the rule rather than the exception. In April, the geese lay their clutch of four to five eggs in 48 hourly intervals and, as a rule, incubate them quite reliably. Geese which have grown to maturity in preserves are remarkably trusting and quiet and allow keepers to examine their eggs. Goslings are reared by the parents on lawns with short grass; the goslings are robust and not sensitive to cold. Losses of eggs and young birds are rare. Probably goslings reach sexual maturity in the third year of life.

Hybridization: Not very marked and, because they are usually kept in separate enclosures, in any case unlikely. However, hybridizing has been known to occur with the barnacle goose as well as with the New Zealand and Australian shelduck.

Ruddy-headed Goose
Chloephaga rubidiceps Sclater

Comparative Size: Smaller than Magellan and white-fronted goose.

Plumage: M. in adult plumage see plate 39; sexes differ mainly in behaviour and voice, less in coloration; juveniles rather like adults in coloration, but more dull and with typical wings of a young bird. Voices begin showing sexual variation after the eighth month.

NATURAL HABIT

Status: No comprehensive research has been carried out so that it is not really possible to give an estimate of the size of the total population. However, an approximate impression may be obtained, since ruddy-headed geese have only small breeding populations. On the one hand, an increase of cattle and sheep rearing has changed the former forests into grasslands, and these give the ruddy-headed geese new habitats. On the other hand, farmers tend to regard the ruddy-headed geese as food competitors for sheep and have therefore decimated their numbers.

Habitat: Similar to that of the Magellan goose in moist areas of the grass steppes, but they also like fairly high plateaux of gently rolling valleys. In certain localities the ruddy-headed geese are referred to as mountain or valley goose in contrast to the Magellan goose which is also called upland goose.

Breeding Biology: After heated territory fights nesting sites are occupied and the nests are built underneath thick grass cover. A normal clutch consists of five to six shining, brownish eggs; incubation takes 30 days. Families graze on damp tracts of meadows where tender grasses grow, but they also dig up roots and feed on seed pods.

Migration: The majority of ruddy-headed geese winters in the Province of Buenos Aires; many stay in areas further to the South, some stay in their breeding grounds.

Yearly Cycle: Breeding takes place during the southern summer months; eggs are laid from September/October. The young are reared in November and December; large flocks form in January.

Climate: Cold, sub-arctic weather conditions with average temperatures of 10°C during the summer; the climate is not unlike that of the northern tundra.

AVICULTURE

Among the sheldgeese, together with the Kelp goose, ruddy-headed geese—even at present—are among the least imported, most dificult to keep and most rarely seen in preserves. They are also the smallest of the sheldgeese. However, ruddy-headed geese are rarely missing in the more impressive collections of private enthusiasts. Their behaviour is quiet and trusting, they are fairly hardy, withstand winters well—but they are also aggressive. They can be recommended to breeders with grounds in mountainous regions with a cold, rough climate.

Housing: They are best kept in solitary enclosures, or they may inhabit large grounds with plenty of space for spreading out, in company with swans and large geese. Ruddy-headed geese like grazing and swim relatively rarely. A small pond should be provided for them. Copulation takes place on land (if at all).

Food: See other sheldgeese.

Breeding: First imported by London's Zoo in 1860; later, in 1872, by the Berlin Zoo. First breeding result also by London Zoo circa 1865. After 1930 BLAAUW, Amsterdam, made some serious attempts to breed the goose; since 1950 it has been bred at an increasing rate in western Europe and North America.

Amongst the wildfowl inhabiting preserves in western Europe the proportion of captured and imported ruddy-headed geese is relatively high. It is only to be expected that these breed less easily than geese reared in captivity; on the other hand they do not take as much time to become established and find mates as wild northern geese do. For nesting places they should be given huts or large, shallow nest holes. In the Wildfowl Trust eggs are laid between March 25th and mid-May, mainly in April. As with other sheldgeese it is best to leave incubation and rearing to the parents; if the female does not incubate a second clutch may be expected.

Hybridization: Apparently not at all marked; only with the Magellan goose is a case of interbreeding known to have taken place.

Cereopsis

Cereopsis novaehollandiae Latham

Comparative Size: Considerably larger and more massive than white-fronted goose and greylag.

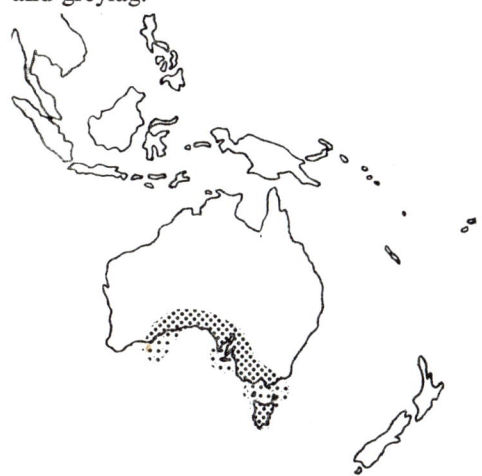

Plumage: Adults in plumage for all seasons see plate 42; juvenile plumage darker and less clearly coloured on the whole (although this does not apply to inhabitants of preserves), forehead and middle of the head cream-brown to light-grey; in adults white; adult F. always smaller than M.

NATURAL HABIT

Status: Species threatened with extinction. Total population only 5,000 to 6,000 birds. Breeding grounds are restricted to a few small islands; in 1960 protective laws were passed and this has resulted in a slight increase of stock.

Habitat: Small, low islands covered with short grass, sparse shrubs or hard bunches of grass. Large islands, inhabited by man, are rarely occupied by the geese. Outside the breeding season pastures in the lowlands.

Breeding Biology: Cereopsis are very definitely grazing birds that only rarely seek out the waters. They are monogamous and pair for life and—during the breeding season—they are extremely aggressive. Nests are built by both mates in areas of grassland (not near the water), and they contain a clutch of 3–6 rough-shelled, white eggs. Incubation roughly 35 days. The young birds grow very slowly and the parents look after them for many weeks in the breeding territory. Afterwards the young geese form flocks while the parent birds moult.

Migration: When they are not breeding, the cereopsis fly to the Australian mainland and to N. E. Tasmania; apparently some of them stay on their breeding islands throughout the year.

Yearly Cycle: Dependent on the rainfall (vegetation period of the grass) the cereopsis are distinct winter breeders. Arrival on breeding islands in February, breeding period May to August, rearing the young until October and—in the latter month—formation of flocks and moult of the adults; in November migration to summer quarters.

Climate: Cool sea climate with average temperatures of 18°C in January and 10°C in June; winter rain predominant.

Aviculture

Cereopsis are much desired waterfowl, but because of their small total population they are not often offered for sale. Only some large zoological gardens and bird sanctuaries as well as some special breeders own a few of these precious birds. Most of those kept nowadays in Europe and North America are presumably bred in captivity and therefore well acclimatized and of a robust constitution.

Housing: As the birds are extremely aggressive, particularly while they are breeding, they should be housed in very spacious separate enclosures. The latter should have good turf, but a pond or lake is of minor importance. As second clutches are likely to be laid in the winter, their shelter should have adequate room and in unfavourable climatic conditions it should be heated.

Food: Entirely vegetarian; apart from corn they should always be given fresh greenstuff and—in the winter—additionally carrots, cabbage, raw potatoes and sprouting grain.

Breeding: Cereopsis are normally sexually mature when they are three to four years old; as a general rule they are monogamous and pair for life. Decreasing daylight hours make them come into condition for breeding. In the Prague Zoo the cereopsis start laying in November when the daylight lasts just 10 hours; they have done so for more than 15 years. In the Wildfowl Trust at Slimbridge, on the other hand, laying begins in January. Copulation takes place on land exclusively. Under cover a nest foundation is made of straw and twigs. The gander guards the incubating female and examination of the nest while the eggs are being brooded is only sometimes possible because the birds are vicious (the female will help the male in an attack). Both parents guide their young and brood them; their rearing is not without trouble owing to the late winter weather. In contrast to the adult cereopsis goslings like swimming and are clever at it; the adults bathe standing on the shore, and they swim further out only to escape an enemy. Goslings are given fresh lettuce and sprouting grain as part of their diet.

Hybridization: None is known to have occurred so far.

Common Shelduck
Tadorna tadorna (L.)

Comparative Size: Like a medium-sized goose.

Plumage: F. and young see plate 44; in eclipse plumage little change in coloration, red knob at base of bill hardly noticeable. Juvenile males recognisable by red-brown and dark-green scapular and patina green speculum feathers; in juvenile females these are grey-brown and grey-green instead.

Natural Habit

Status: Comprehensive protective laws as well as a ban on hunting common shelducks have led to a noticeable increase of populations in many European countries during the last two decades. The central Asiatic zones are only sparsely populated.

Habitat: In Europe they breed by preference on stretches of the coast (more recently also inland), in central Asia near saline or brackish lakes of the steppes. Moulting areas (e. g. Great Knechtsand in Heligoland Bight) are on coastal tidal stretches.

Breeding Biology: After they have paired the common shelducks arrive in small groups in their breeding grounds where their most determined courtship display, territory defence and choice of a nesting site takes place. Nests are made in a hole in the ground (rabbit holes), only rarely in the vegetation on the beach, at times between stones or in hollow trees. A normal clutch consists of 7–12 eggs; it is by no means rare for several females to lay into one nest. Incubation takes 29–30 days. The young are taken by both parents to shallow places on the beach, sheltered from wind; they find sufficient food at the tide line.

Migration: Asiatic breeding birds spend the winters along the coasts of Japan and as far as India and the Caspian Sea. The northern European population moults on Great Knechtsand (approximately 100,000 birds), then remains on the mud flats of the North Sea; periods of severe frost send the birds to the coasts of Great Britain and further southwards as far as Portugal.

Yearly Cycle: Arrival in European breeding grounds from February/March, egg laying usually in May, rearing of young in June/July. Afterwards migration to moulting areas and subsequent stay in winter quarters.

Climate: The climatic distribution of common shelducks is very varied; the birds may live in a cool-temperate sea climate, or the dry-hot climate of the steppes, or even in humid tropical weather. The European population, from which the birds in captivity have descended, are relatively well adjusted to cold.

AVICULTURE

Common shelducks are beautifully coloured throughout the year; nowadays they are inhabitants of all zoos, bird preserves and the grounds of breeders. In some ways they resemble the mandarin duck — they are pleasant to look at, are rarely sickly and their breeding and rearing are quite easy.

Housing: Normally a few pairs of common shelducks are kept on a communal pond with other species. Outside the breeding season they are not likely to cause any trouble. But during the breeding season the drakes may turn into veritable tyrants (a behaviour which intensifies until the young are led from the nest). They are likely to disturb the breeding cycle of all other ducks on the pond. Such aggressive pairs are best housed in solitary pens during this period. During the winter they will thrive quite well as long as there is no ice on the water. In times of severe, prolonged frost they should be given an enclosed and dry room.

Food: Grain up to the size of wheat, food mixed with animal protein (shrimp and animal protein meal) as well as duckweed. At times they like accepting small pieces of fish. Ducklings are given a finely minced nourishing food mixture and plenty of duckweed.

Breeding: They reach sexual maturity in the second year; well-matched birds form a strong pair bond and stay together for life. For nesting they should be offered huts, nest boxes of artificially constructed earth burrows. Common shelducks also like making nests indoors (e. g. in their winter house). Egg laying may begin at the end of March but is more usual in April; in the Wildfowl Trust at Slimbridge eggs are laid end-April, beginning of May. Many females incubate quietly and reliably; guiding the newly hatched ducklings is the job of both parent birds. When young common shelducks are three weeks old their shoulders and flanks become feathered; at seven weeks they are almost the size of the adult female. At that age there are distinct differences between the sexes regarding colouring and voice. They begin moulting into the coloration of the post-juvenile plumage at two to three months.

Hybridization: Fairly marked within the *Tadorna* group; interbreeding is known to have occurred with the Egyptian goose, the eider duck and the mallard.

Radjah Shelduck

Tadorna radjah (Lesson)

Comparative Size: Smaller than other *Tadorna* species.

Plumage: Adult in eclipse plumage see plate 45; no seasonal dimorphism. The coloration of the upper side varies between black and dark red-brown (according to sub-species). Sexes recognisable by difference in voices. Up to the first full moult juvenile wings are different from those of adults; wing coverts are a washed-out grey-white, speculum has little sheen and scapular feathers are a dirty red-brown.

39 ↑ Ruddy-headed Goose
40 ↗ Andean Goose
41 ↓ Magellan Goose

42 ↑ Cereopsis
43 ↓ Ashy-headed Goose F. and young

44 ↑ Common Shelduck F. and young
45 ↓ Radjah Shelduck

46 ↑ Australian Shelduck M.
47 ↗ Ruddy Shelduck M.
48 ↓ New Zealand Shelduck F. and young

49 ↑ Cape Shelduck
50 ↓ Egyptian Goose

51 ↑ Chiloe Wigeon
52 ↗ European Wigeon
53 ↓ American Wigeon M.

54 ↑ Baikal Teal F.
55 ↗ Baikal Teal M.
56 ↓ Falcated Duck

57 ↑ Pintail M.
58 ↓ Green-winged Teal

Natural Habit

Status: Because the area in which the radjah shelducks occur is very confined, and even within it they only make use of areas with a very specific ecology, the total population is small. However, it is neither endangered nor threatened with extinction.

Habitat: Meandering river courses in wooded plains with adjacent lakes and swamps; along the coasts in mangrove woods and estuarine zones.

Breeding Biology: Except for family groups, which stay together for a long time, most of the radjah shelducks have been observed as single pairs. Nests are in hollow trees near the water or in flooded, boggy woods. Full clutches contain 6–12 cream-white eggs; incubation takes approximately 30 days. The hatched ducklings jump down from their nest burrows and are then looked after by both parents.

Migration: During the dry season in North Australia, many plains and river beds dry out completely. Radjah shelducks inhabiting these areas wander off to nearby lakes, river courses or to the coast. All other radjahs are residents throughout the year.

Yearly Cycle: Courtship display and selection of nest territory start when the rainy season begins (from November onwards); on the other hand, eggs are laid at the end of the rainy season (usually in May and June) when the highest water level has gone down. While the young are being reared they find most of their food in the shallow waters of very small pools.

Climate: Tropical warm climate with plenty of summer monsoon rain followed by drought.

Aviculture

For a long time radjah shelducks have belonged to the most rarely imported but most sought after waterfowl in Europe and North America despite their delicate constitution. Even at present they can only be viewed in a few zoos, preserves or breeders' grounds. While they are becoming acclimatized during the first few years the rate of mortality is very high and thus there are few prolific broods reared in captivity. However, with the building of large tropical halls in zoos and preserves the chances are now somewhat better and it is hoped that it will be possible to breed the radjah shelduck successfully in captivity.

Housing: Sunny sheltered preserves with shallow, warm ponds where the birds can filter out part of their diet. Although the radjah shelducks are aggressive in the breeding season it is not essential to confine them in solitary enclosures; nonetheless it is advisable to do so to make certain that they receive a maximum amount of food. They should spend the winters in heated shelters with a temperature of 10°C. On sunny days without frost they should be allowed runs outside in the fresh air.

Food: Small grain, enriched with animal protein; but they should also be given wheat, millet, ground shrimps, meal worms and—particularly—duckweed (compare with common shelduck).

Breeding: Radjah shelducks are just as difficult to breed now as they have always been. Only a few yearbooks and articles in magazines report breeding results for the birds; even the British Wildfowl Trust managed to rear very few of them. A few West European and North American breeders have had slightly better results, but the rate of success has been very limited; in preserves the radjah duck may just about keep up its numbers but they do not increase. Their breeding cycle is about the same as that of the common shelduck. Eggs are laid in the early summer months; chicks need much warmth and sun; juveniles are sexually mature in the second year of their life.

Hybridziation: The two sub-species of the radjah shelduck (red and black-backed) are much interbred among birds in captivity. There are obviously no isolating mechanisms breeders can resort to. Tendencies to interbreed with other *Tadorna* species have also been observed.

Ruddy Shelduck
Tadorna ferruginea (Pallas)

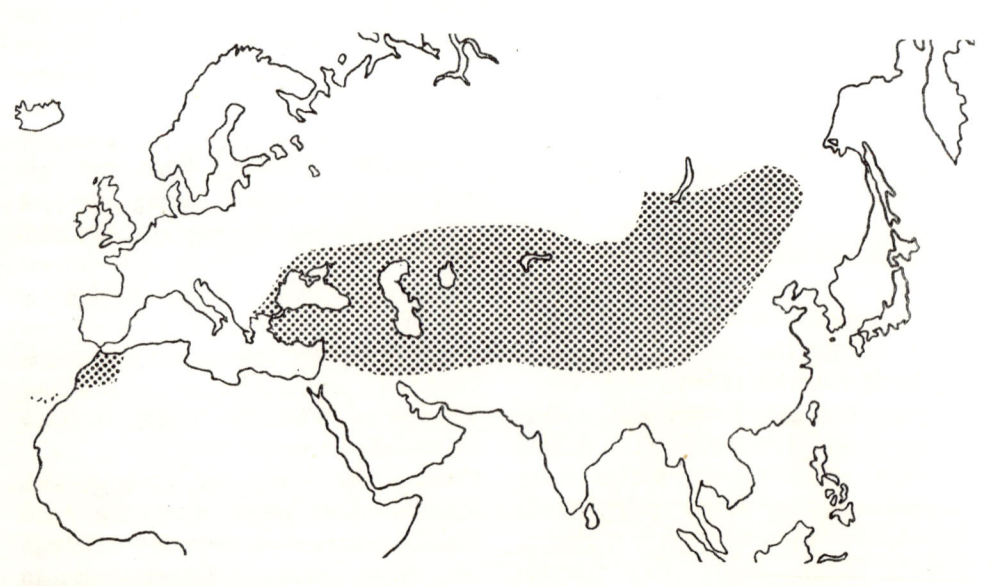

Comparative Size: Like a medium-sized goose.

Plumage: M. in breeding plumage see plate 47; eclipse plumage somewhat lighter; black ring around the middle of neck missing. Juveniles' plumage washed-out light-brown colour throughout; sexes recognisable by differences in voice and size.

Natural Habit

Status: Rapid decline in southern and south-eastern Europe since the turn of the century; only a few pairs may be found breeding in very few places. Their most common area of distribution today is in central Asia and from Turkey to Turkestan.

Habitat: Coasts of Asiatic inland seas; fresh-water, brackish water and saline water lakes of steppes and high plateaux — poor in vegetation growth; also wide river valleys with gravel banks. For feeding and breeding they often **inhabit** grass steppes and semi-deserts, far away from the water.

Breeding Biology: Ruddy shelducks arrive in their breeding grounds already paired and occupy very large nesting sites. For that reason nests are often built many kilometres away from the waters on which they later rear the goslings, for instance in the burrows of small mammals, tree holes and old buildings. Full clutches consist of 8–11 smoothshelled yellowish eggs; incubation takes 28–30 days. When they have hatched, the young are taken by the parents to the nearest water; they have to undertake quite long marches to get there and jump off cliffs and rocky walls on the way. While the young shelducks grow up on the water the parent birds moult.

Migration: Predominantly migratory birds which winter on shallow lakes with poor vegetation and stony river courses of southern Asia. During their autumnal migration they gather in especially large swarms in eastern Turkey and Afghanistan.

Yearly Cycle: In high altitudes with short periods of summer the ruddy shelducks arrive just as the snow is thawing; eggs are laid from early May; migration to wintering grounds together with the juveniles approximately middle of August. Ruddy shelducks inhabiting lower regions start breeding after the beginning of March.

Climate: Not at all uniform within the breeding area (ranging from cold high mountain to hot desert climate); differences between day and night temperatures vary greatly.

AVICULTURE

Ruddy shelducks are among the hardiest and most easily bred waterfowl; thus they are kept by all zoos, bird preserves and breeders. However, the frequent very loud calls of the females together with their aggressiveness are not particularly pleasant. Before and during breeding, many pairs become really vicious so that in smaller preserves other species may suffer because of them.

Housing: During the breeding season it is best to house them in separate enclosures, preferably with a small pond and—if necessary—a shelter to protect them from predatory game; a nesting box may be placed in the shelter. On the really large lakes of zoos and preserves several pairs of ruddy shelducks are normally kept as a group in which case they neither quarrel among themselves nor with other species.

Food: Their main diet is wheat, a simple food-mix, or a mixture consisting of soaked bread, bran and green rye flour. They are very partial to duckweed and while the young are being reared this should always be given.

Breeding: The reproductive potential of the ruddy shelducks which have inhabited preserves for many generations is unusually high and far above that of other shelduck species. Frequent calling and agitated behaviour by the female are an indication that she is ready to breed; copulation soon follows and then the female inspects the ready-made nesting boxes or shelters and burrows for their suitability. Egg-laying may be expected from end-March onwards (in 48 hour intervals). Most females are reliable breeders and both parent birds guide their young, whom they defend bravely against all enemies (such as dogs, cats and crows), even against their keepers. During the first few days the young have the typical characteristics of ducks. They start growing feathers on shoulders and flanks in the third week of their life and when they are eight to nine weeks old they have most of their feathers. The post-nestling moult sets in shortly afterwards so that after the late autumn, one-year old shelducks are very like the adults in coloration. They are sexually mature when they are two years old.

Hybridization: Apart from interbreeding with the members of the *Tadorna* group they may hybridize with the Egyptian goose and the large *Anas* species.

Cape Shelduck
Tadorna cana (Gmelin)

Comparative Size: Like a medium-sized goose.

Plumage: Adult birds and young see plate 49; size of white patches on the head varied in individual females; eclipse plumage somewhat darker than breeding plumage; juvenile females moult the white feathers around eyes and base of bill when they are 10 weeks old while juvenile males moult the grey-brown plumage of the head into grey at the same age.

Natural Habit

Status: Widely distributed in landscapes with the right type of ecology, the Cape shelduck is most common in the Cape Province. It has been observed repeatedly that the birds tend to form a loose bond with domestic waterfowl.

Habitat: Warm shallow inland lakes with a wealth of vegetation and small fauna, also river plains, reservoirs and shallow coastal waters—they are all favoured habitats.

Breeding Biology: After display and pair formation the Cape shelducks occupy their breeding territory and they defend their nest site against all members of their own species. Nests are often far from the water and they are usually in holes in the ground, more rarely between stones or in hollow trees. The clutch consists of 10–14 yellow eggs; there is an interval of 48 hours between each laying. Incubation by the female takes 30–31 days. Parents and young spend their time in the shallow water which is full of nourishment for them.

Migration: Infrequent migrants; outside the breeding season they often form into small flocks for moulting or wintering. Some of the breeding grounds are left only during the dry season—or not at all.

Yearly Cycle: The whole of the breeding cycle is dependent on the rainfall rather than the temperatures. The breeding season starts with the onset of the rainy season or—in areas with rainfall throughout the year—at the time of the southern spring.

Climate: Predominantly periodic rainfall with sub-tropical temperatures; in some parts of Cape Province, these may go down to freezing point during the winter months.

Aviculture

Cape shelducks were not among the early imported birds in Europe. It was not until 1930 that they became generally known and from 1960 they could be found in most zoos and breeding preserves. Of all the *Tadorna* species they are the hardiest but unfortunately the most quarrelsome; they are also the noisiest.

Housing: The private enthusiast will be able to enjoy the possession of Cape shelducks without any reservation only if he can offer them a separate pen. A shelter is not needed except in unfavourable climatic conditions or as a protection from predators during the night. The birds are quite able to stand up to cold and snow.

Food: See ruddy shelduck.

Breeding: It is just as easy to breed the Cape shelduck as the ruddy and common shelduck. The birds display and—from January onwards—they copulate; a very short time afterwards they look for suitable breeding holes. Egg laying starts in the second half of March so that the young are ready to be hatched at the beginning of May. The ducklings are just as hardy and impervious to cold as the parent birds. In my preserve five ducklings left their brood hole at 6 o'clock in the morning when the temperature was 4°C (the grass was still covered by night frost); they were led to the water by the parents and it was not for another hour that they were briefly brooded and warmed;

eight to ten days later the female brooded the ducklings only during the night.

Rearing the young Cape shelducks is not particularly difficult. If they are given plenty of duckweed and a suitable food-mix the do thrive indeed. At barely one month the first wing quills may be seen on their shoulders and—when they are two months old—they have most of their feathers. They moult their plumage shortly afterwards and from then onwards have their first adult plumage. Differences between sexes now show up not only in markings on the head (see plumage) but also in the pitch of voices.

Hybridization: As breeders tend to keep Cape shelducks in separate enclosures they are unlikely to have hybrids. In zoos and large preserves interbreeding with other *Tadorna* species and the Egyptian goose is not uncommon.

New Zealand Shelduck

Tadorna variegata (Gmelin)

Comparative Size: Like medium-sized goose.

Plumage: F. and young see plate 48; at the end of the breeding season a full moult results in a plumage which is hardly different from the eclipse plumage. The juvenile males have mat black-brown heads, those of females are white, at least at the base of the bill; immediately after the birds become fully feathered they have another moult and afterwards their first adult plumage appears, when all brown feathers of the head are replaced by white ones.

Natural Habit

Status: Total population relatively small owing to the limited area of distribution; however, the species is not threatened with extinction. The birds adapt themselves very easily to all kinds of different ecological conditions; they find food on cultivated land and they have settled on the pastureland of New Zealand's North Island after drastic wood clearance.

Habitat: Their original habitat used to be mountain streams, river courses lined by old trees, lakes of the plains and some coastal areas. Nowadays their favourite nesting grounds are in the cultivated areas of the plains where they have good pasture; since 1908 these have been much expanded. Occupation of a specific area by the birds depends largely on the existence of large, old trees near the water.

Breeding Biology: In August and September winter flocks disperse and pairs occupy their nest territory. If the nest is on agricultural land it will almost certainly be placed in a large hole of a tree, up to 10 m high. In older literature

(OLIVER 1930) nests were described as being placed either on the ground under cover of vegetation or between rocky stones. Clutch consists of eight to eleven light cream-coloured eggs; incubation takes roughly 30 days. The ducklings jump down from their nest when they are one day old and they are then immediately taken to the water by their parents.

Migration: As soon as the ducklings are able to fly, the families leave their breeding grounds and form flocks on a large, nearby lake where they undergo a complete moult. The majority of birds do not migrate further than 80 km at most.

Yearly Cycle: Breeding season is during the southern spring (October to December), moult is in February and March and afterwards loosely-knit flocks join up for the winter.

Climate: On the South Island it is temperate; the North Island has a sub-tropical maritime climate with rainfall throughout the year.

AVICULTURE

Of all the shelducks the New Zealand shelduck is perhaps the one most suitable for being kept by a private breeder. The reasons are as follows: it is attractively coloured; does not disturb with noisy, obtrusive calls; is hardy in winter; is easy to breed—much easier than the Australian shelduck for example—and, most of all, it is good tempered (even breeding birds are not aggressive towards other ducks).

Housing: Equally suited to large communal preserves as to small separate enclosures. Outside the breeding season New Zealand shelducks are completely non-aggressive. During the breeding season they defend solely the immediate vicinity of their nest site.

Food: See ruddy shelduck.

Breeding: Results of breeding quite promising but not equal to the ruddy shelduck. Large, hollow tree trunks, huts and pipes in the ground are all satisfactory places for making nests. In Germany eggs are normally laid at end-March/early April, at Slimbridge in the Wildfowl Trust usually between mid-April and mid-May. Incubation and rearing of the ducklings are like those of other shelducks. If the parent birds are left to look after their own young difficulties do not normally arise and losses are very rare.

The fledglings moult the whole plumage of the body between August and November; afterwards—up to the following summer—they can be recognised as juveniles by their wings, which have brown-grey coverts and unusually long scapular feathers in contrast to mature birds. In the second year of their life they are sexually mature.

Hybridization: In large preserves of zoological gardens unpaired New Zealand shelducks may find a mate among one of the other shelducks; interbreeding with any other species is rare. In breeding preserves hybridization is quite insignificant.

Australian Shelduck

Tadorna tadornoides (Jardine & Selby)

Comparative Size: Like a medium-sized goose.

Plumage: Adult M. in breeding plumage see plate 46; the amount of white around eyes and bill in females is varied; little change in eclipse plumage of either M. or F. except for some minor colour variations on parts of the body; juveniles very similar to adult M., juvenile F. initially without white on the head (this appears after the first moult of body plumage in the autumn).

Natural Habit

Status: Still quite common in many areas of their range, although being hunted and regarded as a competitor for food of the sheep.

Habitat: During the breeding season on ponds surrounded by old trees, at river courses and at watering places for cattle in grass and bush landscapes. Later they stay on large inland lakes (up to the time of the complete moult), on estuaries and brackish and saline water lagoons along the coasts.

Breeding Biology: When the breeding season begins the shelducks separate from the flock and occupy their nesting site where they do not tolerate a second pair. For preference they like laying their eggs in large hollow trees, or more rarely, in rabbit burrows or among rocks. A full clutch consists of 10 to 14 creamy white eggs. Incubation takes 30–33 days. The young jump down from the nest and are then looked after by both parents. The latter maintain the pair bond throughout the year, even within the moulting and summer flocks.

Migration: At the end of the breeding season, moult—migrations to the large inland lakes of southern Australia; during the summer they stay along the coasts.

Yearly Cycle: Australian shelducks return to their inland breeding grounds towards the end of summer (normally after March), clutches have been found between July and September. From September onwards flocks of young shelducks form, the adults moult in November, and the summer flocks stay together in coastal zones until February.

Climate: Temperate to sub-tropical; average temperatures in the winter are 12°C, in the summer approximately 22°C; rain is predominant in the winter.

Aviculture

The Australian shelduck was imported for the first time by the London Zoo in approximately; 1860 after 1872 the Berlin Zoo followed with regular imports of the birds, and since the turn of the century they have been kept in many places. The first breeding result was obtained in 1939 by DELACOUR at Clères in France. After the Australian government banned the export of animals from their homeland, the number of Australian shelducks in European and North American preserves decreased sharply. Nowadays, together with the radjah shelduck, they are among the rare birds of the *Tadorna* group.

The Australian shelduck is just as robust, long-lived and cold resistant as their New Zealand and African kindred. HEINROTH (1910) reported on their utter peaceableness towards all species of ducks, but it may be taken that this applies, in the main, to non-breeding pairs.

Housing: Grass grown separate enclosures or communal preserves, in the latter together with *Anser* species and large ducks, but preferably not with other species of *Tadorna*. They need very spacious winter quarters, because they reach breeding condition in the winter—if at all.

Food: See ruddy shelduck; breeding pairs must be given a sufficient amount of green or sprouting vegetation.

Breeding: After 1939 and again after 1955, several juvenile Australian shelducks were reared to maturity in western Europe, especially in Great Britain, but even at present a successful brood of the birds is considered a remarkable achievement. Even the Wildfowl Trust has not managed to breed any Australian shelducks to date. Like the cereopsis, the Australian shelducks reach breeding condition during our winter months; they copulate (provided their winter quarters contain a sufficiently large area of water) and their behaviour becomes broody, possibly to quite a marked degree; generally towards the spring their breeding impulse disappears. In known successful broods the female started laying in February every time.

WIENANDS (personal communication) bred Australian shelducks repeatedly during the last few years, one brood was from a clutch in 1974 out of which he reared 11 young birds. Despite the seasonal cold, rearing of the ducklings was not particularly difficult.

Hybridization: Interbreeding has taken place with the common shelduck, the ruddy shelduck, the domestic duck, the bar-headed goose and the Cape shelduck.

Egyptian Goose
Alopochen aegyptiacus (L.)

Comparative Size: Only a little smaller than white-fronted or greylag goose.

Plumage: Adult M. and F. with juveniles see plate 50; eclipse plumage is unchanged in colouring. In wild birds colour of back feathers has variations (from red-brown to pale grey) as has the size of the black spot on the lower chest. Birds in preserves are somewhere in between these colour variants. Mutation has produced a pale-cream, almost white Egyptian goose which is fertile. Sexes (even fully grown juveniles) have different calls, the M. a hoarse throaty call, the F. a loud, high-pitched shriek.

NATURAL HABIT

Status: Quite common South of the Sahara, particularly on freshwater lakes; it is less common in the tropical rain forest of West Africa.

Habitat: In almost equal frequency the birds inhabit inland lakes, river courses, coastal lagoons and—during the rainy season—flooded meadows.

Breeding Biology: Egyptian geese breed in various places: in the vegetation on the ground, in hollow trees, between rocks, and also in trees in nests deserted by their former occupants. During the breeding season one pair takes charge of a large territory which the gander defends aggressively. A normal clutch consists of eight to ten white eggs; time of incubation is 30 days. The goslings are looked after by both parents; either in river shallows or on the gravel banks of large rivers; at nine to ten weeks the goslings are able to fly. However, the families stay together for many more months.

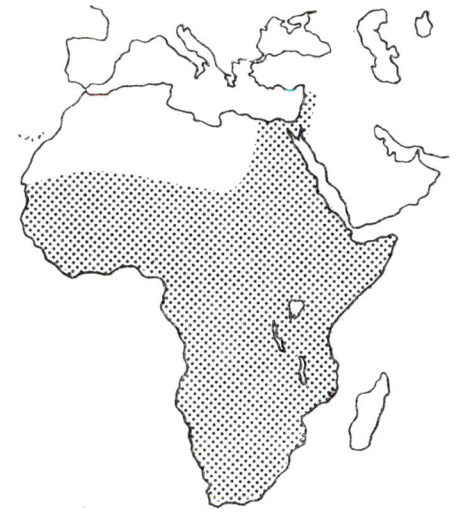

Migration: Where food and water exists in sufficient quantities the Egyptian geese are stationary residents; in areas of possible drought they are infrequent migrants.

Yearly Cycle: Breeding season in South and East Africa fairly uniform—between July and December. In areas with periodic strong rainfall eggs are laid before the end of the rainy season.

Climate: In the whole area of distribution temperatures are far above freezing point during all seasons; the greatest density of breeding birds, however, can be found in the dry-hot climate of the steppes and savannas.

AVICULTURE

Egyptian geese were already well known as ornamental waterfowl in Old Egypt, Old Greece and the Roman Empire. Since the 17th century they have become known in western Europe. For the last 100 years they have been kept by many bird lovers, in zoos and on lakes in parks, and they are among the most popular ornamental geese. In certain areas of Great Britain and the Netherlands there are some small wild populations made up of birds which have escaped from preserves, and vagrants. In spite of their tropical origin Egyptian geese are very hardy in the winter; alas, they are very aggressive and quarrelsome. During the breeding season, mature birds attack even swans and other large geese; weaker birds may even be killed by beating from their wings.

Housing: They are very suited to being kept on lakes of parks and towns where they look very interesting and decorative. The present day breeder is particularly keen on the lighter-coloured mutants among them. They should always be housed in separate enclosures to stop their vicious biting of others. In the winter, Egyptian geese are usually peaceable on densely populated lakes. They are able to spend the cold months without having a shelter at their disposal.

Food: If they have enough green food they only need some grain mixture additionally. Goslings are reared on duckweed and not very high protein starter crumbs.

Breeding: They are easily bred. Well paired Egyptian geese get into condition for breeding in the second or third year of their life. They can rear their young without any particular help from the keeper. Eggs are laid in dense cover or artificial 'bowers', in large nesting boxes or inside stables. A full clutch contains up to eight eggs. The parent birds should be left to do the incubating and rearing of the young: these strong birds are well able to protect their brood from enemies. Unpinioned young birds tend to wander off in the autumn; quite a few leave the water on which they have been bred for ever unless they have their wings clipped. Moulting to the adult plumage starts in late autumn and is finished, with the moult of the flight feathers, in the following summer.

As a rule the breeding results of the light coloured mutants are less prolific than those of the darker coloured geese.

Hybridization: Rather pronounced; they have interbred (amongst others) with Muscovy ducks, greylags, marine and sheldgeese; with nearly all species of *Tadorna* and also spur-winged and maned geese.

European Wigeon
Anas penelope L.

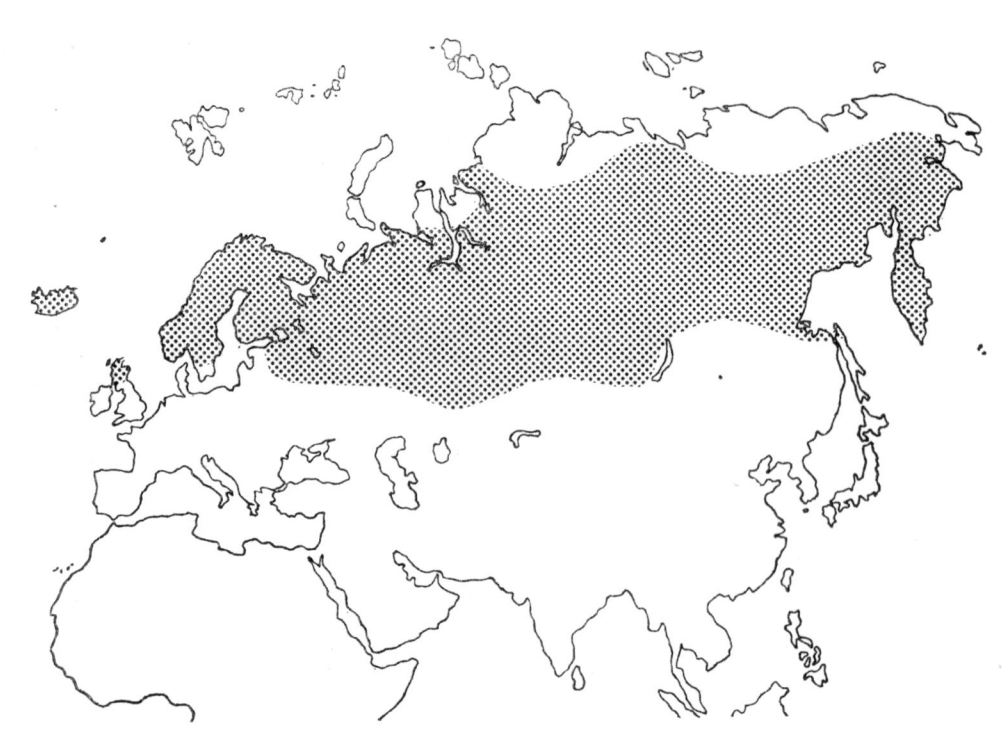

Comparative Size: Smaller than a mallard.
Plumage: M. and F. in breeding plumage see plate 52; drake in eclipse plumage similar in colour to F., but has a richer chestnut brown on the upperside; juveniles also resemble females, but M. differs from F. of the same age by having lighter coloured wing coverts.

Natural Habit

Status: Abundant as a breeding bird in the spacious zones of northern Eurasia; however, over the last few decades, in Mecklenburg, Schleswig Holstein, the Netherlands and the southern half of Great Britain they have become a sporadic to rare breeding bird.

Habitat: During the breeding season they inhabit fairly large lakes, river plains and coastal sites; they avoid boggy lowlands, still ponds and forest pools. Later they migrate further along the coasts to estuarine mud flats, and they like to spend the spring on flooded meadows.

Breeding Biology: Pair formation during the last third of the winter; there is no distinctive courtship display. Nesting site—evidently chosen by the female—under good cover among reeds, under small bushes or in the heather. Full clutches consist of seven to ten cream-coloured to red-brown eggs; incubation 23–25 days. The female incubates the eggs and looks after the young. The male leaves the breeding site before beginning his full moult.

Migration: Predominantly migratory birds; they winter along the west European coastal zones; in Africa southwards as far as the Equator; in Asia as far as Burma and India. Normally they join up in very large flocks; in the southern Soviet Union the drakes undertake a moult migration.

Yearly Cycle: Laying begins end-April (Scotland) and up to the end of June (Siberia); moult migration of drakes in July; migration from breeding to winter grounds from September. Their main migratory flights through central Europe are in October/November and March/April.

Climate: Most of the breeding sites are in regions of cool boreal or inhospitable tundra climate with low summer temperatures. A few of the birds breed in dry-hot parts of central Asia.

Aviculture

Wigeons are among the most strikingly coloured ducks. Therefore it is not surprising that they have been known as ornamental birds for a long time (according to DELACOUR (1956) even in Old Egypt). Their non-aggressive behaviour—even if several pairs inhabit a pond—their hardiness in the winter and their undemanding food requirements are all reasons why wigeons are kept in nearly all zoos and bird preserves. In fact the breeder has only recently become aware of the beauty of the species.

Housing: The best way to house them is on large communal ponds with an adjoining area of healthy grass (wigeons graze in the manner of geese) and some small bushes. Breeding results, however, have been obtained, too, in small separate pens with a water basin. They can winter in the open or in an unheated shelter.

Food: Grain and a simple duckfood mixture; if breeding results are desired, wigeons should be given plenty of green stuff in spring (duckweed and dandelion leaves).

Breeding: A few years ago the animal trade was offered—and bought—ducks caught in duck decoys; it was the cheapest way of obtaining them. But the birds captured in this way were wild, very shy and always concerned for their safety; either they did not breed at all or it took a very long time before they did. Nowadays most of the wigeons in preserves are reared in captivity and although their breeding is by no means very common there is a much better chance of it.

Central European wigeons always make their nests on the ground, under cover of vegetation and far distant from a pond. Eggs are laid in May usually, although in the Wildfowl Trust at Slimbridge this occasionally takes place from March onwards. Inverval between laying is 24 hours. Undisturbed females are good breeders, but they and their eggs are always endangered by hedgehogs and other predators; it is often necessary to have the eggs incubated some other way. Rearing of the young wigeons is not particulalrly difficult. Three week old young are feathered on the underside; at six weeks they are fully feathered. A year later they are sexually mature.

Hybridization: GRAY (1958) reported of 11 different *Anas* species as well as North American wood ducks, tufted ducks and red-crested pochards which hybridized with European wigeons; however, I myself, am of the opinion that the European wigeon does not interbreed extensively.

American Wigeon
Anas americana Gmelin

Habitat: Large inland lakes and water-rich plains in an open landscape, also lakes in prairies and waters of the tundra. During the winter mainly areas of freshwater such as river courses (in plains), rice fields and flooded pastureland.

Breeding Biology: The birds breed in a very similar manner to the Eurasian species. Nests are in reeds, under bushes, in the dry prairie grass or on small grassy islands. A full clutch consists of nine to ten cream-white or red eggs which look exactly like those of the European wigeon. Incubation takes 23–25 days.

Migration: Migratory bird; winters southwards as far as Colombia, but the majority fly to the Southern States of the USA. A few American wigeons cross the North Atlantic and winter in the west of Great Britain or in Ireland.

Yearly Cycle: Depending on their arrival in the breeding grounds between mid-May (prairies) and end-May (Alaska), the birds lay eggs from May to July. In the north autumnal migration begins at the end of August and in early September.

Climate: In the breeding grounds, the typical boreal climate with rather changing temperatures; spring starts late and there are often early frosts in autumn.

Comparative Size: Smaller than a mallard.
Plumage: M. in breeding plumage see plate 53; plumage of juveniles and M. in eclipse plumage very like adult females in colouring; differences between sexes quite distinguishable however. According to GLUTZ VON BLOTZHEIM et al. (1968), the females differ from Eurasian wigeons as follows:
"Speculum with less or no green but correspondingly more black; the second inner secondary with light-grey tinted scapulars; wing bars white outside with grey-brown undersides and broad velvety black tips (in *penelope* grey or sepia-brown instead with grey-white outer border and narrow black-brown horizontal stripe)."

NATURAL HABIT

Status: Large area of distribution; abundant as a breeding bird with a big total population.

AVICULTURE

North American and Eurasian wigeons have much in common regarding behaviour, basic needs and possible breeding results. Therefore, the American wigeon may be discussed in a few words, particularly as it is not as commonly kept as its Eurasian relatives.

Housing and Food: See European wigeon.
Breeding: Compared with the European wigeons the *Anas americana* is far less attractively coloured and in its behaviour

rather quiet. It is not often found in private preserves, but many zoos and bird sanctuaries. Breeding results tended to be very rare for a long time; many captured birds showed no inclination to breed at all. Most of the birds kept in western Europe at present are those which have been reared in preserves and are therefore far more likely to breed. In spacious and not very populated enclosures there is a real chance of breeding success with most pairs. Within the last ten years, more than 90 American wigeons have been bred and reared to maturity in the British Wildfowl Trust at Slimbridge, and breeding results have also been achieved at Peakirk where they begin egg laying between mid-May and mid-June. Incubation, rearing of the young and their development very closely resemble both other types of wigeon.

Hybridization: Very pronounced tendencies to hybridize exist and interbreeding is known to have taken place with approximately 20 different species. Hybrid descendants of *penelope* appear to be fertile.

Chiloe Wigeon

Anas sibilatrix Poeppig

Comparative Size: Smaller than a mallard.
Plumage: M. and F. see plate 51; no seasonal dimorphism; juveniles in type of colouring like adults, but darker. In young males scapular feathers white bordered in black, flight feathers velvety black; in juvenile female scapulars and middle wing coverts faded grey-white, all outer wing feathers lighter in tone.

NATURAL HABIT

Status: Widely distributed and—according to older literature—quite common. Nowadays, hunting has decimated numbers in certain areas.

Habitat: In the interior of Argentina, shallow lakes with rich vegetation and valleys of slow-running rivers in regions of the steppes; water reservoirs in the lower mountains adjoining the Andes; in coastal and wintering grounds also brackish and saline lakes.

Habits: As typical dabbling ducks their behaviour is analogous to that of many of our species (e. g. gadwalls, pintails); they winter on large lakes together with other species of ducks; during the breeding season they live in pairs in the shore vegetation of the lakes, and nests are made among the reed grasses; clutches consist of six to nine cream-coloured (almost white) eggs; incubation takes 25 days. The male does not leave the incubating female and later takes an active part in rearing the young. After the moult the birds live predominantly near and on open zones of water.

Migration: Migratory birds or infrequent migrants; they migrate to northern areas with good rainfall along the coasts.

Yearly Cycle: They have their breeding season at the time of the southern spring, from September onwards, depending on local variations of climate and rainfall. Winter swarms can be seen in the Province of Buenos Aires and central Chile after February and March.

Climate: Chiloe wigeons winter in areas with a marked regional difference as regards rainfall and altitude. They breed in sub-arctic as well as in temperate climatic zones.

AVICULTURE

Chiloe wigeons have been bred and reared in Europe for the last 100 years. The species is colourful throughout the year and they are also very hardy. Together with the mandarin duck and the North American wood duck they have found their place among the ornamental waterfowl kept in captivity. They are common inhabitants of zoos, bird preserves and breeding preserves alike.

Housing: As the majority of Chiloe wigeons tend to become aggressive while they are breeding it is recommended that they are either housed on large communal ponds—where threatened birds can get out of their way—or by themselves in small enclosures. Furthermore, many drakes have an undesirable habit of 'raping' unrelated species of female ducks which can lead to unwanted hybrids. This kind of behaviour is, however, not as pronounced as it is in mallards, spotbills and red-crested pochards. Chiloe wigeons enjoy grazing on short grass; they are undemanding with regard to housing and the quality of the water of their pond. They are well able to withstand the cold of the winter and do not need a shelter; the water has to be free from ice.

Food: The same as other dabbling ducks.

Breeding: The birds are sexually mature after one or two years. Eggs are laid in nest boxes, preferably on islands or near the water. The females are reliable breeders. Occasionally they produce three clutches. Eggs can be incubated quite easily in an incubator. The pretty, brown ducklings are very lively right from the beginning and accept food immediately, even without prior parental guidance. Many breeders like keeping these wigeon ducklings in their grounds so that other ducklings can learn from them. On the whole, young ducklings are fully feathered when they are five to six weeks old; at that time the drakes start practising their typical whistling sounds. Change of coloration into that of a mature bird takes place in September.

Hybridization: As Chiloe wigeons enjoy courtship and breeding, unmated drakes will often copulate with a female of a different species. However, once a drake has really paired with a female Chiloe wigeon, the ducks can be kept quite safely in a mixed collection of waterfowl.

Falcated Duck
Anas falcata Georgi

Comparative Size: Almost the size of a mallard.

Plumage: M. and F. in breeding plumage see plate 56; in eclipse plumage similar in looks to wigeons because of the high crown, but darker and different colouring of wings (light-grey instead of white wing coverts, for instance) makes them quite easily distinguishable. Juveniles in coloration similar to females, speculum has less sheen.

NATURAL HABIT

Status: Although no specific data are at hand, it is supposed that a large total population exists. In wintering grounds the falcated ducks are often the most numerous members of the flocks.

Habitat: During the breeding season in similar locations as gadwalls: freshwater lakes with adjoining swampy plains; forested and reed-grown river banks. During the migratory period middle and lower courses of large streams; wintering by preference on inland lakes and in quiet coastal bays.

Breeding Biology: Pair formation in their winter quarters. Nests are built in the typical fashion of the dabbling ducks, on banks near the water, with dense vegetation and occasional bushes and trees. Full clutches contain seven to nine brownish eggs; incubation takes 24–26 days. Rearing of the young appears to be done only by the female. Before the autumnal migration small flocks are formed and the birds join up with other *Anas* species.

Migration: Bird of passage; it spends winters in Japan or southern China, also in S. E. Asia and westwards as far as India.

Yearly Cycle: Courtship and pairing begin just after December, spring migration along the Ussuri river is in March-April, arrival in the breeding grounds normally in May, and eggs are laid in June. The breeding grounds are left as early as September and from November onwards the birds are winter guests on the lakes of Japan or southern China.

Climate: In the breeding grounds winters are extremely hard (temperatures as low $-50°C$); in April/May temperatures rise quickly and a short warm summer follows with maximal temperatures of $25°C$ in July. In the main wintering quarters temperatures are normally near freezing point.

AVICULTURE

Rarely imported in former decades, at one time the falcated duck could be seen only in large zoological gardens; few breeders kept them. Nowadays, a stable preserve population has developed in western Europe; breeding successes and some new imports are the responsible factors. As a result the colourful species which is also quite easy to keep can be seen in many private collections and zoos, and numbers are increasing steadily.

Housing: It is best to keep them on communal ponds with adjoining stretches of grass as a run. But it is also quite possible to give them quite small enclosures or keep them on the densely populated display lakes of zoos and birds preserves. Falcated ducks are peaceable throughout the year and, naturally, they are hardy in the winter.

Food: Normal food for dabbling ducks.

Breeding: If breeding results are desired, falcated ducks should be put into a spacious, not very populated grassy enclosure, perhaps as fellow occupants of preserves in which geese breed. There the female can find for herself a quiet nesting place on the ground in the cover of vegetation; she chooses a site far distant from the pond if possible. Only a few prefer making the nest in a burrow, for instance on the island of the pond. In central and western European countries eggs are laid more or less at the same time—between mid-May and mid-June—in the Wildfowl Trust at Slimbridge, exceptionally in the second half of April. As the breeding ducks and their clutches on the grass are always endangered by predators the breeder would be well advised to have the eggs hatched in an incubator or to use other birds to foster them. The rearing of the ducklings without parents to guide them is no problem and some of the females lay second clutches if the eggs are removed. It is generally assumed that falcated ducks reach sexual maturity when they are two years old but one-year old birds have been known to breed.

Hybridization: Relatively pronounced within the genus *Anas* and particularly with other wigeons. Descendants are quite often fertile. Apparently a ruddy shelduck M. interbred successfully with a falcated duck F. in the 19th century, and since then this hybridization has been mentioned by a number of authors.

Baikal Teal
Anas formosa Georgi

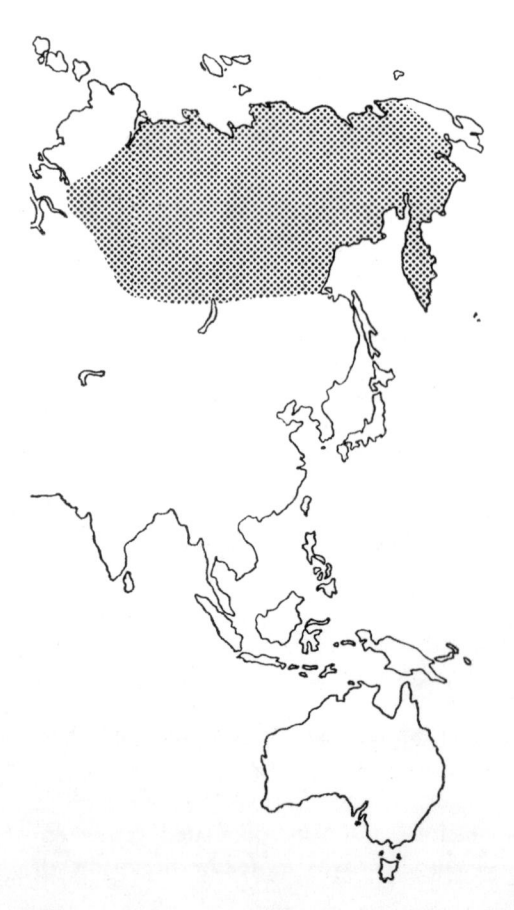

Comparative Size: A little larger than the green-winged teal.
Plumage: M. in breeding plumage see plate 55, F. plate 54; in eclipse plumage both sexes have yellow-brown bodies and are distinguished by a pale straw-coloured spot on either side of the base of the bill.

Natural Habit

Status: In east Siberia one of the most common—or perhaps the most common duck species. Large numbers of Baikal teal can still be observed during migration or in their winter quarters.
Habitat: Baikal teal breed on eutrophic lakes, also along the banks of oxbows of rivers, in swampy plains of the taiga and the southern tundra; they spend the winters on large inland lakes, reservoirs, rice paddies and in quiet oceanic bays of the Japanese islands.
Breeding Biology: Courtship and pairing take place during the spring migration. Nests have been found under the cover of reed grasses or low-growing bushes. Full clutches contain six to ten pale grey-

green eggs (similar to those of the green-winged teal) and incubation takes circa 24 days. Little else is known of the breeding biology of free-living Baikal teal.

Migration: Once incubation has begun the males undertake a moult migration to the estuaries of the rivers running northwards and, in the autumn, they migrate with the females and juveniles southwards to Japan, eastern and southeastern China; just a few find their way to Alaska, western Siberia and southeastern Asia.

Yearly Cycle: The majority of Baikal teal stay in their Japanese winter quarters from October to March; spring migration in Trans Baikal is in May; they remain in the breeding grounds from June to September. Moulting grounds are visited in July.

Climate: Very similar to the conditions under which falcated ducks live. In the more northerly breeding grounds of the Baikal teal the summer is even shorter and, particularly in the coastal zones, considerably cooler.

AVICULTURE

The Baikal teal is one of the most beautifully coloured ducks, its shining ornamental plumes and colour pattern being perfectly balanced. It was imported to Great Britain from Japan as early as 1840 and, in our century, large numbers of them have been kept at times. Until very recently Baikal teal were considered as almost impossible to breed; for that reason these lovely ducks have often been seen in zoos and bird preserves but only rarely in private parks.

Housing: Like all northern *Anas* species Baikal teals are quite easy to care for; they are not at all difficult to feed, and they are paeceable and long-lived. I, myself, know of birds which have been kept by bird lovers for 20 years (or even longer) and their condition remained satisfactory throughout. They can be kept in small as well as in communal preserves, on lakes of parks and in zoos. Breeding results can be expected only from birds bred in captivity whose requirements are no higher than, for instance, those of the wigeons and falcated ducks.

Food: Ordinary dabbling duck food.

Breeding: Of all the northern *Anas* species, the Baikal teal is the one least often bred, even in present times. Many theories have been developed for the low rate of reproduction in captivity, but the actual reasons are not really known.

How satisfying, therefore, to learn of a whole series of successful Baikal teal broods from WESSJOHANN who reported (written communication): caught as wild birds, a pair lived in a small enclosure for four years. They became quite tame and, in 1971, they were put into a spacious enclosure (more than 1 hectare); a first clutch of eggs was laid in June 1972 (not fertile). After the breeding season the male was replaced by a younger drake, caught wild. Eight fertile eggs were laid in a small spruce-wood between June 15 and 24, 1973. The female used to leave the nest briefly just before the evening twilight, and incubation took 23–24 days. The eight ducklings grew just like other ducklings, presented no difficulties and were fed on food dropped on the water and on pellets used for rearing chicks. At six to seven weeks the young Baikal teal had most of their feathers. The body of the juvenile male was a deeper brown than that of the juvenile female, i. e. similar to the eclipse plumage of the adults. After the beginning of May 1974, the adult female laid seven eggs, and two females fledged the previous year laid ten eggs each; altogether 20 young birds were reared to maturity—proof indeed that the Baikal teal can be bred in captivity. The adult female actually built her nest in a stall. Another breeder wrote to me and informed me that his

Baikal teal which grew to maturity in the summer of 1974 showed all the symptoms of intense courtship display from December onwards.

Hybridization: GRAY (1958) mentioned interbreeding with five different *Anas* species as well as with the red-crested pochard. In the majority of cases only the Baikal teal drakes hybridized, but in 1914 a bird was reared through interbreeding by a Baikal teal female and a versicolor drake.

Mallard
Anas platyrhynchos L.

Arrows (from left to right): Laysan, Hawaiian, Mexican, Florida and Greenland Mallard

Comparative Size: One of the largest of the dabbling ducks; M. weighs 1,000 to 1,400 g, F. 800 to 1,200 g.

Plumage: M. and F. in breeding plumage see plate 59; the eclipse plumage of the M. is darker than that of the F. and the bill lacks the orange markings; juveniles are similar to adult females.

NATURAL HABIT

Status: In Europe, large areas of Asia and parts of North America the most abundant duck. On the other hand, there are only relatively small populations of all sub-species, which in many cases are threatened with extinction.

Habitat: They inhabit areas with very divergent ecological conditions: the sea coast on the one hand, the lake in the park on the other; swampy plains as well as small mountain streams; the fiords of Greenland but also lakes of steppes and prairies.

Breeding Biology: Courtship display and pairing start in the autumn reaching a climax in October and also in January. On the whole, birds pair for one season only (tame and half-tame ducks may pair for life). Both male and female search for a nest site; locations are very variable. Nests may be made in reeds—a favourite place—or at times in trees and even on roofs of houses. Nest building, incubation and rearing of the young are done by the female. Normal clutches contain seven to eleven olive-green eggs; incubation takes 24–28 days. Young mallards are fully feathered when they are eight weeks old, by which time they are able to fly; wild birds inhabit almost exclusively marshy areas where they find plenty of vegetation while the young are flightless.

Migration: They are birds of passage, infrequent migrants and also stationary residents. Mallards winter wherever water is free of ice and thus gives them their basic needs; recently they have tended increasingly to stay on lakes and ponds within large townships. Many of the males undertake moult migrations (Volga delta, prairie lakes).

Yearly Cycle: This is staggered according to geographical location and regional climate; in central Europe breeding grounds are occupied from February onwards, eggs are laid from March onwards, followed by incubation. Young mallards able to fly can be seen in July and August. Males start to moult in May (non-breeders), females moult as soon as the young are fledged. The male moults into his breeding plumage after the beginning of September.

Climate: As a breeding bird the real mallard (nominate race) is missing only in arctic, sub-tropical and tropical zones where it is represented by sub-species.

Aviculture
(in Breeding Preserves and Parks)

Mallards are among the most beautiful of all ducks; if they were not so large and so abundant, doubtless, they would be the most popular inhabitants of a bird preserve. As they are very adaptable and easy to breed they have been domesticated quite early on in history and made use of by man. Nowadays, because of increasing urbanization and the countless numbers of half-tame mallards on the lakes and water areas of large towns, the birds are confronted by humans for a second time. Might it not be a modern form of domestication?

Breeding preserves keep the mallards rarely. What makes them troublesome is their undesirable habit of 'raping' females belonging to other species; even firmly paired females of numerous species are 'raped' by them (the female of a pair is not defended by her mate in such cases); invariably, undesired hybrids are the result.

Occasionally female mallard ducks are kept as foster mothers for the broods of others. They are quite suitable for the purpose but, unfortunately, they are likely to attract wild drakes. Because of the sexual behaviour of the latter and the possibility that they might carry infections of parasites, ornamental waterfowl preserves are not at all keen on having them. If a lake in a park is to have a population of mallards for the first time, the following procedure can be recommended: a group of young mallards should be pinioned and then left free on the lake where they should be supplied with plentiful food throughout the year. In the first winter wild birds will arrive and partake of the food; some of them will mate with the pinioned birds and breed on the same lake. If this does not happen, at least the wing-clipped ducks will breed and rear young ducklings which need not be pinioned later on. As long as the mallards are given a sufficient quantity of food very few of them will wander off elsewhere; in all probability they will be joined by others which will settle down with them.

It is not advisable to put grey ducks, spotbills and domestic ducks together with the mallards. They would interbreed, and eventually a mixed, unattractively coloured population would be created.

Hybridization: Tendencies very pronounced indeed: hybrid descendants are often fertile. GRAY (1958) named approximately 50 types of waterfowl—the mallard interbred with all of them.

Grey Duck

Anas superciliosa Gmelin

Comparative Size: Approximately the same as a mallard.

Plumage: New Zealand grey duck see plate 61; face is yellow-brown with a black-brown eye stripe, the rest of the body is mud-coloured and the feathers have a narrow border at the tips; speculum has a green sheen. The difference between the sexes shows up in the cloaca test, but they also have different voices. Juveniles have a paler colouring with a wider border on their feather tips until the autumn; afterwards they moult into the adult plumage.

NATURAL HABIT

Status: The grey duck is the ecological counterpart of the mallard in New Zealand and Australia. The birds are very abundant in many places and at the same time they are the ducks most frequently hunted. But, even the smaller island populations (Palau grey ducks) are apparently not endangered.

Habitat: Any type of waters as long as they offer sufficient nourishment and the right places for making a nest; favourite habitats are fairly large, shallow lakes, river plains, flooded areas and coastal lagoons.

Breeding Biology: Courtship display is not very impressive; pairing starts shortly before eggs are laid. Nests are made on the ground under cover of vegetation, in hollow stumps of trees (in flooded, tree-grown meadows) and also in deserted birds' nests. Full clutch consists of eight to ten greenish-white eggs, incubation takes 26–28 days. In New Zealand females were observed with 14–17 ducklings (either very large clutches or the young of two females?). Juveniles are able to fly when they are seven to eight weeks old and, in the following year, they are sexually mature.

Migration: When the dry period sets in, the Australian grey ducks start roaming the continent in huge swarms. They fly to inland lakes which permanently carry water and to rivers, but also to the coasts. Wherever periods of rainfall give them good living conditions they can be found in large numbers. The birds belonging to the other sub-species are permanent residents.

Yearly Cycle: Breeding season in Australia at the beginning of the regional rainy seasons; in New South Wales eggs are laid from May to November, in the Northern Territory from February to September, in New Zealand at springtime (approximately from November onwards).

Climate: Habitats are predominantly in the zones of dry-hot tropic and savanna climates and extend to the temperate areas of New Zealand and Tasmania.

AVICULTURE

Grey ducks have been shown in European zoos for more than 100 years (in Berlin since 1874) and they have been bred for almost as long. The Australian sub-species, in particular, had been imported, but nowadays all three types of grey duck are being kept. As the Palau grey duck is very much smaller than the other two it is regarded with even greater interest.

Housing: Because of their large size and their rather plain colouring plus their tendency to hybridize, Australian and New Zealand grey ducks are only rarely kept by breeders in private preserves (the differences between the two ducks— *A. s. rogersi* and *A. s. superciliosa*—can only be determined up to a certain degree). On the other hand they are very suitable for the lakes in parks, but in the manner of the spotbills they tend to interbreed with the other ducks. The Palau grey duck, *A. s. pelewensis*, can be recommended as an inhabitant of breeding preserves, but care has to be taken that they do not have the opportunity to hybridize (even with larger species).

Food: Like mallard.
Breeding: The two large sub-species breed freely in captivity; unfavourable conditions do not deter them (such as disturbances, predators and periods of poor weather); the females still manage to rear many ducklings. In the British Wildfowl Trust eggs are laid between the beginning of March and June, as a rule two weeks later than the mallards'. Nests are made in shelters, nesting boxes and baskets, only rarely on the ground under cover of vegetation.

The Palau grey duck first reached Europe around 1967 (Tierpark, Berlin and Wildfowl Trust, amongst other places) and, since 1968, it has been breeding in the Trust on a regular basis and with success.
Hybridization: Strong tendency within the mallard group (compare with spotbill). The majority of nesting birds are presumably no longer pure breeds.

Spotbill

Anas poecilorhyncha Forster

Comparative Size: Like mallard.
Plumage: Adults see plate 64; no seasonal dimorphism; M. and F. have the same colouring. The dominant colour tone of the body is a light silver grey (particularly in Indian spotbills), the speculum green with a black and white border. Middle part of bill black, base red, towards tip yellowish. Juveniles more brown in coloration, speculum almost without sheen, bill without red.

Natural Habit

Status: Just as the grey duck is the subspecies representing the mallard in New Zealand and Australia, the spotbill represents it in South-East Asia. In many places spotbills occur with the abundance of mallards.
Habitat: In southern breeding grounds the birds inhabit rice paddies, marshy plains, ponds overgrown with sedge, and river meadows. In Siberia spotbills breed in the reed banks of oxbows and ponds. In some areas of Japan they have a tendency of urbanization.
Breeding Biology: On the whole spotbills breed like mallards. Nests have been found almost exclusively on reed banks or in rice fields (especially on the slopes of dams). Clutches consist of eight to fourteen pale brown or green eggs; incubation takes 26–28 days. The female alone looks after the young.
Migration: Indian and Burmese populations are either stationary residents or infrequent migrants; those inhabiting more northerly are migratory. Even in Japan only a few of the birds spend the winters there.
Yearly Cycle: On the Indian sub-continent

only the breeding season depends on the rainfall. Main season in the North between July and October, in the South November/December. In China and Japan egg laying starts in April, in Trans Baikal at the end of May, perhaps two weeks later than mallards and pintails.

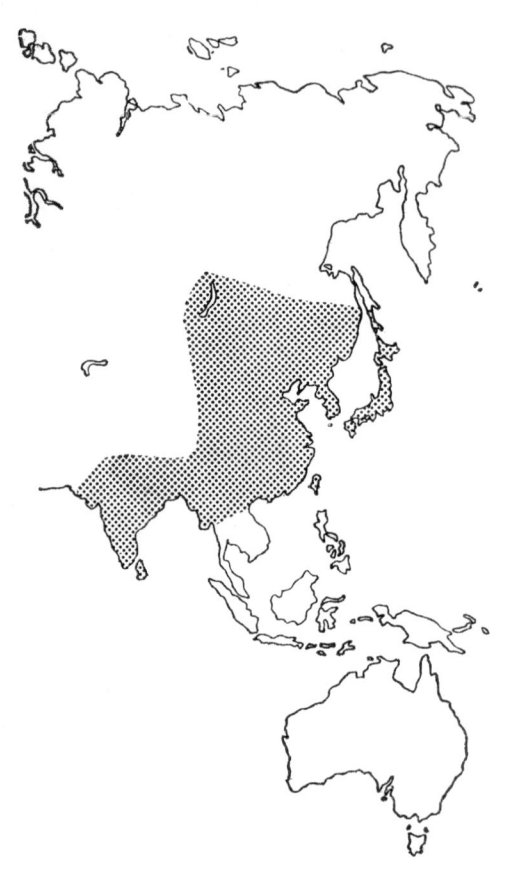

Climate: Indian spotbills kept in central Europe normally come from areas with hot savanna and monsoon climates throughout the year.

Aviculture

In Europe, the first spotbills could be seen in the London Zoo in 1870 and in the Berlin Zoo in 1875; first breeding results were obtained in 1874 and 1881 respectively. Later on, Indian spotbills were imported quite often and could frequently be seen in zoological gardens, on lakes in parks and towns and, at times, they have been bred and reared by private enthusiasts. In spite of their tropical origin the ducks are robust, hardy in the winter and undemanding in their requirements.

Housing: Because of their size and tendency to interbreed their inclusion in private collections is not always advisable. On lakes in parks they may be kept rather like the mallards and can be left free. There is little danger of them wandering off as long as they are given enough grain to feed on in all seasons.

Food: See mallard.

Breeding: Easy to breed, they normally have a high rate of reproduction. They attain sexual maturity after one year; pairs form in late autumn, eggs are laid between mid-April and mid-May which is later than the mallard. Spotbill males 'rape' females of other species, whereas spotbill females are 'raped' by mallard and grey duck drakes. Today only very few pure breeding stocks of spotbills are left.

Hybridization: Within the mallard group obviously no intrinsic mating barriers exist. Even where birds are firmly paired, the female may be 'raped' by a strange drake, and thus numerous hybrids will be members of the next generation; these, in turn, are fully fertile. If mallards inhabit the lake of a park and, additionally, grey ducks and spotbills are kept on it, not many years will pass before the lake is so full of mixed breeds that the only pure species are new immigrant mallards. For this reason it is advisable to make it a rule never to keep any spotbills, grey or Philippine ducks on a park lake. These three species should be kept in small preserves which are able to produce pure-bred species and cut out unwanted hybridization.

Philippine Duck

Anas luzonica Frazer

Comparative Size: A little smaller than a mallard.

Plumage: Adults see plate 66; no seasonal dimorphism; sides of the head cinnamon brown, body grey-brown with feathers having lighter edges. Wings have a green speculum with a black and white border. Bill blue-grey, that of the male has a black line at the base. Juveniles much like adults.

NATURAL HABIT

Status: Although no exact population count exists, it is certain that the Philippine duck which inhabits the 7,000 or more islands of the archipelago is not an endangered species. It is fairly rare on the main island, Luzon, but flocks of up to 2,000 birds have been observed on Mindoro (TEMME by letter, September 1974).

Habitat: TEMME has found the Philippine duck on large salt water basins where salt is extracted, in rice fields, on rivers and lakes as well as on ponds and pools, even where these are surrounded by dense jungle.

Breeding Biology: Behaviour corresponds very much with that of the mallard. Display, however, is less conspicuous and the breeding season lasts eight months. Nests have been found on the ground under cover of vegetation and they have contained eight to ten (sometimes even more) white eggs. Incubation takes 26–27 days, and sometimes both parents guide the ducklings.

Migration: The Philippine Islands are never left, neither during nor after the breeding season; the various populations undertake short wandering flights only.

Yearly Cycle: According to written communication by TEMME the breeding season lasts from April to November, being at its height in July and August.

Climate: High temperatures and an enormous amount of rainfall (monsoon rain) throughout the year cause great humidity (tropical rain forest climate).

AVICULTURE

Philippine ducks are simply coloured; as such they are waterfowl which have not been of great interest to breeders in the past. DE LAVEAGA (California) received the first import of the ducks in 1935; with them he managed to rear only a few hybrids. Between 1948 and 1950 a few of the ducks were acquired by D. RIPLEY (USA) and a little later by the British Wildfowl Trust. After excellent breeding results by JONES, Leckford (UK), zoos and breeders in western Europe and the USA paid them attention and took them up in the mid-1950s. Nowadays, Philippine ducks are kept by zoos

and bird preserves with really good waterfowl collections. They are rarely included in private collections because of their less attractive colouring.
Housing: Like all ducks of the mallard type the Philippines are undemanding in their requirements and, in spite of their tropical origin, they are robust and fairly hardy in the winter.
Food: Like mallard.
Breeding: RIPLEY (1951) was the first who managed to get a clutch of four eggs at New Haven, Connecticut, at the end of June 1950. Supported by the experiences of one ornithologist in the Philippines, it was at first believed that a full clutch consisted of not more than four eggs. Such is not the case, however, as numerous clutches in our preserves have shown; as a rule they contain seven to ten eggs. TEMME always found that wild birds laid white eggs whereas those of birds kept in preserves are greenish.
The breeding of Philippine ducks is not particularly difficult. The birds are assumed to be sexually mature when they are one year old, but they rarely start laying for another year or even two years. Nests are made in shelters or in baskets. Eggs are laid in mid-May, in the Wildfowl Trust already after mid-April; the latter is exceptional. Rearing of the young is very much as with other species of ducks.
Hybridization: Particularly pronounced tendencies within the group of mallard ducks. Compare with spotbill.

Chestnut Teal

Anas castanea (Eyton)

Comparative Size: Considerably smaller and slimmer than mallard.
Plumage: M. and F. in breeding plumage see plate 65; head of M. with green gloss, body chestnut brown; F. dark grey-brown; eclipse plumage of M. darker than at breeding time, head black-green; F. in eclipse hardly changed. Juveniles differ from F. mainly by having speculum with hardly any brightness.

NATURAL HABIT

Status: They are fairly common within the small Australian area of distribution, but they are far behind the population of grey ducks and grey teal. The very similar Auckland teal inhabits New Zealand where the population is small but not especially endangered; on the neighbouring islands, however, these birds have been almost exterminated.
Habitat: In Australia, during the breeding season, the birds prefer coastal lagoons, mangrove swamps, river deltas, and islands off the coasts to inland lakes. In Tasmania, chestnut teal nest along the coasts, on inland lakes, river courses and marshy plains; between these habitats their numbers are fairly evenly divided.
Breeding Biology: After a very pronounced courtship display within the winter flocks, the paired birds spread out along the water zones where they breed. Nests are made in dense reeds, sometimes in tree hollows and—where available—in nesting boxes. Clutch is seven to ten very pale brown eggs; incubation takes up to 28 days. Many of the drakes take an active part in rearing the young; juveniles are fully able to fly when they are eight weeks old.
Migration: Breeding birds of a particular area congregate on large lakes and river estuaries of their own region; only a few of them wander off further than 500 km.
Yearly Cycle: It corresponds with the seasons of the southern hemisphere; display and pairing activities develop

in August and September. Clutches are found from October (in lesser numbers up to December); rearing of the young and moult of adults during the summer and, from March onwards the formation of winter flocks may be observed.

Climate: Southern Australia has a warm mediterranean and mild climate; winter temperatures average 8–12°C; conditions are roughly similar to those of southern Europe.

AVICULTURE

The beautiful chestnut teal have been very popular inhabitants of private preserves and animal parks for many decades; they were shown for the first time in Europe by the London Zoo in 1870. Looking after them is rather easy, they are quite hardy and, nowadays, chances of breeding results are reasonably good. For the above reasons these pretty ducks deserve to be recommended for inclusion in a waterfowl collection. Opinions on their temperament vary, but in my own experiences they are not aggressive and are well suited for collections of smaller species of ducks.

Housing: The breeder keeps the species on communal ponds or in small enclosures together with two or three other pairs of ducks. In cold, unfavourable weather they need a dry, draught-free shelter for the night; heated houses for the winter are not necessary.

Food: They are easy to feed and have no special requirements.

Breeding: Chestnut teal now inhabiting European and American preserves are almost certainly birds bred and reared in captivity. Therefore it should not be difficult to obtain further breeding results with them. However, their urge to breed is far below that of the mallard group. Without doubt, one year old chestnut teals are sexually mature, though many females only start laying in the second or third year of their life; some do not get broody at all. Females which are good breeders manage up to three full clutches in one summer, but only if the eggs are removed before the birds start incubating them. In the northern spring months, eggs are usually laid from March onwards, in the Wildfowl Trust normally in the second half of April; they like laying in nest boxes; the ducklings can be reared quite easily together with other young ducks.

Hybridization: Numerous hybrid breeds are known to exist; however firmly paired drakes only rarely mate with females of another species.

Green-winged Teal
Anas crecca L.

Comparative Size: Total length 34–36 cm, wing span 170–190 cm, weight 250–440 g. Smallest northern dabbling duck.

Plumage: Adults in breeding plumage see plate 58; M. in eclipse and juveniles similar in coloration to F. Sexes in young birds are distinguishable with a degree of certainty because of different markings on the wings, but the cloaca test is more reliable. The male of the

American sub-species can be distinguished quite easily by the vertical white line on either side of the chest.

NATURAL HABIT

Status: In the large area of their distribution and in suitable places they are quite common; in central and western Europe, however, they are rare breeding birds.

Habitat: During breeding season shallow ponds with good vegetation as well as eutrophic shallow lakes, also marshes, moors, forest lakes; large inland lakes, coastal waters, river courses and lagoons at migration time and as winter quarters.

Breeding Biology: When the green-winged teal return to their breeding grounds in the spring they are usually firmly paired and soon lead a secluded life on the shores under dense cover. They make their well concealed nests under bushes, in sedge and scrub, even in the heather and in woods far distant from any water. A full clutch contains eight to twelve cream coloured, slightly green eggs. Incubation takes 21–23 days. The females look after the young under the concealing vegetation of shallow waters.

Migration: Bird of passage, infrequent migrant as well as stationary resident which mainly winters to the south of its breeding grounds — in Europe particularly in Great Britain, Holland, Switzerland, and the Mediterranean countries; the North American populations wander southwards as far as Honduras and the Lesser Antilles.

Yearly Cycle: Eggs are laid between beginning of April (western Europe) and June (N. E. Europe and Siberia). Incubation, rearing of young and moult take approximately three months; afterwards small summer groups congregate and, in central Europe, they migrate to their wintering quarters from October onwards.

Climate: They breed in many countries with different climatic conditions, ranging from Arctic to temperate as well as mediterranean and northern boreal climate zones. During the winter they may even be found in the tropics.

AVICULTURE

A number of breeders pay little attention to the small, beautifully coloured and undemanding ducks (probably because so many captured birds are offered for sale by animal dealers). Undoubtedly, captured adult birds remain shy, usually try to hide and rarely want to breed. Those bred in captivity, on the other hand, are quite different. They are very suitable for waterfowl enthusiasts with little experience and limited space for the needs of their birds. Within the last few years the American green-winged teal is increasingly kept and bred. It is slightly larger than the palearctic species. M. – like Baikal Teal – with cream-white band on the chest.

Housing: Green-winged teal are equally suitable for accomodation in aviaries, small enclosures and on communal ponds. In preserves with little cover from growing plants they get tame within a short time. However, if breeding results are the aim, they should be provided with lakes with plenty of shore-vegetation and also low, dense ground cover. As long as ponds are not frozen the birds can stay on them during the winter; in periods of frost they need a good shelter. Green-winged teal are not sensitive to cold on the whole.

Food: Normal food for surface-feeding ducks dropped on the water and plenty of duckweed.

Breeding: If a bird enthusiast keeps several pairs of green-winged teal, he should accommodate them on a fairly large lake during the winter months. Here the drakes will display and call unceasingly from December until well into spring time. Afterwards the pairs should be put into solitary (smaller) enclosures where they can breed.

In their search for a suitable nesting site a pair takes an enormous amount of trouble; everything is examined and turned over. If there is the tiniest hole in ae fenc the birds are certain to find it and will probably wander off. Nests are usually made on the ground under dense cover of vegetation, but also in nesting boxes. Eggs are rarely laid before the beginning of May; if the female is left undisturbed she will breed quite reliably; if eggs are removed second clutches may be expected. Rearing of the young— whether by the female or in conditions of artificially applied warmth—is quite easy. The young birds are fully feathered and able to fly when they are six weeks old; they moult into their first breeding plumage during the first autumn.

Hybridization: Not very marked; green-winged teal may be kept on ponds together with other small species without having to worry about their interbreeding (perhaps with the exception of the Chilean teal).

Chilean Teal

Anas flavirostris Vieillot

Comparative Size: Little larger than green-winged teal.

Plumage: M. in adult plumage see plate 62; body predominantly grey-brown, wings with bright green speculum and light brown coverts. Overall appearance, minor colour variations and different voice distinguish M. from F. Juveniles similar to F.

Natural Habit

Status: Apart from yellow-tailed pintail the most common species of ducks in many parts of South America; since they inhabit small water bodies they are thus widely distributed.

Habitat: All sorts of waters with rich vegetation in the coastal plains, but also lakes, small pools and river courses in the Andes up to 3,000 m high.

Breeding Biology: Small groups separate from the winter flocks; after an inconspicuous courtship display pairs leave the groups and occupy their nest sites. Only some nests are on the ground, under cover of vegetation; they are also made in niches of walls and houses; many Chilean teal make use of the deserted tree nests of birds of prey and the large stick nests of green parakeets (the latter breed a few months later than Chilean teal). A full clutch contains five to six cream or pale red-brown eggs; brooding takes 26 days. Both parents guide the young ducklings and—whilst they are being reared—the adult birds moult.

Migration: Bird of passage, infrequent migrant as well as stationary resident. The southern populations migrate northwards as far as the Buenos Aires Province, those of the periodically dry interior of the country undertake roaming flights, and the breeding birds of the lakes in the Andes (e. g. Sharp-winged Teal, *A. f. oxyptera*) are stationary residents.

Yearly Cycle: Main breeding time is in October and November, migration to winter quarters in January and February, or during the rainy period of the respective area.

Climate: Chilean teal breed in sub-arctic as well as in alpine temperate and tropical climatic zones.

AVICULTURE

Although the Chilean teal are not very gaily coloured they were introduced in Europe a long time ago (first breeding result 1909); nowadays they are not only kept in many places but also very often bred. During the last few years a few alpine sharp-winged teal were imported into Europe. They are a sub-species which is a little larger and distinguishable from the main species by being more sparsely speckled on chest and flanks which gives them a lighter appearance. Chilean teal have the merit of a quiet and peaceable behaviour; they are not as shy as the green-winged teal and less demanding in accommodation requirements, especially regarding the vegetation of their enclosure.

Housing: Chilean teal are particularly suitable for being kept in small preserves and among collections of small species of ducks. Once they have become adapted to their surroundings they are not very sensitive to cold and they are hardy; it is quite easy to keep them on large lakes in zoological gardens. Ground cover of vegetation or other means to hide are unnecessary. They can winter on ice-free water or in a shelter.

Food: Normal food for dabbling ducks.

Breeding: Chilean teal belong to those species of small ducks which are very easily bred in captivity. Making up pairs of birds is not difficult (not even in the case of mature birds). Eggs are laid in nest boxes, in central Europe rarely before the beginning of May, but in Great Britain as early as from end-March onwards. The females may produce one or even two further clutches, but they also brood reliably if they are left undisturbed. Rearing of the ducklings is normally without losses; the young are sexually mature at the end of the first year of their life.

Hybridization: Interbreeding with other small dabbling ducks by both drake and female is known to have occurred; it is fairly rare, however.

Pintail

Anas acuta L.

Comparative Size: Only a little smaller than a mallard.

Plumage: M. in breeding plumage see plate 57; in eclipse plumage upper side of M. slightly darker than that of F., middle tail streamers not elongated. Juveniles distinguishable from adults by immature wings.

Natural Habit

Status: Very large populations in Eurasia and North America but only a sporadic and fairly rare breeding bird in central Europe.

Habitat: Shallow bays of large inland lakes in open plains; extensive river plains; coastal, prairie and tundra waters.

Breeding Biology: Pair formation and display begin during the winter. Males take an active part in the selection of the nest territory, keep contact with the female during the time of incubation and, initially, help with rearing of the young. The nest is always on dry ground with more or less good cover. A full clutch contains seven to eleven greenish or cream coloured eggs. Incubation takes 22–23 days. The young pintails are able to fly when they are seven weeks old, moult into their breeding plumage in their first year and are sexually mature at ten months although many of them do not pair and breed until well into their second year.

Migration: They are all birds of passage: they migrate not only in a southerly direction but also far to the East and to the West (for instance some of them are known to have crossed the Atlantic and the Pacific).

Yearly Cycle: Varying from South to North which they have in common with many other species. In central Europe: arrival in breeding grounds mid-March, beginning of laying period mid-April, and autumnal migration in October/November.

Climate: The majority of pintails breed in somewhat cooler and rougher climatic conditions than the western European populations; their breeding occurs as far as the arctic tundra. In contrast they migrate far into the tropics in the winter (central Africa, Sri Lanka and Colombia).

Aviculture

Pintails are robust, easy to care for and very attractively coloured birds; they are not aggressive and, of course, they are hardy in the winter. They are equally suitable for keeping on large lakes of zoos, bird preserves and parks; they can also be looked after by a bird lover with little experience.

The Kerguelen pintails, too, a small sub-species from the southern Indian Ocean—coloured like female pintails—and imported into Europe for the first time in 1951, are equally easy to keep and breed. They are also fairly insensitive to cold in the winter.

Housing: Pintails which are kept entirely for show are equally suitable for very populated concrete-pools (e. g. in zoos) or even rather small enclosures. If breeding results are expected, however, they need a fairly large pond, preferably with well-covered shores and an adjoining area as a run.

Food: No special requirements.

Breeding: In quarters which are not too confined and offer plenty of good cover, breeding results are quite common. The drakes' very pronounced courtship display goes on throughout most of the spring; it decreases gradually shortly before egg laying begins in April. Nests are either on grass in the open or in nesting boxes. The females' breeding habit is quiet and reliable; if they are prevented from incubating they lay a second clutch. Rearing of the ducklings is just as easy as with other species of ducks.

Broods of Kerguelen pintails can also be very productive; females lay their seven to nine ochre coloured eggs in nesting boxes or small shelters during the spring months. Incubation takes 24–25 days; duckling losses are are. Sexes are distinguished by different voices.

Hybridization: Pintails interbreed with other *Anas* species and sometimes with species of quite different tribes, but the number of hybrids they produce, even in communal preserves, is at a tolerable level. The first Kerguelen pintails received by the Wildfowl Trust at Slimbridge were all drakes; they were crossbred with female pintails, and—applying the principles of backcrossing—the Trust has been able to establish Kerguelen pintail breeding.

Bahama Pintail

Anas bahamensis L.

Comparative Size: Considerably smaller than mallard.

Plumage: M. and F. see plate 80; no seasonal dimorphism; sexes distinguishable from each other by overall appearance as well as voice. Juvenile F. has even, pale edges to lanceolated shoulder and flank feathers, but juvenile M. has yellow-brown tips on otherwise dark feathers.

NATURAL HABIT

Status: Nowadays the northern Bahama pintail is rare on the islands of the Caribbean, so is the Galapagos pintail. The southern Bahama pintail is widely distributed on the South American continent.

Habitat: Warm eutrophic lakes with a wealth of emergent vegetation, and shores grown with sedge and reeds and single bushes; also in zones bordering the river mouths; shallow coastal lagoons, and on the edge of mangrove swamps.

Breeding Biology: Like many other dabbling ducks they display and pair among the winter flocks; afterwards single pairs occupy a small nest territory; the female accompanied by the male chooses a site, preferably in the vicinity of bushes, and makes the nest with blades of grasses she finds nearby. A full clutch contains eight to twelve light-brown eggs; incubation takes 25–26 days; it is believed that the male helps to guide the ducklings.

Migration: Island populations are normally stationary residents. Southern Bahama pintail look for suitable winter sites in accordance with the rainy and dry periods; southern populations are entirely birds of passage.

Yearly Cycle: Breeding seasons vary and depend on local conditions. In Argentina and Chile the breeding season begins at the time of the southern spring (October/November); it is irregular in the tropics and may be after the rainy season sets in; on the islands of Central America it is influenced by the seasons of the northern year.

Climate: On the whole, breeding grounds are in tropical to temperate warm climates with periodic rainfall; there are some exceptions where specific, local conditions prevail.

AVICULTURE

Of the three sub-species mentioned earlier on, it has been mainly the southern Bahama pintail which has been imported recently. Occasionally a few Galapagos pintails have been imported in North America and western Europe. Owing to mutation, a not very stable breeding form developed after 1930, and again—more recently—after 1950. Some of the mutants are still offered for sale by the animal trade under the name of silver Bahama pintail.

Bahama pintails have a reputation for being non-aggressive, easily bred and kept ornamental waterfowl, and they are inhabitants of pracitcally all zoos, bird trusts and private preserves. They are the result of interbreeding by the two sub-species—the northern and southern Bahama pintails. Considering that they are birds with a tropical origin they are remarkably insensitive to cold and, as long as the water is not frozen, they can spend winters out in the open.

Housing: In zoos and bird preserves they are usually kept on smaller display ponds. A breeder has them on communal lakes, and likes to include them in a collection of small duck species; he can also house them in a small enclosure together with one or two other species. They should spend winters in the open only if the water area at their disposal is sufficiently large, otherwise in shelters.

Food: A simple grain or mixed food as well as duckweed.

Breeding: Sexual maturity is attained at the age of one year or in the second year. The male uses attractive display poses for courting the female. Most of the eggs are laid in nesting boxes, less frequently on the ground, under cover of vegetation. Laying may begin in April but is mostly in May. The females are reliable in brooding and guiding their young; they lay second clutches if the first one is removed. I made some notes on the ducklings' development as follows: when they were 16 days old the first tail quills could be seen; flank, shoulder and tail feathers appeared on the 20th day. Four weeks old ducklings have nearly all their feathers except in the middle of the back; when they are six to seven weeks old they should

be able to fly. From October onwards the moult into adult plumage.
Hybridization: They have no pronounced tendencies, but interbreeding with yellow-billed pintails and Chilean teal among others is known to have occurred. If Bahama pintails are firmly paired they very rarely interbreed.

Red-billed Pintail
Anas erythrorhyncha Gmelin

Comparative Size: Noticeably larger than green-winged teal.
Plumage: Adults see plate 81; no seasonal dimorphism; within the species no colour variants, M. and F. very similar in coloration, distinguishable from each other by slight nuances and different voices. Juvenile plumage rather mat and less clearly marked (particularly markings of the face), shoulders without violet gloss, bill dark red.

NATURAL HABIT

Status: Of all ducks in Africa red-billed pintails probably have the largest total population; on numerous waters they form the majority of swimming birds.
Habitat: All sorts of different water areas; during the breeding seasons the birds prefer lakes with plenty of emergent vegetation, or pools and ditches of low-lying swamps; afterwards they migrate to larger lakes (particularly in the African rift valleys), but also to river courses, and to freshwater as well as brackish water lagoons.
Breeding Biology: In most areas of Africa the beginning of the rainy season induces the breeding instinct of the red-billed pintails. They occupy their nest territory in pairs or small groups. The female makes a nest in the reeds of the shore vegetation; she lines it with grass and—later on—with down. A clutch contains five to ten (up to twelve) pale brown eggs; incubation takes 25–27 days. Ducklings are looked after by the female, sometimes helped by the male.
Migration: Predominantly stationary residents or infrequent migrants; some populations undertake regular roaming flights within the breeding grounds during the dry season—from South Africa to the Ethiopian region, for instance.
Yearly Cycle: Eggs are laid at the beginning of the rainy period means that there are considerable variations in laying times. In many areas the breeding season is spread over several months, in Rhodesia from September to May.
Climate: Temperatures are very hot throughout the year. During the dry period of roughly six months, many lakes evaporate while vegetation becomes sparse; a rainy season of almost equal lenght follows when vegetation is again plentiful. North of the equator the heaviest rainfall is between June and September, in South

59 ↑ Mallard

60 ↑ Laysan Teal   61 ↓ Grey Duck

62 ↑ Chilean Teal M.
63 ↓ Cape Teal F.

64 ↑   Spotbill

65 ↑ Chestnut Teal								66 ↓ Philippine Duck

67 ↑   Marbled Teal F.

68 ↑ Garganey M.					69 ↓ Blue-winged Teal

70 ↑   Cinnamon Teal
71 ↓   Brazilian Teal

72 ↑   European Pochard M.

73 ↑   Canvasback M.   74 ↓   Common White-eye

75 ↑ Tufted Duck

76 ↑ Ring-necked Duck   77 ↓ Lesser Scaup

78 ↑ Red and white Crake
79 ↓ Moorhen

Africa from November until March. The alternating seasons influence the yearly cycle of many African bird species.

AVICULTURE

Whereas the Bahama pintails possess glowing colours and are very lively, the red-billed pintails are sedate in manner, rather dull coloured and therefore far less popular than the former. The first to take any notice of them was the London Zoo (about 1850) and, later, the Berlin Zoo (1882). Since then, up to the present numerous birds have been imported from Africa. Nowadays they are on show in practically all zoos and bird preserves. But only a few red-billed pintails have ever been kept by breeders.

Housing: Caring for the small, undemanding red-billed pintails is quite easy in all kinds of preserves; it is best to put them on shallow, warm ponds together with other small species of ducks. They should spend winters in a closed shelter if there are periods of persistent cold weather, particularly if they are newly imported; acclimatized red-billed pintails can be kept in the open as long as their pond is not frozen.

Food: No special requirements.

Breeding: Red-billed pintails belong to the most easily bred species of ducks, but—to the best of my knowledge—pairs rarely breed before the second or third year. They are actually sexually mature at the age of one year; certainly wild birds are. They display and pair in a far less conspicuous manner than the closely related Bahama pintails. In central Europe eggs are normally laid in May, exceptionally in April; in the British Wildfowl Trust predominantly in June/July, more rarely in May or April. Nests are made in nesting boxes or holes. Rearing of the young, either by the parents or in conditions of artificial warmth is quite easy, as a rule.

Hybridization: Obviously no pronounced tendency; the only interbreeding ever mentioned in ornithological literature is that of red-billed pintail and yellow-billed duck, *A. undulata*.

Versicolor Teal

Anas versicolor Vieillot

Comparative Size: A little larger than green-winged teal.

Plumage: M. and F. see plate 82; no seasonal dimorphism; M. several years old slightly larger, hind third of the body more finely freckled and flanks more broadly barred than F. In juveniles only minor colour variations compared with adults, markings of bill always paler.

The very similar Andean puna is larger and can be recognised because of its strikingly long, straight bill.

NATURAL HABIT

Status: According to reports on South American ducks, the versicolor teal population is spread over large areas of the sub-continents; the birds are fairly common but not as abundant as some other species, particularly the yellow-billed pintail and Chilean teal.

Habitat: Shallow waters with good vegetation in open grasslands and also in cultivated areas. The Andean puna breeds in the shallow lakes grown with rushes in the high plateaux of the Andes (Puna Zone).

Breeding Biology: Pairs of versicolor teal find themselves a place in the sedge grown margins of small ponds or pools where they are not very noticeable. They make their nests among tussocks of grasses or dead rushes.

A full clutch consists of ten cream-coloured eggs; incubation takes 24–25 days. The young are reared by both parents on the water's shore where they have plenty of vegetation.

Migration: Southern breeding birds wander as far as the Province of Buenos Aires where they join up with Chilean and yellow-billed pintails on larger lakes and costal lagoons.

Yearly Cycle: The breeding season begins at the time of the southern spring, approximately from October onwards; in northern regions it depends partly on the rainfall. Andean punas' breeding habits are spread over the whole year.

Climate: The majority of versicolor teal inhabit sub-tropical and temperate climatic zones; temperatures averaged 7°C during the breeding season on the Falkland Islands in 1970/71, and frost was registered during 25 nights (WELLER 1972).

AVICULTURE

Versicolor teal inhabit the same areas as Chilean teal, Chiloe wigeons and yellow-billed pintails but are far less often imported in Europe and North America than the others. Until 1975 they were rarely offered for sale by animal dealers. I got it confirmed by many breeders that many versicolor teal, kept in Western Europe during this time, showed all the symptoms of inbreeding such as: low rate of reproductive activity: small clutches; high rate of unfertilized eggs; many losses in rearing the young. Successful keeping and breeding are both more likely as far as the Andean puna is concerned; it has been imported a number of times in recent years.

Housing: Versicolor teal are attractive and always active; a waterfowl enthusiast keeps them in a fairly small, communal enclosure with a warm, sunny pond and lets them spend the winter in a place free of frost. When they are several years old and well acclimatized they are not nearly as sensitive to cold as is often believed; my own breeding birds are given the opportunity to bathe in the open, even in conditions of snow and frost.

Food: The same as species of dabbling ducks; they should be offered as much duckweed as possible.

Breeding: The breeding of versicolor teal, affected—more or less—by inbreeding is not very productive. Many females of pairs do not start egg-laying until the second or thire year, if at all. In my enclosure eggs have been laid in the first half of April, in the Wildfowl Trust about mid-April. I find it remarkable that versicolor teal—in contrast to ringed teal—do not stop laying during periods of cold weather. As they usually nest in nesting boxes, the female can brood there without being disturbed; females which are good for breeding purposes may well produce one or two further clutches if the first one is removed. Once the young have hatched they should be put into an incubator for rearing; in that case the breeder has the additional advantage that he can observe exactly what progress the young versicolor teal are making and give them the best food

possible (e. g. ant larvae and particularly duckweed).
Hybridization: Manifestly insignificant: GRAY (1958) noted down only one case of interbreeding with the Baikal teal.

On the other hand, cross-breeding of versicolor teal with Andean puna is to be expected, but should be strictly avoided in order to keep the species pure.

Hottentot Teal

Anas punctata Burchell

Comparative Size: Smaller than green-winged teal.
Plumage: Adults see plate 83; no seasonal dimorphism; the Hottentot teal is a smaller version of the versicolor teal with darker and warmer colour tones. In appearance M. and F. difficult to distinguish from each other, but voices differ. Plumage of juveniles looks more faded and underparts patchy pale-brown.

NATURAL HABIT

Status: They have a patchy distribution; they are common in tropical East Africa and Madagaskar, but in all other areas they are fairly rare and inhabit some localitites only.

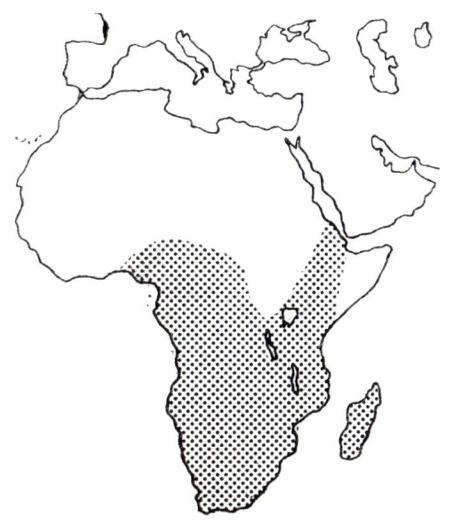

Habitat: Muddy inland waters where reeds and rushes grow, also marshes and flooded meadows of the savanna and coastal regions; large lakes and lagoons are only inhabited in the shore region with aquatic and reed vegetation.

Breeding Biology: Hottentot teal live either in pairs or in small groups. After a short, inconspicuous courtship display and choice of nest territory the female makes the nest on the shore, or she may prefer building it on tussocks of sedge in shallow water; the nest is rather carelessly constructed. Brooding the six to eight cream-coloured eggs takes 23–24 days. The female alone rears the young under the protective cover of plants which grow on the shores.

Migration: In the main stationary residents; the birds wander to nearby larger lakes only where waters dry out in the periods of no rainfall.

Yearly Cycle: This is another species whose breeding instinct is influenced by the rainy season. In the whole area of distribution, beginning of egg-laying ranges over all the months of the year.

Climate: See red-billed pintail.

AVICULTURE

It seems remarkable that Hottentot teal did not reach Europe before 1930 approximately, although they are by no means rare in Africa, as mentioned above. Initially, newly imported birds need a great deal of warmth, and they are rather frail. Once they are well established, however, they are hardly more difficult to keep than cinnamon or ringed teal. A breeder in Leipzig has had two Hottentot teal, caught wild, in his preserve for the last eleven years.

Housing: Hottentot teal should be put only into enclosures which are sunny and well sheltered and have a shallow, warm pond; rims of concrete basins should be covered over with wooden boards. They should spend winters indoors, in an even temperature. In modern bird preserves and zoos, Hottentot teal are kept in large tropical halls with temperatures of 20°C, either throughout the year or—at least—during the cool season (October to April).

Food: No specific requirements, but they should be given a fairly fine-grained food and—always—duckweed.

Breeding: After the first breeding results in the end 1930s, Kooy of t'Zand (Holland) and Jones of Leckford (UK) achieved renewed successes with the birds after 1960. Thereafter, chances of breeding Hottentot teal improved; progress has been slow but continuous. Nowadays these small dabbling ducks are bred by many private breeders of Western Europe as well as North America; in the Wildfowl Trust they have been bred quite regularly since 1967.

Pairs kept out in the open display breeding behaviour at the height of summer; eggs are normally laid in July—in the tropical hall of the Wildfowl Trust birds laid after February 12th in 1971. Even when the teal appear to feel well, their need for warmth should not be underestimated. The young also need a great deal of warmth and it is best to rear them without the parents under a heat-giving lamp.

Hybridization: Experiences from which generalisations can be drawn about Hottentot teal are not available so far; in ornithological literature one case of interbreeding is mentioned: that of a Hottentot teal with a North American wood duck (approximately 1935, in England).

Cape Teal

Anas capensis Gmelin

Comparative Size: Noticeably larger than green-winged teal.

Plumage: F. see plate 63; no seasonal dimorphism; M. and F. predominantly pale grey; feather centres grey-brown, black-brown on the back. Irides and bill pael red, base of bill black. Sexes distinguishable by differences in voices. Plumage of juveniles darker and browner.

Natural Habit

Status: They are distributed over all Africa, but numbers vary greatly in different areas. It is well known that Cape teal are most abundant in South Africa ('Cape' teal refers to South Africa).

Habitat: Shallow lakes with rich vegetation in the lowlands, occasionally flooded grassland; outside the breeding season preferred habitats are: shallow brackish water lagoons in the coastal regions, and salt lakes which are rich in plankton (e. g. Lake Nakuru, Kenya).

Breeding Biology: It is assumed that the pair bond is very strong in many pairs for several years. Nevertheless, the males gather in groups for courtship display, which is simple yet intensive, at the beginning of the breeding season. Nests are on dry ground, either in the open on the grass or underneath bushes, and contain clutches of six to nine brownish or yellowish eggs. Incubation takes 27 days. While the female broods the drake guards the nest site; later on he takes an active part in guiding the young.

Migration: Many populations roam in an irregular manner in their search for suitable waters; other populations migrate far to the North.

Yearly Cycle: Periods of reproduction are not at all uniform, even within the limits of an area; heavy rainfall can be very irregular; the onset of rain triggers off the birds' breeding instinct, and thus they are able to breed in any season.

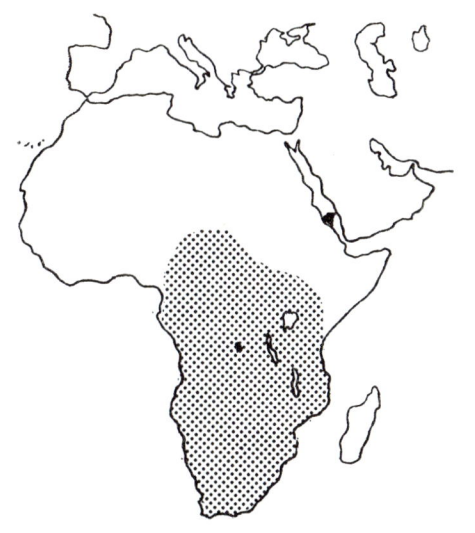

Climate: See red-billed pintail. South Africa with the largest population of Cape teal has a cooler climate, but even there temperatures average 18–20 °C during the coldest months of the year.

AVICULTURE

Like the Bahama pintail, chestnut teal and red-billed pintail, Cape teal belong to the group of medium-sized species of southern ducks. Keeping and breeding them follows much the same pattern. They are equally suitable to being kept on the communal ponds of breeders as well as in the display enclosures of zoos and bird preserves. Cape teal excel in agility and liveliness which compensates for their simple, grey plumage.

Housing: Zoos and bird preserves keep Cape teal in small groups which allows the birds to develop their particular intensive courtship display and other interesting traits. People who breed birds as a hobby usually keep a pair of Cape teal either in a larger or small communal enclosure or by themselves. During winter they should be housed indoors, in a dry, draught-free place; slight heating is necessary only in periods of prolonged frost.

Food: Grain and mixed food as fed to other species of ducks; additionally, Cape teal should be given freshwater molluscs, and crushed insects or shrimps should be dropped on the water for them (Cape teal's feeding habits are similar to those of common shelducks and common shovelers).

Breeding: Not particularly difficult; the majority of pairs appears to be remarkably productive. The first breeding result was obtained by McLean (UK) in 1938—with two drakes and four females which he had been sent from South Africa in the same year. I myself know of females who managed to produce up to three clutches in one year.

The breeding cycle of Cape teal differs little from that of the other species. One point worth mentioning is that at least some of the mature birds moult their flight feathers in the spring and immediately afterwards begin their courtship display.

Beginning of egg-laying is irregular, not only in the birds' natural environment but also in captivity. In Germany, females normally lay eggs between mid-April and end-May; in the Wildfowl Trust the laying period covers a span of several months—from February until June. After the particularly cold winter of 1939 McLean found a clutch of eight Cape teal eggs on February 25th; it was produced by one of the birds he had imported a year before. Nests are made in holes or on the grass. Brooding and rearing the young are quite easy in an incubator. If the eggs of ducklings are not supplied with sufficient warmth they may die.

Hybridization: Tendencies are average; Cape teal interbreed with some *Anas* species hybridization is known to have occurred with tufted ducks and Brazilian teal.

Marbled Teal

Anas angustirostris Ménétries

Comparative Size: Larger than green-winged teal.

Plumage: Adults in breeding plumage see plate 67; M. and F. light grey-brown with cream-yellow feather tips on the upperside and dark grey-brown barring on feathers of the underside; wings lack speculum. Some Ms. slightly crested on back of the neck; in coloration and voice M. not always distinguishable from F. Eclipse and juvenile plumage rather similar to breeding plumage.

Natural Habit

Status: There has been a considerable decline in numbers in the western Paleoarctic region since the turn of the century (southern Spain several thousand pairs in 1900, 100–200 pairs only in 1960); the European breeding population is regarded as endangered. The populations of the Near East are more stable; winter swarms of 2,000 birds have been observed in Turkey.

Habitat: Shallow, very overgrown fresh-water lakes; also shallow lagoons with salt water content and wide regions of dense vegetation consisting of rushes, grasses and small aquatic saltwater plants (Salicornia etc.). Ponds with only either reed or sedge banks are avoided.

Breeding Biology: Not very much is known about the wild marbled teal's breeding habits. Presumably the birds pair in their winter quarters. Nests have been found on the ground, well hidden by dense vegetation of sedge, aquatic salt water plants and grasses; also in tamarisk bushes, and even on grass-thatched roofs of huts. Clutches contain seven to ten eggs; incubation takes 23–24 days.

Migration: They are infrequent migrants and birds of passage; at times there are invasion-like migratory movements which do not take the birds much beyond the southern and south-western limits of their breeding area.

Yearly Cycle: Laying begins at much the same times—in May and June—over the whole area of the birds' distribution. When many of the waters dry out in the breeding grounds at the height of summer, marbled teal undertake short, irregular flights and also roam northwards (as far as southern France, Hungary and Roumania).

Climate: Dry-hot mediterranean and desert climate with little rainfall. In some local areas of wintering grounds, temperatures sometimes sink to frost level.

AVICULTURE

While not many marbled teal were kept in preserves in former decades, they are now inhabitants of numerous private parks, bird preserves and zoos where they are also bred. The British Wildfowl Trust imported marbled teal from southern Iraq in 1948, and the Trust as well as JONES (Leckford) achieved excellent breeding results with them as early as 1950. Marbled teal bred at Slimbridge in 1969 were released into the wild in the Lal Suhanra Bird Preserve (Pakistan); there they could re-occupy their natural environment in which they had become nearly extinct as a result of being overhunted.

Housing: No specific provision has to be made for the care and breeding of marbled teal; they can be kept quite easily together with other species in all kinds of different enclosures. However, they are at their best if ponds have shallow, well-grown shores and adjoining areas planted with short sedge and other grasses. They should spend winters in draught-free shelters which may need sight heating at times.

Flood: Grain and food given to other *Anas* species; additionally animal foods such as shrimps, earth and meal worm.

Breeding: They yield of breeding can be very good indeed; in the Wildfowl Trust, for instance, more than 40 young marbled teal have been reared to maturity over a number of years. On the other hand, there may be a marked lack of success with some pairs; either they do not breed at all, or—if they do—after several years only. An additional difficulty is that of distinguishing sexes from each other, so that many 'pairs' are in fact birds of the same sex.

Display, pairing and choice of nest site are quite inconspicuous. Many females lay in nesting boxes or make a nest amongst grasses, at some distance from the pond. They start laying in the second half of May, in the Wildfowl Trust during the first years at the beginning of May, nowadays even some in the second half of April. The young are very timid for the first few days after they have hatched and—like mandarin ducklings—try to jump or climb out of their nest box. Once the ducklings have settled down, however, their rearing is not difficult.

Hybridization: Although tendencies to interbreed are not at all marked there are some that marbled teal may hybridize not only with other *Anas* but also with *Netta* and *Aythya* species.

Garganey
Anas querquedula L.

Comparative Size: Little larger than green-winged teal.

Plumage: M. in breeding see plate 58; in eclipse plumage similar to F. but distinguishable by unchanged coloration of wings. Juvenile M. has pale grey-brown wing coverts and greenish speculum, juvenile F. brown upper feathers and pale-brown wing feathers.

NATURAL HABIT

Status: The highest concentration of breeding birds is in Eastern Europe and Central Asia; in other parts of Europe—the western periphery of the birds' breeding area—limits of areas as well as size of populations are subject to fluctuation; population increase and wider distribution follow upon long periods of warm weather.

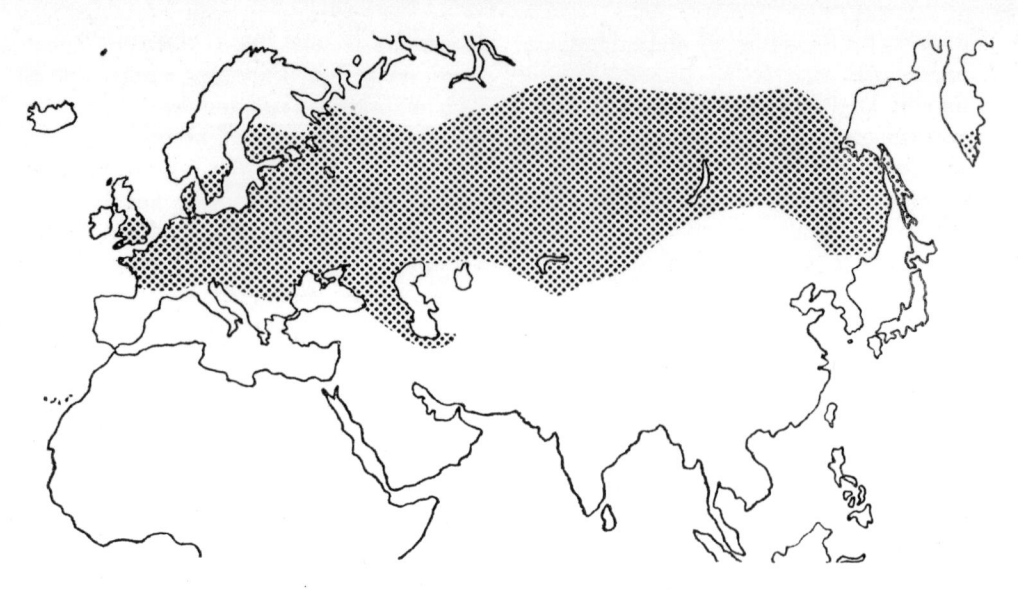

Habitat: Eutrophic lakes with wide reed and rush shores and adjoining expanse of either grass or pasture; also oxbows and small pools in marshes and lowlands. Whilst migrating the birds like to rest and feed on flooded meadows.

Breeding Biology: Gargeney pair in their winter quarters. In breeding grounds, troops of birds initially stay on open water surfaces; later on, pairs separate and spread out over their breeding territory. They nest on reeds, meadows and fields. A full clutch contains seven to eleven cream-yellow eggs; incubation takes 21–23 days. The female alone rears the young in the shore vegetation. Afterwards new troops form; they are made up of the moulted adults and the newly fledged ducklings and, once again, the birds take to the open waters.

Migration: Birds of passage; Garganey winter in southern France, Mediterranean regions and — most of all — in West Africa, in the deltas of the Niger and the Senegal. Drakes undertake moult migrations.

Yearly Cycle: The garganey's spring migration is in March and April as they are a species that loves warmth. Eggs are rarely laid before mid-May. From August onwards the birds join up in swarms and then undertake their autumnal migration.

Climate: High summer temperatures prevail in all breeding grounds; northern nesting grounds are always in those areas which are particularly warm in the summer.

AVICULTURE

Garganey are notable for their discreet coloration, easy maintenance and lack of aggressiveness towards other species; thus they are very popular with the breeders who keep them in their preserves. On the other hand, some people disregard them and favour the very similar bluewinged teal. One point worth mentioning: the garganey drake does not begin moulting into his breeding plumage before December so that he wears his complete nuptial plumage only from February until May.

Housing: Garganey always make their nests in the ground vegetation at some distance from the pond. As a consequence they can only be bred in preserves which have either areas of grass or low-growing plants. Quality of water as well as size of pond and enclosure are of minor importance. However, provided that breeding results are not expected, garganey may be kept in densely populated display enclosures. They should be wintered on water which is not frozen and, in periods of prolonged frost, they should be housed in shelters—at least at night.

Food: The same as that of other dabbling ducks.

Breeding: Sexual maturity is attained towards the end of the first year of life. Drakes display and call unceasingly in early spring to stimulate the female in her search for a nest site. The male himself makes several nests in April, sits in one and utters his low-pitched croak; the female sits nearby and behaves as though she is not interested. The female herself then looks for a nest site in May (the male accompanies her but is now inactive) and scratches together a nest, just a few days before she begins laying. Many females are very sensitive to any disturbance of the nest while they are laying. If they are disturbed they are likely to go off and lay their eggs scattered over the preserve. Even brooding females may not return to nests and continue incubating if they are disturbed; it is therefore better to have the eggs incubated by a hen. Whether garganey ducklings are incubated by a hen or in an incubator, once the eggs are hatched it does not take them long to find their food—mixed food and duckweed—in the box in which they are being reared. I have kept young garganey repeatedly with other ducklings, just a few days younger then themselves; the ducklings quickly learnt from the garganey young. Maturing garganey ducklings are also very robust and clever on breeding ponds, and losses are rare.

Hybridization: Tendencies are average; it is not advisable to keep closely related species (blue-winged and cinnamon teal) together with garganey. One of our garganey drakes copulated several times with a laying mandarin female although he had a mate of his own; the birds produced no hybrids.

Blue-winged Teal

Anas discors L.

Comparative Size: Approximately the size of a green-winged teal.

Plumage: M. and F. in breeding plumage see plate 69; in eclipse plumage pale-blue wing coverts and yellow feet distinguish blue-winged teal from garganey, and a stronger grey of the body from cinnamon teal. Juvenile Ms. have less brown in wing coverts of primaries and a slighty brighter speculum than juvenile Fs.

NATURAL HABIT

Status: Widely distributed in North America and, in some areas, the most abundant species of ducks. In North America, blue-winged teal take the place of the garganey.

Habitat: Shallow freshwater lakes, small ponds in low-lying swamps and river plains; also wherever silted-up shore zones have wide reed margins with adjoining areas of grass or pasture. Rice paddies are much liked during the winter.

Breeding Biology: Pairing and height of courtship display take place after arrival in the breeding grounds; normally female alone chooses the nest site. Nests are made on dry grounds, either on the grass or in adjoining fields. Clutch consists of six to fifteen—usually ten—ligth cream coloured eggs; incubation takes 21–23 days. The female looks after the young ducklings in the regions of shallow water. When water recedes families wander off to areas with better ecological conditions where troops of 20–30 mature birds guard the young. The latter are able to fly at the age of six weeks and are sexually mature at ten months.

Migration: Birds of passage; large numbers of blue-winged teal winter in the southern states of the USA and spreda as far as the Guianas and Peru.

Yearly Cycle: Arrival in breeding grounds of USA March/April and Canada in May; eggs are laid between mid-May and end-June (Iowa from end-April onwards); in the north, autumnal migration begins in mid-August. In the wintering grounds of Surinam many blue-winged teal remain from September until April.

Climate: Prevailing temperatures in USA breeding grounds are similar to those of Europe; north-western regions are therefore occupied comparatively late in the year but also left rather early. Wintering grounds are in sub-tropical and tropical zones—the blue-winged teal's love of warmth is similar to that of the garganey.

AVICULTURE

Blue-winged teal have been shown in European zoos since approximately the turn of the century, and they have been bred for almost as long. Nowadays the majority of the birds is bred in the preserves of private waterfowl enthusiasts. Well established blue-winged teal have stamina, on the whole they are not aggressive, and they are easy to keep. As they cannot defend themselves against larger species they are best kept in mixed collections of small ducks (such as ringed and green-winged teal); enclosures need not be spacious but should be easily surveyable.

Housing: Sunny grass-grown preserves with a fairly warm shallow pond (concrete basins with deep water are not really suitable). Fencing should be very solid, at least the lower 20 cm; blue-winged teal searching for a nest site will find the tiniest hole in a fence and leave the preserve if they have the chance (like green-winged teal, garganey and common shovelers). Where climatic conditions are unfavourable they should be wintered in shelters.

Food: See other *Anas* species.

Breeding: As most of the blue-winged teal offered for sale are birds bred in preserves their further breeding is not particularly difficult. Nests are always made on the grass; the breeding female likes some plant cover, but it must be low enough for her to look over it while she is sitting. Eggs are laid in 24 hourly intervals, normally from mid-May onwards, only exceptionally in April. Brooding females and eggs are in constant danger from hedgehogs, predatory mammals and birds of the crow family; it is therefore better either to have the eggs brooded by a hen or to put them into an incubator, particularly as blue-winged teal are then likely to produce one or two further

clutches. Rearing of the ducklings does not differ from that of other *Anas* species.
Hybridization: Tendencies are average; what is remarkable is the blue-winged teal's inclination to interbreed with larger species, such as mallards and wigeons, at times.

Cinnamon Teal

Anas cyanoptera Vieillot

Comparative Size: Rather larger than green-winged teal.
Plumage: M. and F. in breeding plumage see plate 70; M. in eclipse plumage as well as F. and juveniles very similar to blue-winged teal and only distinguishable from them by having slightly more red-brown coloration of the body and a fairly long—and therefore slimmer looking—bill.

NATURAL HABIT

Status: Cinnamon teal are distributed over a wide geographic range and split into a number of races; status in the different areas is therefore uneven. Northern and Argentinian cinnamon teal occur in large populations; the three tropical races inhabit small areas but do not appear to be endangered.
Habitat: In North America similar habitat to that of blue-winged teal: eutrophic shallow waters; in Argentina: lagoons grown with sedge and reeds as well as silted-up lake shores in open landscapes; in the mountains; high plateaux overgrown with grass, including one of the Puna zones.
Breeding Biology: Cinnamon teal's breeding habits are less well known than those of blue-winged teal but, evidently, they have much in common. Nests are always on dry ground, amongst grasses, sedges and herbs. Clutches contain ten to twelve slightly red or yellow, elongated eggs. Incubation takes about 24 days. The female rears the young in the shallow water; afterwards the birds form into flocks. Whilst they are breeding, up to 20 per cent of the cinnamon teal's nourishment consists of animal food.
Migration: North American populations wander southwards as far as Panama and Colombia, those of Argentina northwards to the area around Buenos Aires. The three tropical races appear to be largely stationary residents.
Yearly Cycle: Considerable variations occur within the whole area of their distribution. In California eggs are laid between April and June—generally in May; in Argentina at the time of the southern spring (October-November); in other areas in accordance with local

conditions which depend largely on the amount of rainfall.

Climate: Cinnamon teal kept in Europe are usually of Argentinian stock; a few only come from the western states of USA where it is very hot in the summer, or from the tropical mountains of South America.

AVICULTURE

Cinnamon teal have been imported in Europe for nearly 100 years; according to DELACOUR (1956) the northern race was imported first and the Argentinian shortly afterwards; it was not long before both sub-species interbred. Nowadays the other three races can also be seen in a few zoos and private preserves. As a matter of fact, in captivity it is rarely possible to be absolutely certain of the exact sub-species to which a cinnamon teal belongs. Cinnamon teals are quiet, peace-loving small ducks with a good deal of stamina; they are well worth keeping.

Housing: Rather similar to blue-winged teal. They are kept in collections of small ducks and their enclosure should not be too large and have a sufficient amount of open ground. If danger threatens them (e. g. a cat) they have to be able to save themselves quickly be getting on to the water. The pool in the enclosure should be filled with water which has a well regulated temperature. Good grass is desirable but not absolutely essential (eggs are very often laid in nesting boxes). During winter they should not be exposed to frost and have to be housed indoors.

Food: Like that of other dabbling ducks, but a little more finely grained. In spring and whilst the young are being reared, food should be enriched with animal substances.

Breeding: Successful breeding is just as likely and no more difficult than that of closely related species. Many females lay eggs in nesting boxes, others make nests on the grass. In preserves, the laying period is from early May until July. Many males moult into their eclipse plumage around mid-May; nevertheless later clutches are still fertilised by them. Incubation and rearing of young are carried out in the manner of blue-winged teal and garganey. The young drakes moult into their breeding plumage after early October and, when about one year old, they are sexually mature.

Hybridization: They tend to interbreed with blue-winged teal and common shovelers and should not be kept with them in the same preserve. Cinnamon teal rarely hybridize with other genera or larger species.

Common Shoveler

Anas clypeata L.

Comparative Size: Condiserably larger than green-winged teal.

Plumage: M. and F. in breeding plumage see plate 85; in eclipse plumage easily distinguishable by pale-blu peatch on wings and spatulate bill. Juvenile M. has speculum with slightly stronger green brightness and wing coverts showing more grey-blue than juvenile F. of same age. Newly hatched shoveler ducklings lack spatulate bill.

NATURAL HABIT

Status: On the whole, not rare in areas with favourable ecological conditions; on the western coast of the Baltic Sea shovelers belong to the most common breeding ducks.

Habitat: Shallow inland waters with wide reed areas and adjoining agricultural land; fens and marshes; lakes of steppes with brackish or saline water. Whilst migrating they like to rest and feed on flooded meadows.

Breeding Biology: Pair formation is for one season and takes place during the winter; once breeding territory is occupied the simple courtship display soon comes to an end. The nest is made on dry ground, either in reed-grasses, in meadows or fields. Full clutches contain eight to twelve greenish or cream-coloured eggs; incubation takes 22–25 days. The female rears the ducklings in the region of shallow water and, at that time, the adult birds moult their wings.

Migration: Birds of passage; they winter in Mediterranean countries and in Africa, also in sub-tropical and tropical Asia as well as in Central America.

Yearly Cycle: Common shovelers arrive late in their breeding grounds and leave them early. In central Europe, spring migration begins after April 10th and ends in the last ten days of May; eggs are laid after mid-May. Moult migration of drakes in many areas begins gradually in July and goes on until August. Migration to wintering grounds is in October.

Climate: Breeding grounds range from boreal zones in the North to dry-hot regions of deserts and steppes in the interior of the continents. Shovelers winter in sub-tropical and tropical areas.

AVICULTURE

Because they are attractive and colourful, shovelers are popular inhabitants in bird preserves and, despite their highly specialised food requirements in their natural way of life, they are quite easy to maintain. They are not very sensitive to cold; nevertheless, in periods of prolonged frost, they should be given a shelter. The highly developed lamellae on the edge of the bill may get frozen and the birds may then find it difficult to feed.

Particulars of common shovelers apply in almost equal measure to the other kinds, such as: the very beautifully coloured South American shoveler; the African shoveler, coloured like a female common shoveler; and the Australian-New Zealand shovelers which look less colourful. South American and New Zealand shovelers are quite often imported and bred.

Housing: Preferably warm sunny ponds with shallow, well-grown shores and adjoining areas of grass. But they can also be kept on larger waters in bird preserves and in zoos or—in the latter—in the ditches which surround the sites of mammals on show.

Food: Nutritious but not too coarse; grain should not be larger than wheat;

also duckweed. If the pond provides no natural food (small crustacea and aquatic invertebrates) shovelers should be fed, additionally, on shrimps, bristle worms or other similar animal matter.

Breeding: In open-air preserves which are neither too confined nor over-populated. Breeding results are similar to those of garganey and cinnamon teal. After the beginning of May, the females search for a quiet nest site on the ground, under cover of vegetation which they like to be no higher than they are themselves when standing, so that they can look over it. They scrape together a nest during and begin laying around mid-May—in western Europe from the end of April. The eggs are covered so cleverly that they are barely noticeable. The females are reliable breeders; unfortunately they—and their eggs—are threatened by numerous dangers. It is often necessary, therefore, to remove the eggs for incubation elsewhere. Shoveler ducklings are fed initially on fine particles of food dropped on the water for them. The development of the spatulate bill and growth of feathers take approximately the same length of time; when they are six to seven weeks old the young are able to fly. Young drakes moult into their breeding plumage in the autumn of their first year.

Hybridization: They are known to interbreed with a number of *Anas* species; however, once shovelers are firmly paired they rarely hybridize.

European Eider

Somateria mollissima (L.)

Comparative Size: Considerably larger than mallard; very bulky.

Plumage: M. in breeding plumage see plate 84; eclipse plumage of M. predominantly drab black-brown, normally with some white feathers (intermediate plumages see plate 86). Juvenile M. also darker than F. and, while moulting into breeding plumage, increasingly marked black and white.

Natural Habit

Status: Harvesting of down and eggs caused a considerable decline in numbers up to the turn of the century. Worldwide protective measures have benefited populations which have increased considerably in many places, and also areas of distribution which have become far more extensive (in this century European eiders have expanded their range to the Frisian Islands and Holland, for instance).

Habitat: Gently sloping oceanic coasts, islands, rocky islets and reefs; eiders like wind-sheltered bays and fiords and prefer them to inland lakes. The sea provides the birds with plenty of food (clusters of mussels) and this is the reason why so many of them inhabit coastal areas. Inland lakes and rivers are used as resting places during migration.

Breeding Biology: Eiders nest in loose colonies near the coast, either in dune grass or among large rocks or in meadows. The nest hollow is lined with a thick wall of the much sought after 'eiderdown', just before the beginning of incubation. Clutches contain four to six smooth-shelled olive or grey-green eggs; brooding takes 25–26 days. At the beginning of the incubation period the drakes gather in large flocks offshore or they undertake a moult migration. The females guide the hatched ducklings to the water where the latter form into so-called 'kindergartens'; these are guarded by a few females (which take turns) and look after up to 75 ducklings.

Migration: Stationary residents, infrequent migrants and also birds of passage; eiders move further south only if freezing conditions of their coastal habitat force them to migrate.

Yearly Cylce: Depending on the geographical location of breeding grounds this is liable to be staggered. Along the coasts of the North Sea eiders migrate for the spring from February onwards—concentrating in largest numbers in May; eggs are laid in May, rearing of young and moult take place in June/July; very large flocks of eiders migrate to the North Sea zone in October, coming from further north.

Climate: Breeding and winter grounds farthest to the south are in the temperate zone; all others are in boreal subarctic and arctic climatic zones.

AVICULTURE

Zoological gardens have attempted to keep and maintain European eiders for a long time. The London Zoo is known to have had one breeding result in 1841, and the species was in the Berlin Zoo's possession in about 1888. However, bird enthusiasts who make a hobby of breeding wildfowl were not interested in eiders until a few years ago. The first eiders were reared from eggs collected on the southern coast of the North Sea where the birds were breeding. Nowadays they are bred in many places and it is not only unnecessary to collect wild birds' eggs but it is also an offence since the birds are protected by strict laws. European eiders bred in captivity are very easy to maintain; they are tame, not quarrelsome, and rubost (one bird lived in apreserve for 21 years); but they are extremely greedy. Birds caught wild adapt to their new surroundings fairly easily and are not particularly shy—it is difficult to get them to breed, however.

Housing: It is advisable to keep them on large ponds, more than 1 m deep; the water should be clear and cold; shores should have plenty of shade.

Food: A coarse, high protein mixed food, soaked dog biscuits and grain. Additionally, shrimps, pieces of fish, raw meat and, if possible, mussels or snails (inland, freshwater mussels, *Dreissena polymorpha*, may be given to them).

Breeding: In Europe the nominate race of eiders is kept and bred, in USA the American Eider, *S. m. dresseri*. First results in breeding and keeping are also known of the king and Steller's eider as well as the spectacled eider. Eiders are not sexually mature before the end of the second year, and many attain sexual maturity in the third year of life. Eggs are laid on islands on grass or other plants and in the shore vegetation of ponds, rarely in nesting boxes or baskets. Females lay in May, exceptionally in April, and incubate in a quiet and reliable manner. Nest control underneath brooding eiders is quite easy. It is more practical to rear the ducklings without parents as the latter would gobble all the food themselves. Initially in boxes and—later—on small rearing ponds with clear water eider ducklings develop in much the same way as the young of other diving ducks. It is essential to supply eider ducklings with a sufficient quantity of food.

Hybridization: It is known to have occured with shelduck, mallard and pintail. No doubt the various eider duck races would interbreed freely. One general rule: for the sake of keeping sub-species pure, they should never be kept together.

Rosybill
Netta peposaca (Vieillot)

Comparative Size: Little larger than European pochard.
Plumage: M. see plate 87; F. with young see plate 88; no seasonal dimorphism. Juveniles predominantly dark-brown, some feathers have pale edges. As soon as fully feathered, bill of M. turns pale pink, that of F. remains dark. Moult into adult plumage and coloration from autumn.

NATURAL HABIT

Status: A species with a wide distribution and—in former decades—fairly common. In recent years, a large concentration of breeding birds has been found in the Buenos Aires Province.
Habitat: Nutritious, shallow lakes and lagoons, surrounded by marsh plants, in plains of the interior (Pampas) and in lowlands near the coasts; also brackish and coastal waters.
Breeding Biology: Not much has been published about the rosybill's habits prior to breeding; evidently little is known of them. Nests are in the vegetation of the water—often just above it in bunches of rush. A full clutch contains ten to twelve grey-green eggs. 'Dump' nests have been found on several occasions, two or more females had laid their eggs in them so that one nest contained up to 30 eggs. Incubation takes 27–29 days. There is a lack of specific information about development and rearing of the young; supposedly neither differs much from that of European pochard ducklings.
Migration: Once the breeding period is finished, rosybills migrate either to coastal zones or to the north.
Yearly Cycle: Mainly depends on rainfall; in southern areas it is dependent on the seasonal temperatures. Principal breeding period is in October/November

—in Paraguay February/March. Winter swarms aggregate between March and July.
Climate: Breeding grounds predominantly in areas with temperate and sub-tropical temperatures and very variable amounts of rainfall.

Aviculture

Rosybills—like the closely related red-crested pochards—are kept and bred by many breeders, zoos and bird preserves. The drakes are beautifully coloured throughout the year, and the pairs' courtship display is very pretty to watch; both characteristics combined make caring for rosybills well worthwhile.
Housing: They are diving ducks and, preferably, should be kept on large ponds with a depth of more than 70 cm. Breeding results in small enclosures with shallow basins can be achieved, but at the expense of growing plants which are soon damaged because they are badly bitten by the birds. Rosybills can be wintered out of doors; in periods of prolonged frost they should be offered a shelter.
Food: See red-crested pochard.
Breeding: First breeding results with rosybills became known approximately a century ago; young birds have repeatedly been reared to maturity in the Berlin Zoo since 1882. Imported wild birds have always provided new breeding stock and, as a result, the species has retained a healthy constitution and therefore a normal reproductive activity, up to the present.

One year old rosybills are fully coloured; the drakes court the females and copulate with them, but eggs are not laid before nearly the end of the second year. The female makes the nest in spacious nest holes very close to the water. Laying rarely begins before mid-May, further clutches or second broods are possible until early July. Rosybills brood quietly and reliably and look after their young extremely well. Eggs may also be brooded in incubators and if the young are reared in boxes there are practically no losses. Rosybills have few requirements and are easy to breed; they are not only suitable for being maintained in zoos and on lakes in parks but also by a breeder with little or no previous experience.
Hybridization: Very pronounced tendencies, in particular with the closely related red-crested pochards which should not be kept on one pond together with rosybills; the latter also interbreed with other species of diving ducks.

Red-crested Pochard

Netta rufina (Pallas)

Comparative Size: A little larger than European pochard.
Plumage: M. and F. in breeding plumage see plate 91; in eclipse plumage M. distinguishable from F. by red-brown bill and red irides. Juveniles similar colouring to F., towards the end of feather growth bill of M. reddish, that of F. black-brown.

Natural Habit

Status: Main breeding area is central Asia where they are widely distributed; isolated breeding populations exist in Europe; in Spain (2,000–3,000 pairs); southern France (approximately 500 pairs); German Federal Republic (less than 100 pairs); Holland and Denmark (circa 50 pairs).
Habitat: Warm eutrophic lakes and ponds with well-grown shores; they also need large surfaces of open water. In the southern Soviet Union the steppes' saline lakes (with weak salt content) are favoured habitats.

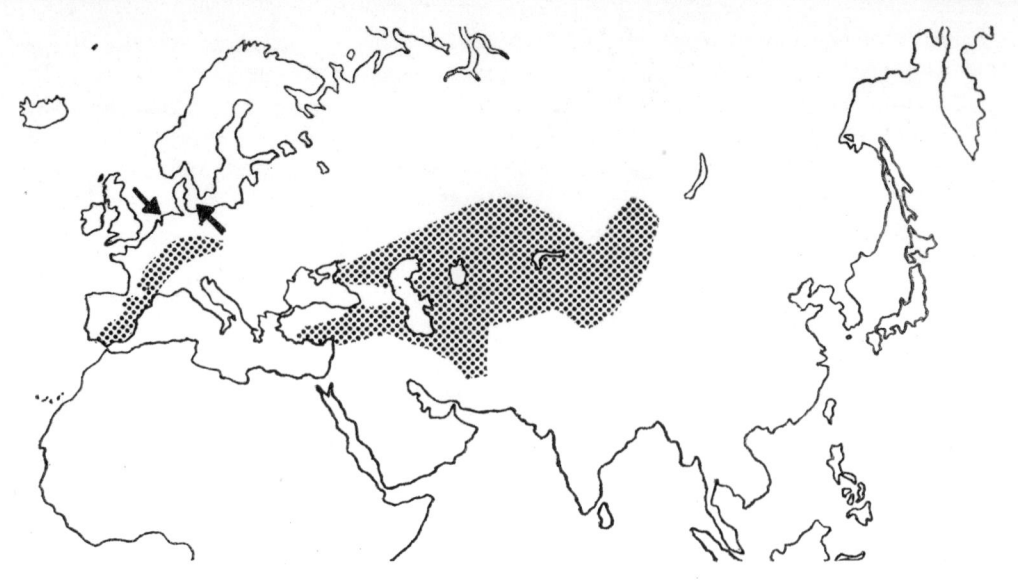

Breeding Biology: Homing troops of birds initially stay on the open water and later occupy their nest sites in the vegetation along the shores. Nests are near the water, in sedge stands or dense reeds, sometimes on islets—always under cover—and often they are large towers. Normal clutches contain six to ten grey-green or ochre-yellow eggs; two females often lay in one nest. Incubation takes 26–28 days. Some males stay with the brooding females and later help a little in guiding the young.

Migration: Predominantly birds of passage. Red-crested pochards winter in the south of the Near East and from southern France (Camargue) to North Africa; they always form large swarms. They also undertake a moult migration (e. g. to Lake Constance).

Yearly Cycle: Brooding begins late (in Europe after May 11th); while the young are being reared and just afterwards, the adult birds migrate to moulting areas (from July—in greater numbers August/September); migration to wintering grounds when frost sets in.

Climate: Red-crested pochards love warmth. In their Asiatic breeding grounds the dry-hot climate of the steppe prevails; in European breeding grounds they begin breeding late in the year in summer weather.

AVICULTURE

Of all diving ducks red-crested pochards are the least demanding with regard to care in preserves; they are also beautifully coloured and it is not surprising that they can be seen in many zoos, bird parks and breeders' preserves. As they are very robust, they are especially suited to being kept on urban waters to which they add considerable liveliness. Red-crested pochards have stamina and are not sensitive to cold; on the other hand their good nature is limited. On small communal ponds the drakes are a danger to females of other species and often rape' them. Therefore, red-crested pochards should only be kept on ponds used by species of the same size or larger.

Housing: As they have few requirements (because they are very adaptable) they can be kept in virtually any kind of enclosure, as long as the water basins are not too small and at least 60–80 cm deep. Red-crested pochards graze in the manner of geese so that a good area of turf is an advantage; in very small preserves the vegetation is soon eaten up.

Food: Their natural food consists mainly of underwater and other aquatic vegetation. In preserves they should be fed on grain, a plain mixed food, duckweed, lettuce, dandelion leaves and other green-food. The green-food is particularly important in the spring and summer.

Breeding: Red-crested pochards are amongst the most easily bred diving ducks. Although it has often been reported that mature birds are difficult to pair there are many examples to the contrary. Eggs are predominantly laid in nesting boxes, rarely among grasses or in shelters. If she can get hold of it the female collects a great deal of nesting material which she builds into a large nest. Under normal conditions the females are very good and quiet brooders and are often used for brooding eggs of other birds and for rearing their young. Red-crested pochard ducklings—whether in the care of parents or in rearing boxes—are full of vitality right from the beginning, accept and eat food put out for them without previous guidance and are easily reared without losses, but they are very aggressive towards other ducklings. The young red-crested pochards are sexually mature when they are one year old.

Hybridization: The drakes often pair with females of other species or 'rape' unrelated females although these may have mates of their own. Interbreeding of red-crested pochards with numerous *Anas* and *Aythya* species has produced many hybrids.

European Pochard
Aythya ferina L.

Comparative Size: Medium-sized diving duck with weight of approximately 1 kg and a total length of 42–46 cm.

Plumage: M. in breeding plumage see plate 72; in eclipse plumage M. similar to F. in coloration but nevertheless distinguishable. Juveniles similar to F., but back of M. more speckled than that of F.; bill of five to seven weeks old M. yellow-orange, that of F. of same age olive which turns brown later on.

NATURAL HABIT

Status: In many places quite common as a breeding bird. Original distribution was westwards to the river Elbe; since the 19th century the breeding range has spread to France and Great Britain.

Habitat: Inland lakes, approximately one metre deep, where the birds can find good nourishment of animal and plant matter; they also like fish ponds and shallow reservoirs and, in central Asia, they are frequently found on saline lakes in steppes. Smaller inland waters are preferred to large lakes and the sea.

Breeding Biology: Display and pairing begin in December and reach a climax in March. Initially the pochards stay in troops on open surfaces of their breeding waters; later on pairs—or just females—separate from the group to find nesting sites, lay eggs and brood. The nest is directly above the water or very close to it, and may be either on islands, or among reeds, willow and alder bushes. Clutches contain six to nine large, olive-green/grey eggs. Incubation takes 24–26 days; only a little down is used to line the nest. The female rears the young on the open water.

Migration: Predominantly birds of passage wintering in western Europe, mediterranean countries and northern India. Moult migrations take the birds to the Volga delta, the Ismaninger Ponds near Munich and other places.

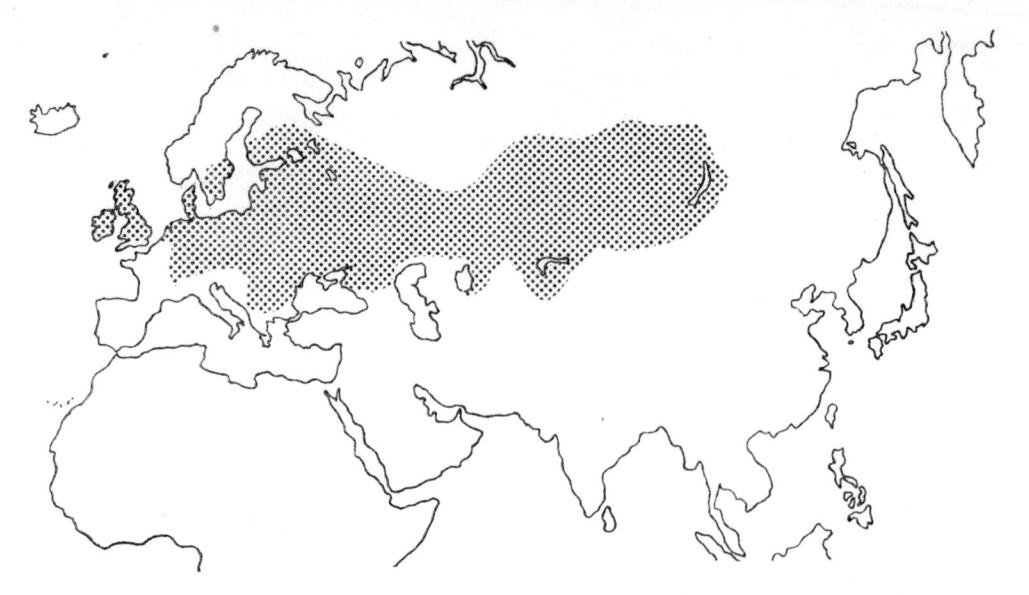

Yearly Cycle: In western and central Europe spring migration between end-February and beginning of May, egg-laying May to June, arrival of males in moulting areas from July onwards—of females in August, autumn migration October and November.

Climate: Pochards breed in the temperate zone, but especially in the dry-hot continental zones of the interior of Asia.

Aviculture

European pochards have few requirements and are easily maintained diving ducks. In the Redhead, *Aythya americana*, they have a close relative in America. They are very active and agile and add considerable liveliness to waters of zoos and preserves as well as many urban and park lakes and ponds.

Breeding them can be particularly recommended to beginners. European pochards are well able to withstand cold in the winter and they are not aggressive towards other ducks. If they are given individual care they soon become tame. What I have found a nuisance is their constant diving which, at times, stirs up the bottom of their pond to such an extent that the water gets muddy[1] and embankments—even with a depth of one metre—are soon badly damaged.

Housing: Ponds have to have a minimum depth of 50–70 cm; pochards do not dive in shallow water where they tend to be rather idle.

Food: See red-crested pochard.

Breeding: European pochards pair for one season; no difficulties with pairing are to be expected, even in the case of mature birds, as long as mates are allowed to be together at the beginning of the year. Eggs are laid in nesting baskets or spacious nesting holes; these should be placed either directly above the water or in the shores' vegetation. Laying seldom starts before the beginning of May. Females breed quietly and reliably, but they are rarely able to keep their roving ducklings together once they have hatched; unfortunately, losses are quite normal (just as in the natural environment). However, ducklings can be reared with the aid of a heat-giving lamp; this is not at all difficult and, where it is

[1] In my own preserve live, among others, velvet scoters and red-breasted mergansers, that is why I attach great importance to completely clear water.

done, losses are rare, the pochard ducklings being full of vitality and cleverness right from the start and considerably less restless than other *Anas* or *Aix* ducklings. If they are given sufficient water for bathing and swimming from the first day they will develop and become feathered quite quickly. The juveniles are fully feathered and able to fly when they are eight to ten weeks old, and they attain sexual maturity towards the end of the first year of life.

Hybridization: Very pronounced tendencies, particularly with Brazilian teal, common white-eyes and tufted ducks, as well as other *Aythya* species.

Canvasback

Aythya valisneria (Wilson)

Comparative Size: Definitely larger than redhead and European pochard.

Plumage: M. in breeding plumage see plate 73; glowing, red irides (yellow in redhead), larger size and pale—almost white—upper parts distinguish M. and the long, dark bill both M. and F. from redhead and European pochard. The long, flat shape of the bill also makes juveniles easily recognisable.

NATURAL HABIT

Status: Canvasbacks have been, and still are, widely distributed over vast parts of North America and—in certain areas—they are by no means uncommon as breeding birds; in general, they have been able to maintain the size of their populations, in spite of considerable hunting pressure.

Habitat: Fairly deep prairie lakes, surrounded by dense reed and containing numerous small islets; also low-lying marshes and fens provided they have areas of deep water. Winters are spent on the coasts.

Breeding Biology: Rather like European pochards, the female canvasback makes a compact nest in the reeds close to the water and later lines it with a small amount of down. A full clutch contains seven to ten olive-grey eggs, incubation takes about 26 days, and the female rears her young in the vicinity of the reed margins; juveniles are able to fly when they are barely 60 days old.

Migration: They winter predominantly on lower courses of rivers carrying fresh and brackish water and in the deltas of the large USA rivers flowing southwards as far as the Gulf of Mexico; also along the Atlantic and Pacific coasts.

Yearly Cycle: Canvasbacks are among the first wildfowl to return to their breeding grounds in the spring; whilst migrating they fly northwards following the route of thawing snow and ice. They usually lay eggs in May and June, as do many other species. In northerly areas,

canvasbacks do not leave breeding grounds before the onset of frost in late autumn.
Climate: In the breeding season temperatures in the prairie are rather high; winters are spent in regions with a temperate sea climate.

AVICULTURE

In common with all other North American diving ducks, the canvasback—often referred to as valisneria duck—did not reach European zoos until fairly late (according to DELACOUR, in 1922) and breeders only after 1960. Even nowadays, this beautiful, attractively coloured duck species is rarely offered for sale in western Europe. The Redhead, *Aythya americana*, differs little from the European pochard, but yellow irides distinguish it quite clearly. At present redheads are frequently kept in western Europe. In North America it takes the place of the European pochard in zoos and on breeders' ponds.

Housing: Like all other diving ducks. If breeding results are the aim, the pond should not be too small and not too densely populated. Wintering possible out of doors; in periods of prolonged frost they should be offered a shelter.

Food: Apart from the normal grain and mixed food, they should be given as much green food as possible (duckweed, dandelion leaves, lettuce).

Breeding: There are very few reports about successful breeding and productive broods of canvasbacks. The *International Zoo Yearbook* has published the figure of redhead broods which is about ten times higher than that of the canvasbacks. Conditions in breeders' preserves are slightly different as they concentrate their efforts on breeding canvasbacks rather than redheads.

The actual breeding of canvasbacks follows much the same course as that of other diving ducks, except that eggs seem to be laid somewhat earlier; in the British Wildfowl Trust they are sometimes laid from end-March, but more usually at the end of April/beginning of May.

Hybridization: Tendencies to interbreed with *Aythya* and *Netta* species are rather pronounced, in particular in preserves which keep redheads and European pochards.

Diving ducks normally pair for just one season, the birds looking for and finding mates at the time of courtship display at the end of the winter. If a breeder wishes to keep his breeding stock pure he should keep one of the three species only on his pond at that time.

Common White-eye
Aythya nyroca (Güldenstädt)

Comparative Size: Smaller than European pochard.
Plumage: M. and F. in breeding plumage see plate 74; coloration of eclipse and juvenile plumage less distinctive and duller; irides of juvenile M. turn pale grey at six to seven weeks, those of juvenile F. stay dark brown.

NATURAL HABIT

Status: In Asia ecological conditions of the steppes' lakes are very variable; population size is therefore fluctuating. In Europe, the breeding range extended to the Netherlands in the 19th century; in the present western limits of breeding (in the region of the GDR) numbers show a general decline.

Habitat: Eutrophic lakes with broad zones of emergent vegetation also—frequently—brackish and saline waters of the steppes; favoured habitats in Europe are shallow, artificial carp ponds. Winter swarms often rest on fairly large inland lakes, rarely on the coasts.

Breeding Biology: In their natural environment pairs of these inconspicuous looking ducks stay in the outer fringe of reed banks or amongst tufts of grasses or other plants. Neither courtship display nor choice of nest site are very remarkable. Nests are in dense sedge in the shallow water zone (often they are very close to each other). Full clutches contain six to ten cream-yellow, rather round eggs. Incubation takes 23–26 days. The female rears her young within the scattered vegetation of marshy plants, seldom on the open water like the European pochard.

Migration: Bird of passage; wintering grounds range from Mediterranean to Caspian Sea regions and, further southwards, to India and central Africa.

Yearly Cycle: Arrival in breeding grounds from end-March, followed by courtship display and pair formation. Egg-laying and brooding take place from mid-May to end-June; afterwards the young are being reared while the adult birds moult. Migration to winter quarters September/October.

Climate: Temperate to dry-hot in the breeding grounds; nevertheless, white-eyes are not very sensitive to cold.

AVICULTURE

Of all European *Aythya* species white-eyes are the one most easily kept in breeding and bird preserves as well as in zoos. They are lively and agile, thus making communal ponds more interesting; they are also very peaceable, even whilst breeding, and they do not destroy natural embankments of their waters to the same degree as do the red-crested and European pochards. Related species which are sometimes kept and bred are: the Australian White-eye, *A. australis*, and Baer's Pochard, *A. baeri*.

Housing: Preferably on ponds with a minimum depth of 50–70 cm and surrounded by embankments with natural shore vegetation (iris, *Acorus calamus*, sedge). Small concrete basins are not really suitable for the birds' needs, although they are rather more likely to breed there than other diving ducks. They should be wintered on ice-free water or in an unheated shelter.

Food: Grain and a simple mixed food; plenty of duckweed, particularly during the summer.

Breeding: It is probably easier to breed common white-eyes than any other diving ducks. The female chooses a nest site in the shore vegetation, using nesting baskets erected directly above the water or nest boxes in isolated places. The drake guards the breeding territory from the water and accompanies the female when she leaves to nest the feed. Eggs are seldom laid before the beginning of May (further clutches up to June) in intervals of 24 hours. In my own preserve, the females have been very quiet whilst incubating and allowed inspection of the nest before the eggs were hatched. The white-eye ducklings are full of vitality right from the start and willingly accept their food (duckweed, pellets shortly afterwards) even without guidance from an adult bird. Their development is as follows: a good three weeks after they have hatched their flanks show the first feathers, two weeks later the first flight feathers appear and at six to seven weeks they have most of their feathers although the wings have not fully developed. By that time the colour of the irides has changed (see plumage) and it is then that the sexes are clearly distinguishable. White-eyes moult into their adult plumage in the autumn of their first year and, at the end of the first year of life, they are sexually mature.

Hybridization: They interbreed freely with other *Aythya* as well as *Anas* species, the three *Netta* species and the goldeneye.

Tufted Duck
Aythya fuligula (L.)

Comparative Size: Smaller than European pochard.
Plumage: M. and F. in breeding plumage see plate 75; dark parts of M. with purple gloss, bill of M. light-grey, that of F. dark-grey, irides of both M. and F. yellow. Feathers around base of bill are brighter in eclipse females, which at that time are easily confused with ring-necked duck and greater scaup females. Juvenile drakes distinguishable by grey flanks from juvenile females, which are dark throughout.

Natural Habit

Status: One of the most abundant Eurasian diving ducks. Approximately one million tufted ducks were counted in the western Paleoarctic region in the winter of 1968.
Habitat: During the breeding season still or slow-flowing inland waters where tufted ducks can find either islets or sedge and reed zones for brooding and rearing young. A depth of water of approximately 2 m is favoured. They winter on oligotrophic lakes and along the coasts.
Breeding Biology: Display and pair formation begin within the winter flocks and are continued on the breeding waters. Nests are on dry ground, often on islands or in the colonies of gulls. Incubation of the eight to eleven grey-green eggs takes 24–25 days; the females rear the young on open water. Juveniles are able to fly at eight to nine weeks and may be sexually mature after one year—though usually after two years.
Migration: Predominantly birds of passage. The European populations winter in the areas of the western Baltic Sea, the Netherlands and on alpine and lower alpine lakes.
Yearly Cycle: As the year begins so do display and pairing; spring migration is during February/March. Within the whole area of distribution eggs are rarely laid before mid-May. In June the drakes gather in small groups and leave the breeding waters in order to moult. Winter visitors and birds passing through arrive

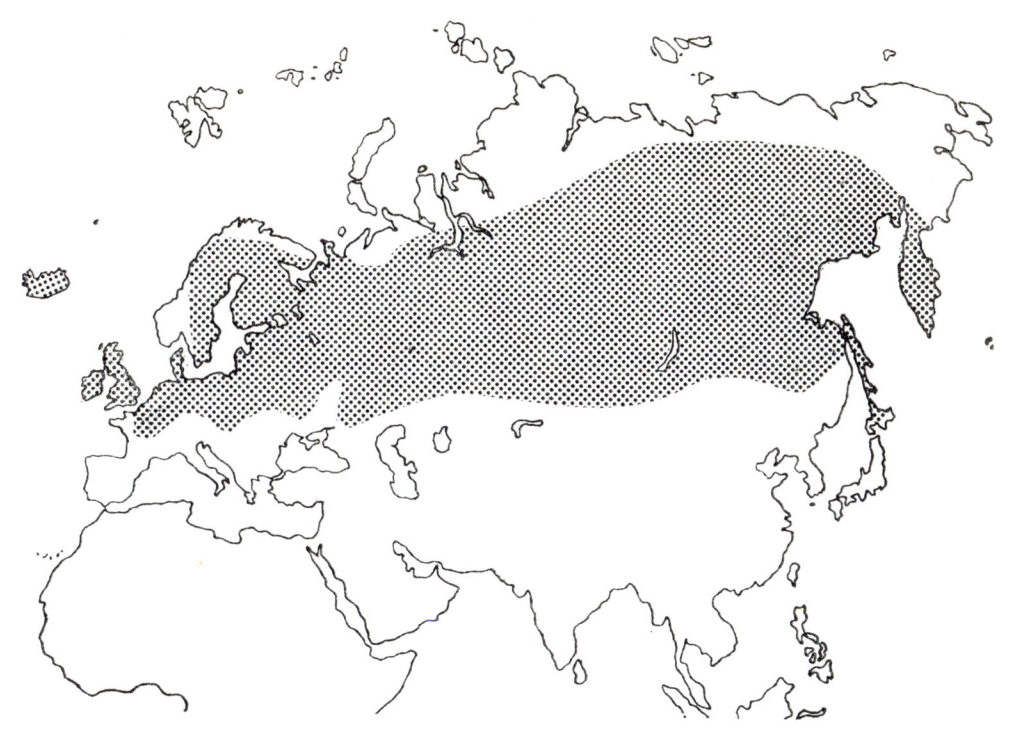

in western Europe from September onwards.
Climate: The majority of tufted ducks breed in arctic and sub-arctic and boreal climatic zones. They also winter further to the north than the other *Aythya* species discussed in this book.

AVICULTURE

Tufted ducks are among the most popular, native ducks: they have been kept and maintained for many decades. Their engaging lively behaviour makes them very likeable wherever they are kept: on lakes of zoos and parks, in display enclosures and breeders' preserves. Birds which are not wing-clipped are inclined to remain faithful to the habitat they are offered. Whilst migrating in the spring, many tufted ducks enjoy a stay on the ponds on which decorative wildfowl are kept and swim to the food trough with the other inhabitants. Some drakes pair with females, even though these may be pinioned.

Housing: Preferably on fairly large lakes, at least 70–80 cm deep, where the tufted ducks can find some of their natural foods for themselves. They have few special requirements and thus are easy to care for on ponds of zoos and parks. They should spend winters on water surfaces which are not frozen; however, being diving ducks, they always find the way back to ice-free spaces, even where there is ice on the water, and there is little danger of them drowning.
Food: Like that of other diving or dabbling ducks. If their water contains no natural nutrients, tufted ducks should be given additional animal matter. They like diving for their food; grain left over by geese and dabbling ducks floats to the bottom where the tufted ducks pick it up.
Breeding: Many of the tufted ducks offered for sale by animal dealers have been caught wild and thus are difficult to breed. Although they become adapted quite soon, they are usually rather timid. Birds bred in captivity do show repro-

ductive activity as long as they are maintained on a sufficiently large lake preferably with natural shore vegetation or islands where they are left in peace. In overpopulated breeding preserves there is little chance of success. Nests are made in the shore vegetation but also in baskets and shallow boxes close to water. Eggs are rarely laid before mid-May. If the female feels secure and is left undisturbed, she will brood reliably, but—on the whole—it is not wise to leave her to rear her brood (except, perhaps, in very small enclosures which can be checked easily or on very large ponds). Diving duck females find it difficult to keep their young close to them and keep them from straying so that losses often occur. On the other hand, rearing the ducklings in boxes under a heat-lamp is quite easy.

In the ducklings the flanks show the first feathers at the beginning of the third week and, normally, they are fully feathered in the fifth week. In the first autumn the drakes moult into their nuptial plumage.

Hybridization: Rather pronounced, particularly with other *Aythya* species.

Ring-necked Duck
Aythya collaris (Donovan)

NATURAL HABIT

Status: Total population smaller than that of the redhead and canvasback as well as the greater and lesser scaup; but the ring-necked ducks are by no means in danger of a decline. During the last few decades, they have occupied large, new breeding grounds to the east of the Great Lakes and concentrated for breeding in large numbers in certain western US areas quite isolated from each other.

Habitat: Waters of the marshes and other similar inland waters surrounded by embankments grown with sedges, pygmy and other low-growing bushes. Outside the breeding season they inhabit large lakes, river estuaries and coastal lagoons.

Comparative Size: Approximately the same as redhead and European pochard.

Plumage: M. and F. in breeding plumage see plate 76; plumage of M. mainly dark, but flanks white and neck has a dark-brown ring; F. is distinguishable from other similarly coloured diving duck Fs. by white face markings—as shown in picture.

Breeding Biology: Ring-necked ducks normally return to their breeding grounds after they have paired. The female makes a simple nest which may be on islets, on sedge stands and in the reeds of the shallow water; she finishes it while she is actually laying. Full clutches contain six to fourteen (an average of nine) dark olive-yellow eggs; incubation takes 26–27 days. Juveniles are able to fly when they are circa 50 days old and, at the age of one year, they are sexually mature.

Migration: Bird of passage which winters in the southern US coastal regions, mainly in Florida and, further southwards, in the West Indies and Guatemala.

Yearly Cycle: Arrival in breeding grounds between end-March (USA, northern states) and beginning of May (central Canada); main laying period in all areas end-May/early June; autumnal migration before winter sets in, between September and November.

Climate: Ring-necked ducks favour climates with warmth throughout the year. Temperatures at times of breeding—on average—like those of Baltic Sea regions; in wintering grounds the climate is comparable with the Mediterranean zone.

Aviculture

Ring-necked ducks are amongst the most beautifully coloured diving ducks. It is therefore remarkable that breeders and zoological experts took little notice of them until fairly late. According to DELACOUR (1956) the first pairs reached Clères (France) and Great Britain in 1935; at that time they were still rarely offered for sale by animal dealers in western Europe and North America. After initial—and gradually increasing—breeding results in the mid-1960s, the stock of preserve birds began to improve. Well established ring-necked ducks are not delicate and are quite easy to maintain. As far as their requirements and habits are concerned they have much in common with the tufted ducks.

Housing: Fairly deep water basins in densely populated display enclosures as well as large lakes in zoos. Where ring-necked ducks are expected to breed they should be put on a reasonably sized pond with plenty of natural vegetation; it is better not to keep them together with other diving ducks capable of breeding. They should spend winters on water free of ice.

Food: A simple grain and mixed food; additionally, the birds like shrimps (dropped on the water) and duckweed.

Breeding: After 1950, a number of American and Canadien breeders took eggs from wild birds, brooded the eggs in incubators and reared the ducklings. This made further broods possible, in only moderate but at least steady numbers.

At Peakirk, one of the British Wildfowl Trust sites, the Trust achieved its first breeding result in 1971 with a pair which had been kept on the Slimbridge ponds since 1966. The female made a well concealed nest on an island close to the water, laid eight eggs from June 2nd, and hatched three ducklings after an incubation which had lasted 26 days. In the following summer ten ring-necked ducklings were reared at Slimbridge and another three at Peakirk.

The safest method to rear the young is in rearing boxes. However, in the field, ornithologists have observed female ring-necked ducks taking care of their broods until they are able to fly; even young adult birds with fully developed wings have been sighted next to the moulting mother bird.

Hybridization: Data which can be generalized are not available so far, but GRAY (1958) gave some interesting information: ring-necked drake interbred with green-winged teal female; they produced one hybrid—a drake which interbred with a tufted duck female which produced fertile eggs. The ring-necked duck also supposedly hybridizes with four *Aythya* species as well as with the red-crested pochard and the mallard.

Lesser Scaup

Aythya affinis (Eyton)

Comparative Size: Hardly smaller than European pochard.

Plumage: M. in breeding plumage see plate 77; feathers of neck and head of M. with violet-blue sheen, in contrast to the greater scaup drake which has green sheen instead. Lesser scaup F. smaller than greater scaup F., also with less white around base of bill. F. very similar to tufted duck F. and may be mistaken for one quite easily. Juvenile M. and F. with very minor differences in coloration; to distinguish sexes with certainty only possible with cloaca test.

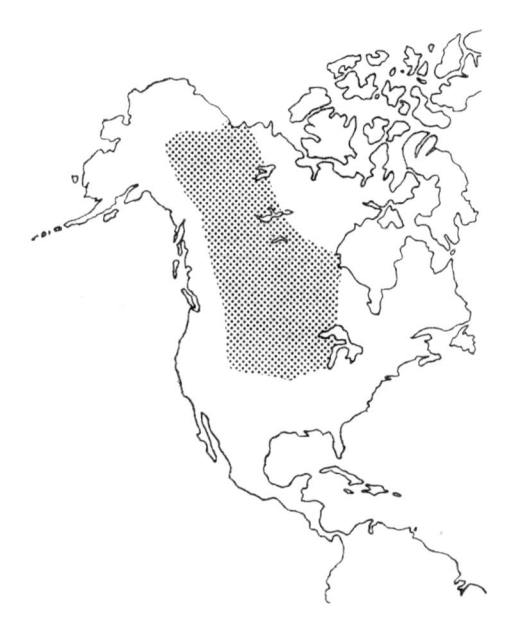

NATURAL HABIT

Status: Common as a breeding bird in the sub-arctic regions of Canada. The lesser, like the greater, scaup (a field ornithologist will find it difficult to distinguish one from the other with exactitude) form large winter flocks on the waters of the USA coastal states.

Habitat: Inland lakes with wide, vegetated shores, islands and adjacent swampy sedge meadows in the open prairie landscapes. At times of migration the lesser scaup inhabits lower river courses, quiet areas of the coasts and large lakes.

Breeding Biology: Pairing and display take place on the open water—near the nest site in the final phase. The female makes the nest on dry ground, among grasses or underneath small bushes, quite often on islands and always near to the shore. The nine to twelve olive-brownish eggs are incubated by the female and are hatched after 26–27 days. The female alone guides the young.

Migration: Lesser scaup flocks breeding inland migrate to areas near the coasts of the central USA states. There they spend winters on low land and brackish water zones of rivers.

Yearly Cycle: When the ice and snow thaw the lesser scaup migrates northwards, coming from the winter quarters. Eggs are laid between May—in the most southerly breeding grounds, and July—in the northern territories. Largest concentration of migrating flocks in the USA state Maryland between mid-November and mid-December.

Climate: In the continental breeding grounds seasonal temperatures show great differences; winters tend to be very cold and, as a result, waters often thaw late. The lesser scaup winters in temperate latitudes.

AVICULTURE

In habits and behaviour the lesser scaup has much in common with its larger relative, the Greater Scaup, *Aythya marila*. Both species are kept nowadays in European zoos and bird preserves; breeders, on the whole, are mainly interested in the lesser scaup which they keep in small numbers. Just like other diving ducks, the scaup is quite easy to look after.

Housing: See tufted and ring-necked duck.

Food: Same requirements as that of above species.

Breeding: If a mature greater scaup is caught and taken from its natural environment, it adapts quickly to preserve surroundings, but only rarely shows reproductive activity. Breeding results are most likely on large zoo lakes. Rearing greater scaup ducklings from fertile eggs, however, is not at all difficult. Rearing the lesser scaup is a different matter. Birds imported in Europe from North America are bred in preserves as there are strict laws forbidding export of wild birds. Anyway, breeding chances with birds bred in preserves are much better and are about equal to those of the tufted duck. In the British Wildfowl Trust alone, 86 lesser scaup were reared to maturity within ten years (1963–1973). The females make well concealed nests in the shore vegetation, showing a decided preference for overgrown islets. Eggs are usually laid in June, exceptionally in May. Further clutches are unlikely as the first one is laid rather late in the year. The ducklings are reared under a heat-lamp. The drakes moult into their nuptial plumage in the autumn of their first year; the scaup is sexually mature in its second year.

Hybridization: Tendencies to interbreed with other *Aythya* species are very pronounced. Particular care should be taken to avoid hybridization between lesser and greater scaup; they produce fulyl fertile hybrids, not easily recognised as such and further breeding leads to undesirable cross-breeds.

African Pygmy Goose
Nettapus auritus (Boddaert)

Comparative Size: Smaller than ringed and green-winged teal.

Plumage: M. and F. see plate 90; no seasonal dimorphism. The green coloration of head and back is typical of all species of pygmy geese. Basal part of the wing is dark patina green, flight feathers have a broad white border. Juveniles are very similar to adult F.

NATURAL HABIT

Status: Distributed over many suitable water habitats; abundant in certain areas, at times.

Habitat: Lakes with permanent fresh water; lowlands and papyrus swamps. Pygmy geese favour staying within the zone of floating aquatic vegetation, or amongst the leaves of water-lilies.

Breeding Biology: Pygmy geese live in pairs or small troops. After a simple courtship in which the green feathers of the head are displayed, a nest site is chosen and eggs are then laid. Nests have been found in tree hollows and on steep slopes, rarely on the ground. Full clutches contain six to nine creamy white eggs; time of incubation of *Nettapus* species is apparently still unknown.

Migration: WILLIAMS (1973) referred to the species as sedentary residents, apparently—at times—very abundant in some areas so that periodic migratory roaming flights cannot be ruled out.

Yearly Cycle: Although African pygmy geese inhabit swamps and lakes with permanent water practically anywhere, their breeding cycle depends on the periods of rainfall. Nevertheless, the span of time during which breeding pairs have been observed, is far greater than that normal in many other duck species.

Climate: The African pygmy geese occur with greatest abundance in equatorial Africa where rainfall is high, and also in hot East Africa. In the cooler South the birds are fairly rare.

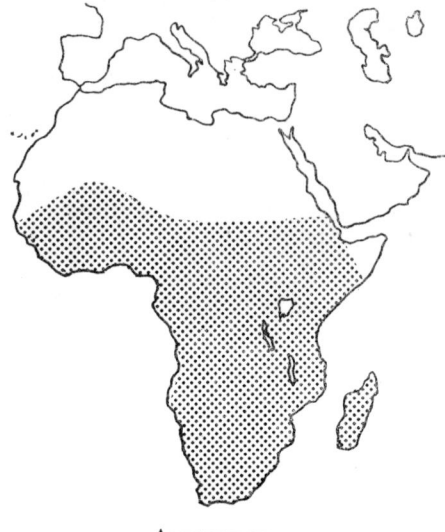

AVICULTURE

For decades European zoos and breeders have attempted to keep pygmy geese successfully. In the 1930s DELACOUR looked after Indian and African pygmy geese in the Zoological Park at Clères (France). The birds had to become adapted to their new environment and, initially, losses were heavy. However, some birds of both species did survive for several years and, in fact, the Indian species proved to be the more robust of the two — one of the females even laid two eggs. In recent years both species have been offered for sale frequently by European and American animal traders, but it is just as difficult to keep them now as it was then. Imported birds are always in an exhausted condition; losses during the period of adaptation are high; the breeding chances are still very poor.

Housing: DELACOUR (1959) recommended that pygmy geese be kept unpinioned in spacious aviaries. Nowadays, the tropical halls of zoos and bird preserves offer new possibilities for successful keeping of these birds and it is more than probable that breeding results will be achieved in the near future.

Although pygmy geese may be kept out in the open — as may ringed teal — until the water freezes, it is nevertheless likely that continued stress from cold upsets their organism and impedes their reproductive activities. Breeders who take pains to keep pygmy geese successfully should house them in light and spacious warm halls from September to May and, during the summer months, in a sunny enclosure containing a pond with good vegetation.

Food: A nutritious finely-grained food; this should be dropped on the water for them — at least until the birds are well established; additionally duckweed and other delicate green food should be given to them, if at all possible throughout the year.

Breeding: No reports of breeding results so far.

Hybridization: GRAY (1958) mentioned one case of interbreeding of an African pygmy goose with a Chiloe wigeon but gave no further details.

Maned Goose

Chenonetta jubata (Latham)

Comparative Size: Larger than a mallard.
Plumage: M. and F. see plate 89; no seasonal dimorphism, no colour variations and no colour change in eclipse plumage. Juveniles initially coloured like F. Juvenile drakes moult into mature plumage in the first year; but the early autumn they are distinguishable from juvenile F. by some single newly moulted feathers.

Natural Habit

Status: Very large total population. Following their very pronounced migratory instinct they move to wherever they find favourable ecological conditions and leave the areas when circumstances change for the worse. The erection of stock dams in the arid interior of the continent has opened up new habitats for the maned geese.

Habitat: Meadows with occasional growth of old trees and in the vicinity of ponds and river courses; also water reservoirs in pasture and arable land. Maned geese avoid low-lying swamps as a habitat.

Breeding Biology: In common with most other *Cairina* species, maned geese pair and display in an inconspicuous manner. Nests have been found in tree hollows—quite often far distant from any water—containing nine to eleven cream coloured eggs. The nest is lined with white down and incubation takes 28–30 days. The young are looked after by both parents on the meadows adjacent to the breeding waters.

Migration: On their extensive migratory flights the maned geese roam all over the continent and stop in areas where good rainfall has created favourable ecological conditions (e. g. flooded pastureland).

Yearly Cycle: The breeding season is largely dependent on rainfall. In Victoria (area with rainfall in the winter) the maned geese breed in the spring months, September and October; in New South Wales between January and March; in the interior of the continent breeding does not depend on the seasons. During the dry period considerable numbers of maned geese form into flocks on the last drying out water surfaces and on larger lakes.

Climate: Tasmania, South and South East Australia lie in the zone of winter rainfall with sub-tropical and mediterranean climates; summer temperatures average circa 20°C and winter temperatures 8–13°C. All other areas have dry-hot desert and steppe climates.

Aviculture

Maned geese have been inhabitants of European zoos and private parks for more than a century. They have few special requirements, maintaining them is not difficult and, nowadays, they are also easy to breed. The poor breeding results of former decades were presumably due to the fact that the maned geese had been imported, and birds taken from their natural environment do not display much reproductive activity as a rule.

Housing: Maned geese like to graze and, like true geese, they should be kept in preserves with good turf. As they are not at all aggressive they are particularly suited to being kept on communal ponds or in collections of smaller ducks. In some preserves it is possible to keep them unpinioned. They need to be wintered in dry, draught-free shelters in prolonged periods of frost only.

Food: Grain and other plain food. If maned geese do not have enough space in which to graze they have to be given a great deal of green food.

Breeding: The Dutchman BLAAUW achieved the first breeding result in 1905, forty years after the first import of the maned goose by the London Zoo. Even in the 1960s successful breeding by maned geese in zoological gardens and breeders' preserves was considered as remarkable. Nowadays breeding results are likely with most pairs, even in fairly small preserves. Eggs are always laid during the northern spring and summer months, sometimes as early as March. At the Wildfowl Trust, Slimbridge, a maned goose female actually started laying her first clutch on February 24 and her fourth clutch on July 9, 1973. Incubation of the eggs and rearing of the young can be left quite safely to the parent birds, but either is equally possible in conditions of artificially applied warmth. The young are very robust and easy to rear. A few weeks after the young have become fully feathered they undergo a post-juvenile moult when the coloration of their immature plumage changes into that of the adult birds. Quite a number of maned geese are sexually mature when they are just over one year old.

Hybridization: Tendencies are not at all marked; a few cases of hybridizing are known to have occurred with the Egyptian and the Magellan goose.

Mandarin Duck

Aix galericulata (L.)

Comparative Size: Considerably smaller than mallard.
Plumage: M. in breeding plumage see plate 95; in eclipse coloration of M. like that of F., but M. has yellow feet and a red bill, F. olive-green feet and grey bill. Feet of juvenile M. yellow-green, those of juvenile F. grey-green. When the drakes are almost fully feathered their bill turns red.

Natural Habit

Status: Because of large-scale deforestation in N. E. China the mandarin duck has become a rare breeding bird there, but in the region of the Ussuri it is still quite common. In Japan many of the birds have taken to urban habitats.
Habitat: Lakes, river courses and reservoirs either surrounded by old trees or situated in high forests (mixed deciduous and larch woods); mandarin ducks avoid swampy lowlands.
Breeding Biology: Eggs are normally laid in hollow trees, often at a great height and far distant from any water; more rarely in rock crevices. Eight to twelve creamy brown eggs are the normal clutch size and incubation takes 31 days. The

80 ↑ Bahama Pintail
81 ↓ Red-billed Pintail

82 ↑ Versicolor Teal
83 ↓ Hottentot Teal

84 ↑ European Eider M.
85 ↗ Common Shoveler
86 ↓ European Eider, one year old, moulting into breeding plumage

87 ↑   Rosybill M.
88 ↓   Rosybill F. and young

89 ↑ Maned Goose
90 ↗ African Pygmy Goose
91 ↓ Red-crested Pochard

92 ↑   Hartlaub's Duck
93 ↓   Ringed Teal

94 ↑   North American Wood Duck
95 ↓   Mandarin Duck

96 ↑ Velvet Scoter
97 ↗ Long-tailed Duck M.
98 ↓ Velvet Scoter M.

newly hatched young jump down from the nest and the female guides them to the water. Whilst the mandarin ducklings are being reared the drakes congregate in small flocks for their moult.

Migration: Bird of passage in most areas; when their home waters freeze mandarins move away in a south-easterly direction.

Yearly Cycle: When waters thaw mandarins return to their breeding grounds from March onwards. Egg-laying at the turn of April/May; arrival in wintering grounds in Japan in October and November.

Climate: In the breeding grounds, periods of heavy rainfall—in higher altitudes short, cool summers—are followed by periods of severe cold in the winter when everything is covered with ice. Even in the south-eastern winter areas temperatures are near freezing point.

Aviculture

The very attractively coloured mandarin ducks were first imported in Europe in the 18th century; nowadays they belong to the most frequently kept ornamental ducks. They are well able to withstand cold, they are robust and very attractive and, thus, they can be seen in many zoos, parks and on urban waters; breeders also pay them a great deal of attention. In some areas, particularly in southern England, feral populations have become established, but these are not very stable.

Housing: They are equally well suited to being kept on breeders' and park ponds, in small enclosures and in aviaries. In very confined spaces, however, the mandarin drakes may impose a severe strain on the females of ground dwellers (rails and waders) and, at times, even on females of their own species. If mandarins are kept in aviaries they should not have their wings clipped. A shelter is needed in severe climates only.

Food: All kinds of grain, a plain mixed food and duckweed.

Breeding: As a rule the rate of reproductivity is high but slightly behind that of the North American wood duck. Display, pairing and copulation take place from October, most of all during the winter months; at that time tree holes are examined as possible nest sites. It is by no means rare that mandarins wintered in slightly heated houses produce a first clutch in February. Normally, egg-laying begins from end-March, but in aviaries often not before May. The females like occupying nest holes arranged for them at some height; they lay eggs every second day. The eggs are slightly more pointed and more strongly cream-coloured than the otherwise very similar eggs of the North American wood duck. The majority of mandarin females incubate quietly and reliably, some tend to be nervous. Their down and contour feathers are very light in colouring, a characteristic they share with other birds that nest in holes. About 24 hours after they are hatched, the ducklings jump out of the nest hole; the female rears them alone. If an enclosure is very small it might be advisable to separate the drake from the family. Rearing of the young, even without parents or foster parents, is quite easy and, generally, losses are very seldom. In the first two days after hatching the young try to escape from their rearing boxes, either by climbing or jumping out; however, they soon calm down and afterwards their progress is satisfactory. When the ducklings are fourteen days old the first quills may be seen; at the age of about six weeks the young are fully feathered and, in the autumn of their first year they moult into their splendid nuptial plumage. One year old birds are sexually mature.

Hybridization: Although mandarin ducks have been observed pairing and copulating with North American wood ducks there appear to be no hybrid descendants (eggs have always been infertile).

North American Wood Duck
Aix sponsa (L.)

Comparative Size: Smaller than a mallard.
Plumage: M. and F. in breeding plumage see plate 94; in eclipse plumage M. resembles F., but he has white markings on the throat and a colourful bill. Juveniles very similar in coloration to eclipse plumage of adult birds; initially, juvenile drakes lack the colourful bill.

Natural Habit

Status: Up to the turn of the century the birds were subjected to great pressure by hunting, stocks had been decimated and many populations exterminated. When protective measures were finally taken, these soon became effective and they have resulted in an overall stabilisation of populations. In 1970 the total number of the birds was estimated at 1.3 million North American wood ducks.
Habitat: Predominantly oligotrophic waters of the plains and lowlands, surrounded by woods of high deciduous trees; North American wood ducks are far less common on lakes and river courses in the boreal coniferous forest zones of the north.
Breeding Biology: As soon as the waters thaw the birds return to their breeding grounds. Eggs are laid in tree holes (which may be up to 10 m high); they readily accept nesting boxes put up for them. Clutch size is between ten and fourteen eggs, rounded off at either end; incubation takes 29–32 days; the ducklings jump down from the nest 24–36 hours after they are hatched and the female rears them in the shore region of the waters. The drake rarely takes an active part in guiding the young.
Migration: Bird of passage, partial migrant and also a sedentary resident. In the autumn they seek waters near areas with a good supply of food (oak, beech or bald cypress woods); when frost sets in they wander to the southern states of the USA.
Yearly Cycle: In the medium latitudes spring migration takes place in March and April, laying begins in April or May (approximately two weeks after arrival in the breeding grounds); the birds undergo a full moult after the beginning of June and move to their winter grounds in October/November.
Climate: Most breeding grounds have a temperate climate, similar to that of western Europe.

Aviculture

Nowadays the North American wood duck and its close relative, the mandarin duck, are among the most frequently kept species. Actually, the North American wood duck was first introduced in Europe as an ornamental waterfowl as early as the 17th century. The birds are notable for their lack of aggressiveness, attractive colouring and modest requirements. Some of them have reared young after they had escaped from preserves; HEINROTH attempted to settle North American wood ducks on the urban waters of Berlin and Dresden in 1900 approximately. But free-living populations able to maintain themselves for any length of time have never developed anywhere in Europe.

Housing: North American wood ducks can be kept and bred in any preserves which are able to meet the requirements of ornamental ducks. The drakes are less aggressive towards the other preserve birds, and in particular, towards their own females, than the mandarin ducks. North American wood ducks are hardy in the winter, but in periods of snow and frost they like to seek the protection of a shelter.

Food: Grain, a simple mixed food and, whilst the young are being reared, duckweed. They like whole acorns in the autumn.

Breeding: Rate of reproductivity is somewhat higher than that of mandarin duck. Eggs are laid in nesting boxes or shelters, in mild weather from March onwards (females may even lay in February if their winter house is overheated); egg-laying continues until the summer months. The females lay in approximately 35 hourly intervals (circa 10 eggs in 15 days) and they incubate very reliably. They may well produce another clutch when they have finished incubating and rearing the first one. The minimum interval between two clutches is 13–15 days. Whether guided by the mother bird or kept in rearing boxes the ducklings develop beautifully and losses are even less likely than they are with mandarin ducklings. At seven to eight weeks the North American wood ducklings are fully feathered and, at that time, the bill of the young drakes—dark during the first weeks—becomes colourful; from September the juveniles moult into their first breeding plumage, although the moult proceeds more slowly than that of the adult birds. The ducklings are sexually mature at the age of nine to ten months.

Hybridization: Tendencies are pronounced. The females allow drakes of numerous species to copulate with them (more than 20 different hybrids are known to exist); they interbreed most frequently with red-crested and European pochard drakes. The North American wood duck males pair less often with females of different species.

Brazilian Teal

Amazonetta brasiliensis (Gmelin)

Comparative Size: Little larger than green-winged teal.

Plumage: M. and F. see plate 71; no seasonal dimorphism; upperparts predominantly brown, the wings are more attractively coloured (velvety black, bottle-green, white), the legs are a glowing red. Bill of M. red-brown, that of F. dark grey. Juvenile M. initially has grey-black bill (like juvenile F.), at the age of three to four weeks the bill of the M. turns horn-brown; thus it is possible to note the differences between the sexes, even before the birds are fully feathered.

NATURAL HABIT

Status: Widely distributed within the whole area of occurence but never in large numbers. In Brazil, attempts have been made to domesticate and breed them, which shows that they are well able to tolerate very variable ecological conditions; the latter would be an advantage for the preservation of their species.

Habitat: Ponds surrounded by woods and bushes; river plains in tropical rain forests and savannas, in the latter especially river courses lined with rows of trees.

Breeding Biology: Display and pairing are inconspicuous and usually take place in the breeding grounds. Most nests are on the ground in the marsh vegetation, more rarely in holes of old trees or old nests. A full clutch contains eight to twelve ochre-yellow eggs; incubation takes 25–26 days. Apparently the drake helps the female to rear the young.

Migration: Only the southern populations are birds of passage migrating northwards to escape the winter's cold. The others roam over wide distances once they have finished breeding and moulting; these wandering flights are determined by the periods of rainfall.

Yearly Cycle: Breeding activities depend less on the yearly seasons than on local conditions which—in turn—are dependent on rainfall.

Climate: Tropical and sub-tropical with high temperatures throughout the year; periods and amount of rainfall are very variable, however.

AVICULTURE

Despite their simple brown plumage Brazilian teal are kept by most wildfowl enthusiasts and zoos. As the birds are small, generally peaceable and make few demands as regards accommodation, quality of water and food, it is not surprising that they are popular.

Housing: It is best to keep them in collections of smaller species of ducks, but they are also quite suitable for large communal enclosures and aviaries. They do not need the ground cover of vegetation. Brazilian teal are fairly hardy in cold weather, but—unlike the northern species of ducks—they do not draw up their legs (which are sensitive to frost) to be covered by their plumage whilst they are resting; thus their toes become frost-bitten on icy ground. A dry shelter or a sufficiently large area of open water has to be at their disposal always.

Food: Normal duck food which may have to be enriched with animal protein, or shrimps can be dropped on the water for them. In the summer they should always be given duckweed and dandelion or lettuce leaves.

Breeding: At least a few of the Brazilian teal are sexually mature towards the end of the first year of life. Eggs are laid in 24 hourly intervals, probably without exception in nest holes. Laying rarely begins before the end of April, further clutches are possible until July. Some drakes defend the nest site and may become quite vicious. The females are good and quiet brooders. The young are robust, not very timid and they are easy to rear; even where they have no parent bird or older ducklings to guide them they soon find their food and the way to a heat-lamp. I made the following notes about their development: at the age of 13 days the first tail quills show; feathering of flanks begins after 17 days, shoulders after 20 days and chest after 22 days.

When they are seven weeks old the young Barzilian teal have most of their feathers and at the age of three months they wear the complete adult plumage.

Hybridization: Brazilian teal drakes mate with females of other species fairly frequently, particularly those of the *Anas* group.

Ringed Teal
Calonetta leucophrys (Vieillot)

Comparative Size: Approximately the size of a green-winged teal.
Plumage: M. and F. see plate 93; no seasonal dimorphism. Blotching on chest may show slight differences in colour intensity, otherwise no colour variants. Sexes of juveniles discernible towards end of feathering—juvenile F. has white face markings (like adult F.), face of M. plain grey, chest barred in varying shades of grey.

NATURAL HABIT

Status: So little has been reported about ringed teal in their natural environment that for a long time it was believed that the birds were becoming extinct. This is nut true, however. REICHHOLF (1975) observed more than 4,000 individual ringed teal on the Pilcomayo lagoons of the Gran Chaco in May, 1970; he remarked that the ringed teal were certainly the most abundant species of ducks in this particular region.
Habitat: Very shallow waters in tropical woods and swamps and sections of slowly flowing rivers.
Breeding Biology: No details are known, the only certainty being that ringed teal nest in tree holes and that five to eight white eggs make up their clutch.
Migration: Evidently permanent residents; REICHHOLF (1975) reported that ringed teal aggregate in swarms within their breeding grounds.
Yearly Cycle: In Paraguay ringed teal breed from September until November.
Climate: High temperatures with few fluctuations prevail in all areas. In some areas rainfall occurs throughout the year, in others it is periodic. Amount ot rainfall is plentiful everywhere so thaf the extensive swampy plains, even in the savanna (Mato Grosso and Gran Chaco), never dry out.

AVICULTURE

Since the first import of ringed teal in 1908, many breeders have attempted to breed these beautiful, small ducks which are easy to maintain. The number of ringed teal imported in Europe appears to be remarkably low and most of the imports have occured in 1908, 1910, and again later after 1950 and 1970. The initial rate of reproduction was high, which led to a rapid increase of ringed teal in breeders' preserves. Typical inbreeding symptoms and resultant stock curtailment became noticeable in the 1930s (KOLBE 1972) and, once more, in certain regions at the end of the 1960s.

Housing: Especially suitable for small, easily surveyable enclosures with warm, sunny ponds. A few pairs of ringed teal can be kept in communal preserves together with other species during the breeding season without causing excessive quarrels amongst the birds. Ringed teal need a shelter in periods of frosty weather. Unpinioned birds are far more likely to breed; they rarely wander off.

Food: They have no special requirements; whilst breeding they particularly like meal-worms and shrimps.

Breeding: One year old ringed teal are fully mature sexually but, as a rule, their clutches are smaller than those of older birds. The female lays her eggs in nesting boxes; unpinioned females prefer laying in nesting holes erected for them at some height. Egg-laying normally begins in May after a spell of warm weather, but eggs may be laid as early as March and as late as June. A sudden period of cold weather often leads to delay or interruption of laying. Incubation takes 26 days. If the female is not disturbed in her nest whilst incubating she will brood reliably and quietly. Both male and female guide their young with great care so that losses of ducklings are rare (the same applies if they are reared in conditions of artificial warmth).

Ringed teal weigh 17–20 grammes when they are hatched; at the age of two weeks the tail quills develop; at three weeks feathers of the belly, flanks and shoulders appear and the flight feathers can be felt. When the ducklings are one month old they are more or less fully feathered and the sexes are dinstinguishable from each other. From then onwards they slowly moult into the coloration of the adult plumage and, at three months, it is difficult to distinguish them from mature birds.

Hybridization: Very little tendency; hybrids of ringed and Brazilian teal have proved to be infertile.

Velvet Scoter
Melanitta fusca (L.)

Comparative Size: Approximately the same as mallard.

Plumage: Adult M. and F. see plate 96 and 98; the black plumage of the M's body has a purple-green sheen, plumage of F. black-brown; both sexes have a large white speculum. Juvenile M. brownish in colouring turning velvety black in autumn, the white eye patch is not moulted until the second winter.

NATURAL HABIT

Status: An abundant total population corresponds with the extensive area over which the velvet scoters are spread. On the European coasts the velvet scoter is a less common winter visitor than, for instance, common scoters, goldeneyes and long-tailed ducks.

Habitat: In North America, during the breeding season, the velvet scoters inhabit oligotrophic lakes in the regions of coniferous forest, and prairie lakes lying further south; in Europe they nest on wooded rocky islets off the coasts of Finland and Estonia; in central Asia they breed on lakes of steppes and mountains. Winters are spent on quiet, shallow seaboards and large inland lakes.

Breeding Biology: Inconspicuous display and pairing take place among the winter flocks. After arrival on their breeding waters, pairs fly over the territory in search of a nest site. The female alone makes the nest on dry ground, either underneath bushes or between stones, often on islands where nests are sometimes only a few metres apart from each other. The nest is lined with very dark down and a clutch consists of eight to ten creamy white eggs. Incubation takes 27–29 days. It is said that the females' impulse to guide their young is not very marked and that they leave ducklings when they are only four to five weeks old (sometimes even earlier).

Migration: The majority of velvet scoters winter on the coasts of the Atlantic and Pacific Oceans and the adjoining seas; some spend winters on the coasts of the Caspian Sea. They stay on ice-free inland waters more frequently than other sea ducks.

Yearly Cycle: Spring starts late in all breeding grounds of the velvet scoters; thus wintering grounds are often not left until April; eggs are laid in June and July; after completed moult and rearing of young rapid migration to the sea.

Climate: Short summers and severe, long winters prevail in all northern breeding grounds and also in the Asiatic mountain areas where the birds are found at altitudes of up to 2,000 m.

AVICULTURE

Because of their dark plumage and high requirements regarding food and maintenance, neither the common nor velvet scoter—in North America also the surf scoter—are species much in demand by wildfowl enthusiasts. Nonetheless, many careful and troublesome attempts have been made to establish these ducks in preserves in the hope that they will breed eventually. The highest rate of success has been achieved in keeping mature wintering birds, caught by chance in fishermen's nets and handed over to bird lovers or zoological experts in a weakened condition or soiled by oil. The scoters experience little difficulty in adapting to a new environment, coping with the proximity of man and accepting food from a trough. What appears to be a greater problem is the birds' inability to maintain the normal functions of metabolism (including moult and maintaining their body's defense mechanisms) for any length of time.

Housing: After the initial period of adaptation, velvet scoters—like all sea ducks (see long-tailed duck)—should be kept on large lakes, more than one metre deep, filled with cold, clear water; they enjoy staying out on the open water. If the ducks remain too long on dry land, e. g. the enclosure where they are first housed whilst becoming established, they develop weal-like sores, inflammations and abnormal horny blisters on the underside of the toes (compare with avocet).

Food: A nutritious prepared food (trout pellets), grain. fish or pieces of meat, shrimps and, if possible, freshwater molluscs which the birds prefer to all other foods. The velvet and common scoters I have maintained myself were initially fed on fish only (herring, cod and freshwater fish); after many weeks they showed a decided preference for mixed food and, later still, preferred wheat to the latter.

Breeding: Very few facts have been reported. *The International Zoo Year Book* quotes one rearing success each for the Washington Zoo, 1960, and for the Helsinki Zoo, 1972, but does not state whether the velvet scoter ducklings were reared from eggs collected from wild birds or from eggs laid by birds in preserves.
Hybridization: Unknown.

Long-tailed Duck
Clangula hyemalis (L.)

Comparative Size: A little smaller than a European pochard.
Plumage: M. in winter plumage see plate 97, M. in breeding plumage (April to June) dark-brown on the upperside, feathers of the back have pale edges, eclipse plumage (August to November) darker still and duller. Plumage of F. rather plain with little colour change throughout the year, although there are individual colour variants. Juveniles similar in coloration to F.

NATURAL HABIT

Status: Most abundant species of ducks in the tundras north of the arctic circle. Despite heavy losses caused by oil pollution and fishing nets which bring about the death by drowning of thousands of birds every year, evidently no stock curtailment has occured so far.
Habitat: During the breeding season small freshwater ponds with numerous small islands in the arctic tundras where the long-tailed ducks move further inland than other sea ducks; they also nest on inhospitable coasts and their offshore islands. They winter on sandy, shallow coasts of the oceans; the largest inland wintering grounds are on the Great Lakes of North America.
Breeding Biology: Display and pairing take place in the wintering grounds and on the homeward migration. Nests are close to the water, often on small islands;

they are made of moss or lichen and are lined with a great deal of down. Six to nine yellow or olive-grey eggs make up a full clutch; incubation takes circa 24 days. The female guides the ducklings to the nearby water; two to three weeks afterwards the birds move to the sea together with the still flightless young. On the inland lakes the long-tailed ducks feed on plankton and, on the sea, almost exclusively on mussels and other molluscs.

Migration: Birds of passage which migrate to the temperate latitudes of the oceans when home grounds become too frozen — in Europe to the western Baltic, in America southwards to Washington and Carolina.

Yearly Cycle: The breeding season begins between end-May and end-June depending on local climate; families' autumn migration is from September onwards. Long-tailed ducks remain on the European coasts from November until April.

Climate: Arctic climate in all breeding grounds with temperatures near freezing point and cold winds.

AVICULTURE

The beautifully coloured long-tailed ducks are not among the species whose maintenance on preserve ponds has yielded satisfacotry results. In Great Britain and North America ducklings have been reared a number of times from eggs collected from wild birds. In the Zoological Park at Clères (France), a drake (received in the winter) lived for eight years and paired with a chestnut teal female at times. My personal experiments in establishing long-tailed ducks which I received in a soiled condition (caused by oil) have been only partially successful but may be of interest to bird lovers living near the coasts. They are as follows:

Treatment of feathers: Several hours after being captured, the oil had seeped right through the ducks' plumage so that it became saturated. It had to be washed a number of times with a paste (designed for hand-washing) which dissolved the oil; afterwards the birds dried themselves underneath a heat-lamp. During the day I offered them the opportunity of staying on a lawn and the possibility of repeated baths on a pond of three square metres. Initially the ducks were completely soaked with water after one minute, were driven out of the water and, without prompting, ran to the sunlight lamp. Little by little, the intervals between baths became shorter and the period of staying on the water became longer until, finally, they were 'waterproof' again.

Food: All the long-tailed ducks were under-nourished when I received them and, because they were so hungry, they immediately accepted, and ate greedily, the pieces of fish they were given. In an astonishingly short period of time they became tame as regards feeding, were remarkably quick in learning and accepted their new environment (sometimes a room in an hotel) as a matter of course and soon found their way everywhere. I fed them on sea-fish, grated mussels, shrimps and, additionally, yeast, vitamins, minerals, and also antibiotics to protect them from pneumonia.

Housing: Once the plumage no longer became soaked with water, the long-tailed ducks were put on a pond with clear water, 250 square metres in area and one metre deep. Pieces if fish were given to them either in a trough or dropped on the water. What appeared to be remarkable was that the ducks never tried to find food for themselves (apart from the pieces of fish they were given) although, at times, they could have found plenty of water insects and small fish in their pond.

Breeding: The long-tailed ducks I myself had salvaged often displayed and called in the spring, but moult and other metabolism disturbances soon became apparent. Mrs. LAMPSON (1973) reported on the first breeding result in Great Britain:

In 1966 eggs collected from wild birds were incubated, the young hatched and were reared. One pair of these ducks inhabited a pond in a park, 0.8 ha in area. The female laid seven infertile eggs in a barrel in 1970; between June 24 and July 1, 1971, she laid another five eggs underneath a bush and two of these were fertile. A hen brooded them and two ducklings were hatched; they grew to maturity without any particular complications. They were fed on similar food given to turkeys: boiled egg yolk, mealworms and some duckweed. Adult long-tailed ducks are fed on chicken and turkey pellets and only occasionally on pieces of fish.

By 1975 no further breeding results had been achieved either with the pair mentioned above or with a younger pair (Mrs. LAMPSON, by letter).

Hybridization: Two ducklings were hatched in the zoological park at Clères in the 1930s after a long-tailed duck had interbred with a chestnut teal, but the ducklings did not live.

Goldeneye
Bucephala clangula (L.)

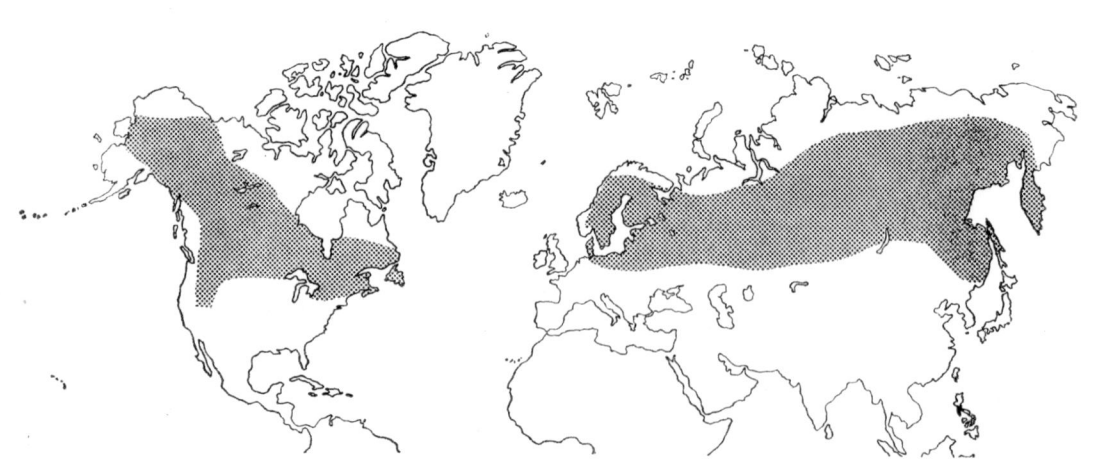

Comparative Size: Approximately the same size as European pochard.
Plumage: M. in breeding plumage see plate 99; M. in eclipse and juvenile M. resemble F. but bill is heavier, and head as well as wing areas are larger.

NATURAL HABIT

Status: As in former times, large populations inhabit Eurasia and North America. Until 1945 the goldeneyes' breeding occurrence extended as far west as the river Elbe; there has been a regression of the breeding range since then.
Habitat: Oligotrophic diluvial lakes and river courses surrounded by old trees in the coniferous forest zone; goldeneyes have spread to the milder deciduous forest zone in central Europe only.
Breeding Biology: As soon as they have moulted into their breeding plumage the drakes begin their courtship display which reaches its climax among the winter flocks and lasts until the time of egg-laying. Tree holes or nest boxes, especially set up in trees, are used as nesting places. Eight to ten large, blue-green eggs make up a normal clutch; incubation takes approximately 30 days. Several females often lay in one nest hole if it seems to

be favourable, but incubation of such over-large clutches seldom yields successful broods. Once the eggs are hatched the female calls to the ducklings and, when they have jumped down from the nest, she leads them to the water. The rate of losses of goldeneye ducklings is remarkably high.

Migration: In many areas drakes undertake moult migrations which often lead them far to the north. Goldeneyes winter on the coasts of the seas adjoining the Atlantic and Pacific (in Europe predominantly on the western Baltic coast) and on large inland lakes: the Caspian Sea, Lake Baikal and the Great Lakes of North America.

Yearly Cycle: Goldeneyes do not leave their breeding and moulting grounds until these freeze, then they move to open oceanic bays and lakes; they return to the breeding grounds as soon as the ice breaks.

Climate: Cool, northern boreal climate during the breeding season; a rough sea climate in the temperate latitudes during the winter.

AVICULTURE

Of all the marine ducks goldeneyes are the ones most frequently kept and bred and, in fact, they are the only sea ducks which are regularly seen on display ponds of zoos and bird preserves. Nonetheless, it is not very easy to keep them, and rearing of the ducklings may cause some difficulties.

Housing: Only on large ponds, not less than 80 cm deep, carrying cold, clear water. If goldeneyes are kept on small communal ponds during the breeding season, the drakes are often so aggressive towards all other species of ducks that the latter avoid the water surface and stop their own breeding cycle. Goldeneyes should be wintered on ice-free water.

Food: Grain and shrimps dropped on the water in the period of acclimatization. Once the goldeneyes are used to taking their food from a trough they should be given nutritious pellets or mixed food, and they gladly accept additionally pieces of fish, meal-worms and duckweed with insects caught up in it, thrown in with the other food. Ducklings are fed on meal-worms, live invertebrates, duckweed and—later—poultry food which can be enriched with minced fish and lean meat (heart).

Breeding: One year old goldeneye drakes have not developed all their courtship display poses and, even at the age of two years, they often do not complete copulation. As a result many eggs are not fertilized. Breeding results are far more likely with pairs which are at least three years old. Eggs are laid in two day intervals and laying takes place after mid-March. Goldeneye females incubate quietly and reliably; if the first clutch of eggs is removed the female is almost certain to produce another clutch. Depending on the facilities he can offer, every breeder has to develop his own method as regards rearing of the ducklings. Just a few words if advice may be given. It is best to rear the ducklings in artificial warmth and keep them separated from other ducklings. After the second day they should be allowed short spells on a bathing pool where they will pick up meal-worms and pieces of fish dropped on the water for them; they will find other food floating on the water surface and soon after they are able to find their way to the feeding trough. The best rearing results are achieved with larger groups of goldeneye ducklings. As they get older they need special rearing ponds which allow them to bathe and dive without restriction.

Hybridization: According to many reports in ornithological literature very pronounced tendencies, in particular with mergansers and diving ducks. However, goldeneyes rarely hybridize in breeding preserves. Presumably, the interesting hybrids have received above average publicity.

Hooded Merganser

Mergus cucullatus L.

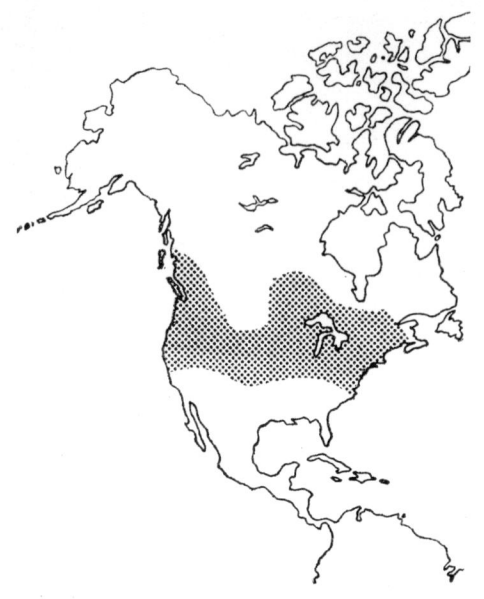

Comparative Size: A small species of mergansers, approximately the same body size as the common white-eye.

Plumage: M. in breeding plumage see plate 101; M. in eclipse plumage resembles F. but can be distinguished by yellow irides. Juveniles' colouring also similar to that of F., but irides of the young drakes gradually turn yellow-brown, those of females stay dark-brown.

Natural Habit

Status: In the extensive North American regions of coniferous forest the hooded mergansers are endangered only in those areas which have undergone drastic deforestation which has robbed the birds of their nesting trees. In any case, other mergansers, goldeneyes, North American wood ducks and buffleheads compete with the hooded mergansers for suitable nest sites. The latter's feeding and ecological requirements are highly specialised, and it is therefore not surprising that the hooded mergansers' breeding density is not as high as that of the *Anas* and *Aythya* species. The total population is estimated to be less than 100,000 individuals.

Habitat: Diluvial lakes, river courses and the quiet causeways beside fast-flowing river streams which are surrounded by old trees. Even outside the breeding seasons hooded mergansers prefer habitats of clear freshwater lakes to oceanic coasts and brackish water.

Breeding Biology: Like many other northern Anatidae, hooded mergansers begin courtship and pairing in their winter grounds; the display reaches its climax during the spring migration and after arrival on the breeding grounds. Once the breeding territory has been selected and is defended from intruders, the display soon dies down. Nests are made in hollow trees where the six to twelve white eggs are incubated for 30–32 days. The hatched ducklings jump down from the nest and are then guided by the female to the outer edge of the shore vegetation where she rears them.

Migration: Cold, continental winters force most populations to migrate in a south-easterly or south-westerly direction. They move as far as the coastal states of the USA. The majority winters south 40° of the northern latitude.

Yearly Cycle: Spring migration begins rather early in the year (mid-February in Virginia), but it also carries on for quite a long time. Main period of egg-laying is between mid-May and mid-June; migration to winter grounds normally between September and November, as soon as frost sets in.

Climate: After long, severe winters, breeding waters and air temperatures gradually become warmer (northern boreal climate). Temperatures near freezing point prevail in the wintering grounds and also at the time of migration.

AVICULTURE

It took a remarkably long time before breeders became interested in the magnificently coloured hooded mergansers with their unusual habits. Pioneering work was carried out by Ch. PILLING of Seattle (USA); he had found injured birds, established them with great care and trouble and, eventually, achieved a breeding result with them (in 1955). Nowadays, of all *Mergus* species, the hooded merganser is the one most frequently kept and bred in preserves—and with very good results.

Housing: Ponds in preserves should contain water of a good quality and they need to be at least 80 cm deep. Concrete basins are no less suitable than natural ponds. Hooded mergansers possibly should spend winters on ice-free water, if not they should be given at least the opportunity of a good, long bathe every day if they cannot remain on their water surface.

Food: Mature birds are fed on nutritious pellets, shrimps, grain and, occasionally, meal-worms; in fact they can be nourished on food containing no fish whatsoever; (WIENANDS, Viersen (FRG) by letter). WILLIAMS, Harpenden (UK), feeds his hooded merganser ducklings on minced ox-heart initially; later he mixes it with dog biscuits and poultry starter crumbs; he also gives them meal-worms and duckweed.

Breeding Biology: Hooded mergansers offered for sale by the present-day animal trade are all birds bred and reared in preserves; they are well adapted by the time they are sold. Several British breeders described planned breeding programmes in the *Avicultural Magazine* and so did WIENANDS in the *Gefiederte Welt*. These reports are no longer as important as they would have been some time ago. WIENANDS wrote in 1974 about hooded mergansers as follows: "Towards the end of the first year of life the drake started moulting into his breeding plumage; the nuptial plumage was completed in that same autumn and the bird started to display and mate. In mid-April of the third year the female began laying. She laid eight eggs in 48 hourly intervals and these were brooded in an incubator. The ducklings accepted the food they were given remarkably quickly (a moist mixture consisting of insects, meat-meal, meal-worms and—a little later—chicken starter crumbs); they thrived very well on the diet. When they were two weeks old they were given the first opportunity of bathing in one of the rearing preserves; at two and a half weeks the first feathers became noticeable, at six weeks they were fully feathered, and at the age of 8 weeks it was possible to tell their sex, the irides of the drakes turning yellow-brown."

Hybridization: Tendencies to interbreed are not marked, but cross-breeding may occur with other mergansers and members of the Anatidae family.

Red-breasted Merganser

Mergus serrator L.

Comparative Size: Smaller and slimmer than mallard.
Plumage: One year old M. see plate 102; M. in eclipse plumage resembles colour of F., M. in breeding plumage has a bottle-green head, red-brown chest and black-grey and white lower back. Juvenile M. distinguishable by strong bill, lighter inner wing feathers and after October by ornamental shoulder feathers; the juvenile F. utters harsh rattling calls.

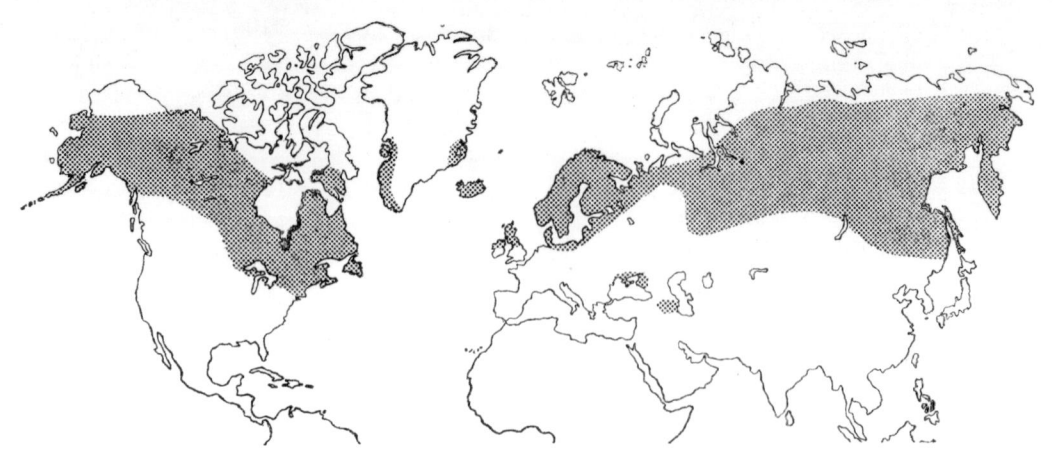

Natural Habit

Status: A very large total population together with a very wide geographical distribution; in northern Europe, including the Baltic Coast, the birds are becoming ever more abundant.

Habitat: Islands and rocky islets off the coasts, also clear inland lakes and similar waters in the tundras and prairies. Red-breasted mergansers are ground breeders and prefer waters of the open landscape to those of woodland areas. Winter swarms use shallow sections of the coasts, up to 10 m deep, as resting places.

Breeding Biology: Display (when the birds 'curtesy' to each other) and pair formation begin in October and November. The red-breasted mergansers arrive in their breeding grounds already paired, but during the breeding season pairs form small flocks with each other. The female makes a well concealed nest, either underneath bushes or among heather and reed grasses. Normal clutch size is eight to twelve large olive-brown eggs; incubation varies between 29 and 32 days. Rearing of the young and moult of the adults take place on the open water near the breeding grounds.

Migration: Dependent on location of breeding and wintering grounds; redbreasted mergansers may be birds of passage, partial migrants or sedentary residents.

Yearly Cycle: Regional conditions are very variable and thus the yearly cycle is not uniform. On the south-western Baltic Sea Coast egg-laying begins after mid-May, normally in June. When the breeding season is finished, fairly large family groups gather and, from September onwards, they join up with the large winter flocks.

Climate: During the time of breeding, red-breasted mergansers predominantly inhabit boreal regions of the north where summer temperatures tend to be lower than those of western Europe.

Aviculture

This interesting duck species did not really come to the notice of zoological experts and breeders until approximately a decade ago. A few attempts at keeping and breeding red-breasted mergansers had been made previously (e. g. Heinroth, Berlin, 1930, and the British Wildfowl Trust, after 1950). Numerous young have since been hatched from wild birds' eggs and subsequently reared; mature birds, caught by chance, have become well established. Among a preserve population red-breasted mergansersare notable for their agility and their remarkable tameness.

Housing: Like goldeneyes they should be kept on a fairly large pond, more than 80 cm deep, and filled with clear water, if possible. Even in winter they have to have access to a bathing pool. In my own preserve, the red-breasted mergansers inhabit a communal pool and always draw the spectators' attention. During the autumn and winter months our mergansers show all the real behavioural traits of flock formation: they swim together, dive together, display in unison and make a concerted dash to the feeding trough. In very windy or dry-cold weather these characteristics are particularly marked.

Food: Freshwater fish and small quantities of sea-fish are their main foods. However, mergansers also accept coarse mixed duck food (up to 30 per cent of their total intake), soaked pellets and small quantities of wheat and duckweed.

Breeding: Less likely to succeed than breeding hooded mergansers and smew. In the British Wildfowl Trust, females laid more than 50 eggs over the last ten years, but very few young birds have been reared to maturity. In my own preserve I have had red-breasted merganser ducklings incubated and reared on several occasions as follows:

At first the ducklings were in a large rearing box with a big water basin but they were put on a pond of two square metres at certain times; not much later they were left on the pond all the time. The young were good swimmers and they dived without becoming too much soaked with water. They were thrown pieces of fish in the water and also in the box. Their mixed food consisted of minced fish and meat, a nutritious, fairly coarse rearing food mixture with pieces of fish, mealworms, shrimps and curd cheese.

When they were three weeks old the flanks became feathered; two-month-old red-breasted mergansers are fully feathered although their wings have not fully developed. I consider it to be of the utmost importance that the ducklings are given the maximum stimulus to bathe on a clean and not too small pool. The difficulty of red-breasted merganser breeding lies not so much in the initial rearing phase but in the rather high rate of losses of mature birds; complications may be caused by metabolism and moult disturbances, aspergillosis and accidents.

Hybridization: One of my red-breasted merganser females copulated (amongst others) with a European pochard, a Chiloe wigeon and a garganey drake. Up to date no eggs have been laid as a result of these cases of interbreeding.

North American Ruddy Duck
Oxyura jamaicensis Gmelin

Comparative Size: Just a little larger than a green-winged teal.

Plumage: M. and F. in breeding plumage see plate 103; M. in eclipse resembles coloration of F., but is nevertheless easily distinguishable. Juveniles are also coloured like F. There still appears to be a lack of information on the finer distinguishing marks between the sexes.

Natural Habit

Status: Three sub-species inhabit the New World from Canada to Tierra del Fuego. The North American ruddy duck described here has its densest breeding population on the prairie lakes of North America; with a population of 47,500 individual birds in these areas it is just as common as the other species of indigenous ducks.

Habitat: Large eutrophic lakes with a wealth of marsh and shore vegetation, vegateted islands and zones or emergents. Brackish water and coastal lagoons outside the breeding season—river mouths in particular.

Breeding Biology: On open surfaces of the breeding waters the males develop a heated courtship display for females and nesting sites. Nests are made in the zone of shallow water, among tussocks of reed grasses or sedge and they look like covered platforms. A full clutch contains five to ten (up to fourteen) very large white eggs; incubation takes approximately 25 days. Initially both parents guide the young, but the family bond lessens before the young are fledged.

Migration: Bird of passage in all northern breeding grounds; in central and southern regions predominantly sedentary or partial migrant.

Yearly Cycle: North American ruddy ducks leave their winter grounds later than other Anatidae—between March and May. The main breeding season is in May and June. Autumnal migration begins in September and in the central states of the USA it is at its height end-October.

Climate: The majority of breeding grounds are situated in the zones of summer-hot, dry continental climates; the birds winter in temperate-warm to tropical latitudes.

AVICULTURE

The North American ruddy duck looks charming and its habits will delight every waterfowl enthusiast, regardless of wheater he himself owns a bird in his preserve or has the opportunity to observe one at close quarters elsewhere. The drakes' colouring is plain, but it is clear and glowing. The North American ruddy ducks' general manner is playful, particularly so when they are showing off in courtship. They are lovable birds and quite different from other ducks. It was not until 1950 that American and British breeders made real efforts to breed the North American ruddy duck, the first representative of its kind in preserves. Nowadays, the ducks may be seen in breeding preserves of waterfowl enthusiasts, bird parks and all good zoos. They are widely distributed although keeping and breeding them is by no means easy.

Housing: Warm, shallow ponds, preferably with natural shore vegetation. It is essential that feeding and nesting places can be reached from the water as the ruddy ducks do not like going on land. They should be wintered on ice-free water; well-established birds are not particularly sensitive to frost, however.

Food: Grain dropped on the water; a feeding trough underneath the water is quite useful. Mixed food together with shrimps, duckweed, and meal-worms should be given to them close to the water. Their natural summer food consists of 90 per cent animal substances.

Breeding: The young North American ruddy ducks are sexually mature when they are ten to twelve months old. The drakes display almost continuously in spring and summer and later defend the chosen nest site. The nest, constructed by the female, is erected in the shore vegetation so that the brooding bird has immediate access to the water. At one time it was believed that the ruddy ducks only started the incubation of the eggs and that the egg embryos later developed by themselves. However, observations in preserves have proved the theory to be wrong. The females incubate just like other ducks, but the eggs are able to withstand long periods of cooling without damage. Laying begins in the British Wildfowl Trust sometimes at the beginning of May, more often after mid-May; second clutches are likely in June and July. The parents themselves should be left to guide their young in small preserves where they have the best chance of rearing a brood in the right conditions. If the young are reared in boxes they have to have a large water basin at their disposal to stimulate their swimming and diving. It is essential to make a careful selection of foods.

Hybridization: Supposedly not at all pronounced.

Rails and their Relatives

The large, diverse group of rails embraces well over 100 species and, although in relationship they are closest to the cranes, in appearance they do not resemble them at all. Many species inhabit in small populations the islands of the Pacific Ocean; over the last 150 years 15 species have become extinct.
Some well-known species will be discussed in the following pages. Rails and their relatives are notable for being enormously mobile and agile and thus they add considerable life to aviaries and open water surfaces. They rarely become really tame and attached to man like the cranes, however. Nonetheless, the small and particularly the tropical species are very interesting nurslings, such as the red and white crake; the Black Crake, *Limnocorax flavirostra*; and the very attractive sunbittern. All the birds display unusual characteristics and their calls are very melodious. An additional advantage is that few of them destroy the ground vegetation of their aviary. Nearly all these rails love warmth and humidity and will soon feel at home and thrive in tropical halls planted with the beautiful and rare flowers which need similar conditions. There the birds can find a habitat for themselves among the plants and doubtless if they can find a mate they will nest.

Red and White Crake
Laterallus leucopyrrhus (Vieillot)

Comparative Size: Considerably smaller than moorhen and water rail (total length 17–19 cm).
Plumage: Adults see plate 78; upperside glowing red-brown, wings and tail olive brown; throat, chest and belly silvery white as are undertail coverts of F.; the latter are glowing white in M. Flanks are barred in a strong black and white. Juveniles dark-grey with brown overtones, underparts lighter, irides dark-brown, feet black-brown, but red later on.

NATURAL HABIT

Status: It is impossible to make an exact population count o fthis swamp inhabiting species. However, their natural environment has undergone little change, and it is quite easy to import the red and white crakes. It may be assumed therefore that the birds are still quite common.
Breeding Biology: Practically no reports are at hand. It is therefore particularly informative to have MEISE'S report

(1934) about two breeding results in a preserve (see under 'Breeding'). Some nests have been found in Argentina, some were half-way up some reed-grasses and others in brushwood and tree undergrowth.
Migration: Presumably sedentary and resident; short periods of roaming flights because of rainfall are quite likely.

Yearly Cycle: Breeding season in Argentina between October and February; the northern populations also breed in other months.
Climate: Tropical climate with high temperatures throughout the year; periods and amounts of rainfall are regionally variable.

AVICULTURE

Nowadays, rails are used as fellow occupants in many different types of preserves, and it is difficult to imagine tropical halls and aviaries of zoos and bird preserves inhabited by unpinioned birds without at least some rails. Particularly the small rails (as for instance the red and white crake) are very active and agile so that something interesting always happens at ground level.
Housing: Bird and glass houses; outdoor aviaries for small birds during the summer.

A water basin with a shallow rim, 5 cm deep, and a small corner with some dense ground vegetation should be at the birds' disposal. If the whole area is closely planted, the birds will hide and lead a timid and withdrawn existence. In houses without too much dense cover they will become quite tame. These small rails are very keen and good climbers so that they should always be housed in fully enclosed spaces. Confinement in cages cannot be recommended; they would impede the birds' great urge for moving about.
Food: A good universal mixed food; additionally meal-worms, minced meat, crushed insects and shrimps. What the red and white crakes especially like is to find some of their own live food in the water (water-fleas and insects).
Breeding: Zoological and technical literature has repeatedly mentioned breeding results of the red and white crake. The following is an excerpt of an article by MEISE (1934):
A pair imported from Argentina was kept in a room during the winter with lowest temperatures ranging from +3 to −5°C; during the summer they were given the opportunity of occupying an adjacent outdoor aviary. This aviary was inhabited by 50 birds.
In February the red and white crake pair made a nest between blades of rush at a height of one metre (a wire contraption served as a base); the pair slept in this nest until end-May; then the female began laying her eggs. A second nest was also made, this time in a conifer, again at a height of one metre. The clutches contained four and two white eggs respectively, laid in 48 hourly intervals and incubated by both parent birds in 21–25 days. When the young of the first clutch were ten days old, building of the second nest began and egg-laying and incubation only a few days later. Initially the parent birds offered food to the young in their

bill. When it actually came to rearing the second brood an eight week old young bird of the first brood helped the parents to look after the nestlings. Parent and young birds spent the nights in the nests for many weeks; in November yet another nest was built for sleeping. To begin with the young crakes were completely black and began to grow feathers when they were 20 days old; on the 30th day approximately flight and tail feathers started to develop and at the age of eight weeks the young were fully able to fly. As soon as the young crakes had all their feathers they immediately moulted into their mature plumage.

Hybridization: None is known.

Moorhen
Gallinula chloropus (L.)

Comparative Size: Considerably smaller than coot.
Plumage: Adults and young see plate 79; M. and F. black-brown with dark brown wings; undertail coverts and a stripe on the flanks white, plate on forehead and bill red, tip of bill yellow. Juveniles grey-brown, lighter throat, bill and plate on forehead olive-green.

NATURAL HABIT

Status: Very widely distributed as a breeding bird. In Europe and North America moorhens have a tendency to urbanization.
Habitat: Zones of emergent plants and shores of nearly all still and slowly flowing waters of the plains; the birds are much less often found in medium and high mountain ranges. Favourite habitats are nutritious ponds; stagnant river waters; recently also gravel pits, park and village ponds.
Breeding Biology: The male alone builds the nest with reeds and rushes on reedbanks and in thickets of shrubs on the

pond's shores. The female busies herself fetching the necessary building materials. Clutches contain eight to ten ochreous eggs, finely speckled with red-brown and black. Both parents incubate the eggs for 19–22 days. The moorhens are praecocial birds; initially the parents hold out food for the young to take. The family bond with the parent birds may come to an end as early as the second week, particularly if the latter are busy with a new brood. The young are sexually mature when they are one year old.

Migration: They move southwards to escape the winter's cold, but they stay within the limits of their breeding grounds. Some moorhens winter in Europe on ice-free water surfaces, particularly on urban and park ponds where swans are being fed.

Yearly Cycle: Moorhens return to theri breeding waters from March onwards and many clutches are completed by the second half of April. Replacement and second clutches may be found until July. At that time the older juveniles wander off; the autumnal migration of the adults takes place between September and November.

Climate: Moorhens inhabit areas with very variable climatic conditions with the exception of northern and alpine zones. It may be assumed, therefore, that they are well able to adapt themselves to temperature variations which also affect their yearly cycle.

AVICULTURE

The quick and lively moorhens add considerable charm to our ponds. On the waters of parks and zoos they soon lose all shyness and gladly accept bread and biscuits thrown to them. While they are migrating in the autumn some moorhens rest on duck rearing ponds for a few days or they may stay as long as the water is not frozen and the ducks are fed outside. Some moorhens passing through on their spring migration may breed in the vicinity of these rearing ponds.

Housing: Not every breeder who likes these rails will be fortunate enough to see them settle on his pond. If he does wish to look after them, he must bear in mind that moorhens climb over all fences and that they will probably migrate elsewhere in autumn. If the moorhens are settled down, then they will probably either stay or return in the spring. Alternatively, it is quite possible to house them in enclosed aviaries; these should be at least three to five square metres in size and contain some bushes and a shallow water basin. A shelter should be provided for the winter.

Food: A good mixed food as given to ducks, such as soaked bread, dog biscuits, green stuff, some grain, meal-worms, pieces of fish and meat.

Breeding: In the spring the moorhens occupy a large duck nesting box which has been placed on the waterfowl pond, stuff it with nesting material (reed grasses) and start to incubate. The breeder need not be concerned about the safety of the young; the parent birds take great care of their brood and losses are extremely rare. As soon as the first young have become fledged the adults start the next brood. The young birds either wander away or they are driven off by their parents later on. It is also very likely that moorhens will breed successfully in aviaries. However, it has been observed that at the beginning of the breeding season the moorhens become very aggressive towards the smaller species (e. g. spotted crakes and water rails) and all other small birds (if they are ground dwellers); the moorhens may actually kill the smaller birds.

Hybridization: Probably does not occur as it is unlikely that related species are kept in the same preserve.

Purple Gallinule
Porphyrio porphyrio (L.)

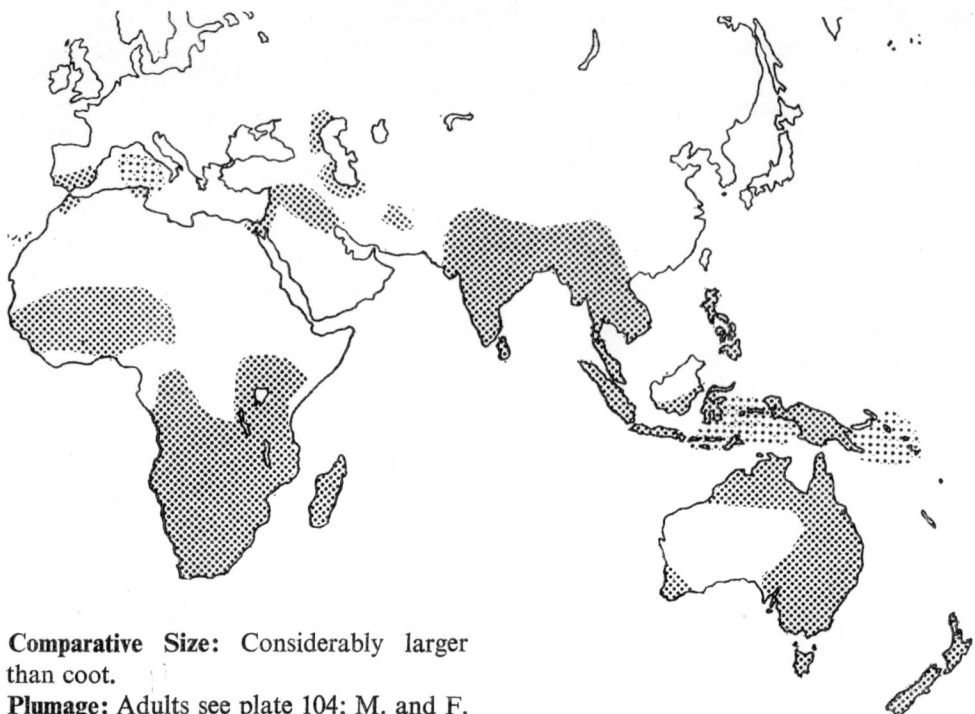

Comparative Size: Considerably larger than coot.

Plumage: Adults see plate 104; M. and F. predominantly dark-brown; particularly the back has purple or green brightness. Basic colour tone and gloss effect are variable (numerous sub-species). Bill and unfeathered plate on forehead shining red. Juveniles grey-blue to grey-brown, gloss effect missing; bill and forehead dark red-brown.

Natural Habit

Status: Due to much hunting (purple gallinules in contrast to coots are supposed to be good to eat) and land drainage of many breeding grounds numbers are declining in the whole area of distribution. During this century most breeding grounds in southern Europe have been deserted.

Habitat: Extensive zones of emergent plants with abundant and diverse swamp vegetation, also reed-banks, rice paddies and zones with plentiful aquatic vegetation (where the birds find a good food supply).

Breeding Biology: Purple gallinules make nests similar to those of the coots; the nests are placed in thickets of reed grasses and the blades above the nests are drawn together to form a type of roof. A full clutch contains three to five eggs; their basic colour is either yellow-brown or cream-pink and they are flecked with grey and lilac and on top red-brown. Both male and female incubate the eggs for 23–25 days (for further details see under breeding). Purple gallinules are praecocial birds; the parents hold food out for the young to take. The adults have only one brood per year.

Migration: Most populations are sedentary and resident. Southern European and north African breeding birds often roam far (also towards the north) and may be seen in arid zones. Purple gallinules have been sighted repeatedly in western and central Europe, but it is likely that they had escaped from preserves; quite a few of these specimens belonged to the exotic sub-species.

Yearly Cycle: The mediterranean nesting birds begin laying end-March and April and wander southwards in late autumn. The African populations breed in accordance with the local rainy and dry period.

Climate: Breeding grounds are in mediterranean to dry zones and, exceptionally only, extend to the temperate zone in the south. The late move to wintering grounds, e. g. in the Volga Delta, suggests a certain climatic hardiness.

AVICULTURE

At the turn of the century many purple gallinules, their numerous sub-species and the smaller, but very similar *Porphyrula* sp. were imported into Europe. More recently, the birds offered for sale by the animal traders have been sub-species with a non-European origin. Purple gallinules very easily become attached to man, far more so than other rails; in preserves they become completely tame, and it is even possible to allow them to run freely in the garden. Unfortunately they tend to be very active in the twilight hours which disturbs the other inhabitants of an aviary.

Housing: Preferably in large aviaries with a water basin, areas of dense ground vegetation and some bushes. Purple gallinules have to be kept warm in the winter. They should not be housed together with weaker species (including common quail and passerine birds); the purple gallinules might kill the weaker birds or, at the very least, rob their nests.

Food: A nutritious mixed food, grain and, as a particular delicacy, pieces of fish and meat, mice, meal-worms, insects and shrimps. There is a report in *Brehms Tierleben* (1911) which says that purple gallinules lie in wait for mice at mouseholes and for sparrows at feeding troughs; when these animals emerge, the gallinules kill them with a thrust of their bill and eat them. Larger items of food they grasp in their foot, in the manner of the parrots, tear off pieces and consume them.

Breeding: HOLYOAK (1970) gave a detailed account of the gallinules' breeding habits in the London Zoo where seven to nine birds had been kept in the very large Snowdon Aviary.

Purple gallinules have no special display poses. Instead the mates pass pieces of food to each other and gently scratch each others neck feathers. It has been observed repeatedly that several males and females (altogether four to six) co-operate collectively in nest building, incubation and caring for the broods. Several females fetch nesting material and one of them makes it into a nest. Eggs are apparently laid by one of the females only, but then all the other members of the community help with incubating and rearing of the young; the leading male—highest in rank—is exempted. The young are offered food by the adults for the first two weeks; afterwards they find their own food supply

Hybridization: Very pronounced within the various sub-species.

Coot

Fulica atra L.

Comparative Size: Approximately the size of a medium-sized duck; rather compact; weight approximately 900 g.

Plumage: Adult and nest see plate 105; in juveniles throat and chest are grey-white, the rest of the plumage is black-grey, plate on forehead narrow and considerably smaller than that of adults. Sexes can be distinguished by different voices.

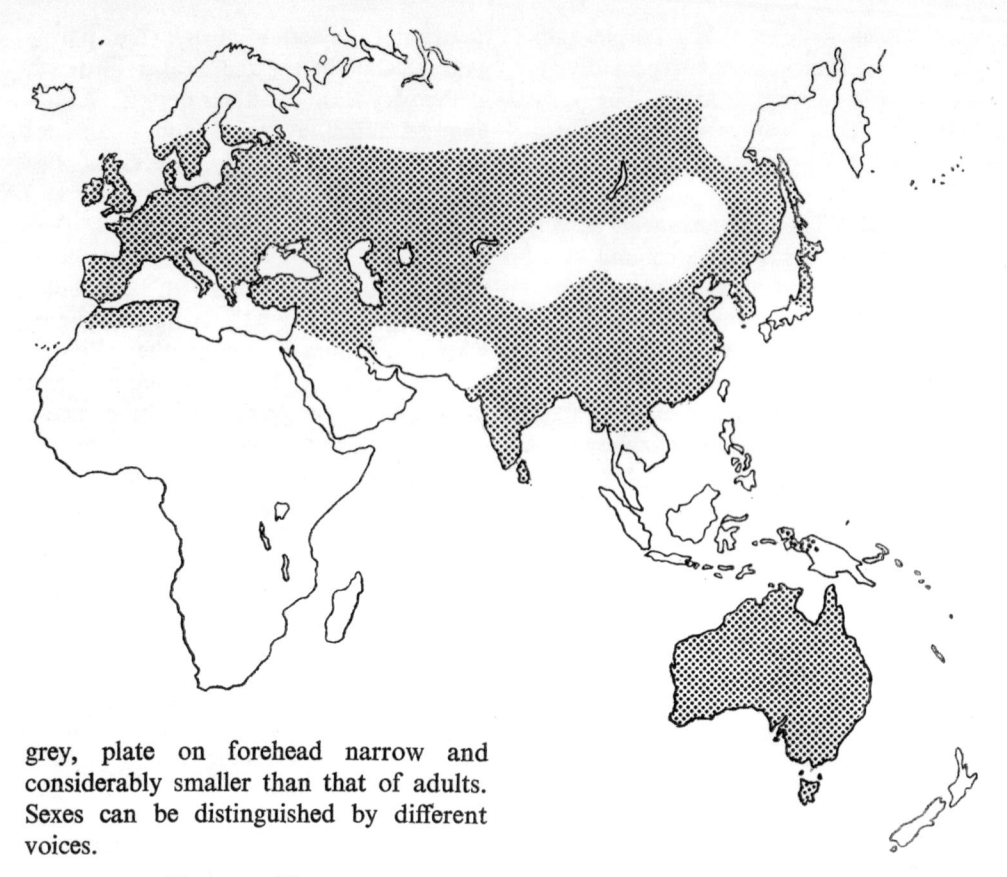

Natural Habit

Status: One of the most abundant waterfowl in extensive areas; breeding density is particularly high in some places. Approximately 4 million coots were counted in the western Paleoarctic region in January 1968.

Habitat: Coots inhabit almost as many different areas as the moorhens, although they prefer larger waters, on the whole. Following in the wake of land cultivation they can be found on many park lakes where they have little flying distance from man.

Breeding Biology: Predominantly the male alone builds the nest; it is compact and placed in sparsely grown thickets of reeds, on islets or on bushes standing in the water; often the nest may be floating on the water. A full clutch consists of six to ten greyish-yellow eggs, finely speckled with black-brown. Both mates incubate for 23–24 days. As the young are autophagous they soon undertake small excursions, some of them join the male and some join the female while they are exploring. But for several days they return to the brood nest or the resting nest, the latter especially built by the male for this purpose (at least for the night). The young are able to fly at the age of eight weeks approximately and after one or two years they are sexually mature.

Migration: They are a very migratory and roaming species; juveniles soon leave the breeding grounds, many non-breeders aggregate on moulting grounds; large swarms collect on ponds with a good food supply during the summer and autumn. Migration to the wintering grounds takes place only with the onset of cold (winter escape).

Yearly Cycle: From the time the ice thaws in late winter until it freezes over again the coots stay on the European waters. Display and pairing take place in early spring, eggs are laid in April and May; first roaming flights and aggregation of swarms from July onwards.

Climate: As America and Africa are also inhabited by closely related species of coots, the American and the crested coot, the birds may be said to have a cosmopolitan climatic distribution, ranging from the cool northern boreal regions to the hot tropical zones.

AVICULTURE

Without particular enticement on the part of man, coots will settle only on very large park and zoo lakes; they breed only exceptionally on the rearing ponds in preserves. When it comes to obtaining nourishment, however, their behaviour is quite different. In farms where ducks are being fattened the coots fly over fences, coming from the water, and consume large quantities of duck food from the ducks' troughs. In severe winters, many coots stay with the flocks of the half-tame mute swans and mallards and accept the food people throw the birds.

If coots are caught as mature birds, they become tame in preserves as regards feeding only; quite a few crawl away under cover and creep to the feeding troughs solely during the twilight hours. With their dagger-like bills they stab at ducks if the latter come too near and they can hurt them quite badly. However, if coots are given a great deal of intensive and personal attention, or if they are reared in a preserve, they may well become really tame and trusting and their expressive voices and interesting behaviour make them into birds well worth caring for.

Housing: On preserve ponds coots have to go through a carefully planned period of adaptation, otherwise they climb over fences or try to leave the preserve by other means. Very large aviaries with water basins and bushes are the best places in which to accommodate them; in zoological gardens they may be put with the herons in large aviaries. As long as the coots are well nourished and the surface of their water is not frozen, they can withstand several degrees below the freezing point. However, they should be offered, as a protection, trusses of dry straw or peat-litter placed underneath the branches of a conifer.

Food: Grain; a coarse food mixture consisting of bread, green rye flour, pellets and, occasionally, meal-worms, pieces of fish or meat and young mice.

Breeding: Little has been reported on breeding results regarding coots. On the whole, a breeder or zoological expert has far less contact with the coots than he has with moorhens. As the coots tend to be somewhat aggressive towards the ornamental ducks, they are not very popular in the preserves which specialise in the care of the Anatidae. If, however, a pair of breeding coots does settle on one of the large breeding lakes, breeding results are more than likely. In the Berlin Zoo (West) some unpinioned pairs breed quite regularly every year on the zoo's lake; the nests are usually completely out in the open, often in the vicinity of much used paths.

Hybridization: There is no doubt that the coots would interbreed with related *Fulica* species if they had the chance; one cross-breeding is known to have taken place, that of a coot with a moorhen.

Sunbittern

Eurypyga helias (Pallas)

Comparative Size: Approximately like a coot, but much slimmer and therefore longer looking.

Plumage: Adults see plate 106. The whole of the upperside, wings and tail of both M. and F. yellow-brown, barred light-grey and black-brown, underside more delicately marked in light and dark-brown. The plumage is as soft as that of the owl because it contains a large quantity of powder down (instead of oil from the uropygial gland). The wing has large white spots in the curve and like the tail it is barred with grey, black and red-brown. Juveniles similar to adults in coloration.

NATURAL HABIT

Status: No generally applicable details are at hand; supposedly the sunbittern is still an inhabitant of unfrequented woodland landscapes.

Habitat: Very dense, half-dark jungels in the vicinity of ditches and small streams. Because of the eternal half-dark there is little ground or herb vegetation and the real habitat of the sunbittern is the leaf-strewn humid jungle soil. On the other hand, the sunbittern has been sighted on light shores of rivers and near small pools.

Breeding Biology: Practically nothing is known of the breeding habits of free living sunbitterns. The sunbittern starts the breeding season with an impressive courtship display in which the colourful feathers of the wings and tail are very effective. The few nests found up to date were in trees at a height of a few metres; they were made of leaves and twigs and glued together with mud or clay. A full clutch appears to consist of two eggs only; their basic colour is mud-brown and they have lilac-grey spotting overlaid with sepia-brown blotches. As the clutches are so small, it is assumed that the birds produce several broods per year.

Migration: Presumably active permanent residents throughout the year.

Yearly Cycle: There is not sufficient evidence. A clutch has been found in Costa Rica in May.

Climate: Total distribution restricted to the tropical plains and here, in turn, to the evergreen rain forests.

AVICULTURE

Beautiful coloration and an interesting behaviour assure the sunbittern of a special position among the rails. The plumage with its butterfly effect and the softness of an owl looks particularly conspicuous in display and threatening poses. The sunbittern's other movements, e. g. when searching for food, more closely resemble those of herons and bitterns than those of rails. It is remarkable how soon newly acquired sunbitterns lose all shyness; quite a few birds in a preserve allow themselves to be handled or they even display to their keeper. On Central

American farms they have been found running around freely with the domestic fowl. One sunbittern lived in the London Zoo for 22 years.

Housing: In temperate latitudes recommended accommodation is in spacious glass houses which can be easily heated; the birds should have an adjacent outdoor aviary at their disposal. The enclosure should be well planted (compare Habitat); it should contain a shallow, but not too small pond and a few thick tree branches or stumps. In zoological gardens and bird preserves sunbitterns are housed in large tropical halls and indoor aviaries.

Food: In the period of adaptation: mealworms, small fish, insects, small frogs and lizards; later on they are fed on a good formulated food mixed with minced meat, pellets and shrimps.

Breeding: The first breeding result was achieved by the London Zoo in 1865 and, subsequently, BARTLETT (1866), published numerous details on the sunbittern's breeding biology; all later authors adopted his account. The Exotarium of the Zoological Garden, Frankfurt on Main, has also had breeding successes; between 1962 and 1970 one pair developed breeding activity every year (altogether five young birds have been reared); although the Zoo's yearly reports have kept the public informed, exact biological details are missing. But BARTLETT wrote earlier (report incorporated in *Brehms Tierleben*, 4th Edn. (1925)):

In May 1865 the pair carried sticks, roots and other building materials from place to place; both searched for muddy substances so that in the end they were offered some mud and clay. They accepted this immediately and a nest was built on a tree stump at a height of three metres. One chick was hatched from a second clutch on May 9th; both parents had incubated the clutch for 27 days. The parent birds fed the chick in the nest and gave it insects and small fishes. On the second day the young bird was able to flutter to the ground. It grew so quickly that after two months it was indistinguishable from the adult birds. The latter began to repair and re-build the nest and collected new mud for it. End-August saw the first egg of the third clutch. The male predominantly brooded while the female looked after the young bird. The second chick hatched on September 28th; it was reared without parents, soon became tame and grew to maturity. (Abbreviated version.)

Hybridization: Manifestly non-existent.

Cranes

Apart from South America and the islands of the South Pacific, the fourteen species of cranes inhabit large parts of the earth. A fact worth noting is that the breeding grounds of several species are minute (e. g. in eastern Asia) and that the total population of these cranes is small and endangered as a result. Five out of the fourteen species are acutely threatened with extinction. Capturing wild cranes and selling them in the animal markets is not justifiable any more, with the exception of a few species, especially in view of the fact that keeping cranes in preserves and the unsatisfactory breeding results have done nothing to maintain further their species as will be shown in the following text. The problem of housing and feeding cranes in captivity has been solved, as is evident from the longevity of many cranes in zoos; 25–30 years may be considered as quite a normal life span for some of the birds; a Siberian White Crane, *Grus leucogeranus,* is said to have lived in a zoo for more than 60 years. But the breeding of cranes is still subject to a number of basic difficulties: recognition of the sexes; low rate of reproductive activity; rearing of the young. As far as present-day knowledge allows judgement, rearing of the young is most likely to be successful if undertaken by the keeper himself without the use of parents or foster parents. However, the maturing birds are then imprinted on humans that further breeding will be even more difficult than with their captured parents.

A number of bird lovers keep single cranes in park-like gardens. A point worth mentioning here is that the northern species particularly—also the small demoiselle cranes—have extremely loud voices and greet the rising sun with loud, trumpeting calls each morning.

Cranes moult their body plumage once a year. Demoiselle and crowned cranes shed their wing feathers gradually so that they are always able to fly, which is important in their steppe habitat where they have little cover. All other species of cranes moult their flight feathers every two years at one and the same time, and for five to six weeks while they are rearing their young they are flightless.

Common Crane

Grus grus (L.)

Comparative Size: Considerably larger than a white stork.

Plumage: Adults see plate 107; M. and F. identical in coloration. Juveniles darker overall, no red on head, scapulars scarcely elongated.

Natural Habit

Status: Because of the common occurrence of *Grus g. lilfordi* east of the Volga the world population is not endangered; however, heavy hunting pressure (before the turn of the century), robbing nests (by 'egg collectors'), and loss of breeding grounds (land drainage) have combined to leave less than 20 breeding pairs west of the river Elbe and 1,100 pairs in central Europe. Stocks of the common cranes in Sweden, Finland and the USSR are satisfactory.

Habitat: Quiet, water-rich lowlands; lakes with wide zones of emergent vegetation and adjoining boggy alder woods; moors and forested swamps. In the North moist depressions in the tree-less high moors and regions of pygmy bushes and birches. After the breeding season, certain cultivated lands and meadows serve as resting places which are visited every year.

Breeding Biology: The cranes pair for life; when they arrive in their breeding grounds they begin their courtship display which is accompanied by dances, jumps and loud trumpeting calls. Afterwards, while they are breeding and rearing their young, they live a very hidden and secretive life. The large nests are in inaccessible places in the vegetation. Two olive-brown eggs, flecked with grey are incubated for 30 days. The chicks leave the nest when they are 24 hours old, but the families stay together. Each parent bird cares for one chick and presents food to it. When the young are nine to ten weeks old they are able to fly. The family bond is broken up in the winter; sexual maturity is attained between the fourth and sixth year of life.

Migration: Bird of passage which leaves Europe flying in V-formation in south-westerly and south/south-easterly direction. The birds fly over mountains and oceans. On their migratory route they frequent resting places where they gather in flocks (e. g. southern Sweden and the Island of Rügen).

Yearly Cycle: Central European cranes arrive in their breeding grounds in mid-March; first clutches have been found as early as end-March. Main laying time in central Europe is approximately in the middle of April and, thus, the majority of the young cranes is able to fly after the end of July. Autumnal migration in Europe takes place in September/October.

Climate: More common as breeding bird in the cooler, moist, northern and temperate latitudes than in the dry-hot steppe zones of Asia.

AVICULTURE

Although their simple, elegant appearance makes the common cranes attractive birds to care for, very few only are kept by bird enthusiasts and large zoos. Because the birds are endangered in their natural habitat they are strictly protected and not many are for sale. On the other hand, the smaller *Grus g. lilfordi* is imported rather more frequently. Both sub-species easily adapt to a new environment; they are not delicate and soon become very attached to their keepers, particularly if there is only one bird.

Housing: Private enthusiasts keep their cranes in large, fenced-in orchards or in spacious grounds with Anatidae. At least a part of the grass area should be kept cut short. Even a single crane creates considerable damage in a smallish flower or vegetable garden. It digs holes in the grounds up to 10 cm deep while it is searching for food (insects, larvae, worms) and numerous plants get uprooted. The cranes have to be provided with a shelter in periods of frost.

Food: Apart from corn (maize, wheat) a nutritious mixed food and shrimps, and additional tidbits which the birds like particularly, such as peanuts, lean meat, ox heart, insects, worms, mice and—unless their enclosure provides them with it—green stuff.

Breeding: Although there are far fewer reports about breeding successes of common cranes and *Grus g. lilfordi* compared with other species of cranes, a few basic facts are known: an increase of display dances and calls as well as a secretive and shy manner are indications of an approaching breeding season. At such times, any kind of disturbances (including those caused by other birds in densely populated preserves) are to be avoided. Anyway, breeding and rearing of young will be successful in very few cases. The rearing of the young is more promising if the keeper undertakes it himself. As the rearing methods for all cranes are very alike, further details about them will be given in the chapters on the Stanley and demoiselle cranes, but HEINROTH's statement (1928) applies to the common crane as well as to all other crane young: "For the first two or three days the chicks are rather helpless and find it difficult to move about on their thick legs. Food has to be held out to them, and it is necessary to be extremely patient, bearing in mind that a mature crane has unlimited time and the foster parent has to be willing to spend an equal amount of time if he wants to be successful."

Hybridization: Highly pronounced within the genus *Grus*. Interbreeding is known to have occurred with the sarus, white-necked, sandhill and Manchurian crane.

Hooded Crane
Grus monacha Temminck

Comparative Size: Approximately the size of a white stork.

Plumage: Adults see plate 110; body dark slate-grey, head and neck white, unfeathered top of head black and red; elongated innermost secondaries sickle shaped, incoherent and consequently rather ragged looking like those of the common crane. Juveniles altogether more brownish in coloration, head and neck pale loam-brown, top of head red-ochre in colour.

Natural Habit

Status: As the breeding grounds of the species are obviously small (breeding west of the Lake Baikal is doubtful, in any case), and as observations in the field are scanty, the conclusion is drawn that the overall population is very small. The International Union for Conservation of Nature (IUCN) refers to the hooded crane as being threatened with extinction. On the other hand, the international animal market does offer the birds—captured in their winter grounds—for sale. SCHUMACHER (1969) reported of hundreds of hooded cranes which he filmed on the South Island of Japan.

Breeding Biology: Nothing is known about the breeding habits of the species from observations in the field (up to date not a single nest has been found); the hooded cranes' breeding habits are assumed to be similar to those of the common crane.

Migration: Some of the areas known to be inhabited as wintering grounds are southern Korea, southern Japan, eastern China and Indo-China. Whilst migrating hooded cranes have been sighted either in small troops or in pairs among *Grus g. lilfordi* in west Siberia and the region of the Ussuri river.

Yearly Cycle: The hooded cranes pass through the Baraba steppe (western Siberia) in May and in August/September; they remain in Japan from approximately November until the beginning of March. The breeding season is assumed to be in June and July.

Climate: Short, wet summers with fluctuating temperatures rarely more than 20°C in July are predominant in the breeding grounds. Climate of the wintering areas is mild, but not without frost or snow at times.

AVICULTURE

The hooded cranes sold in the European and North American animal markets soon become adapted to their new environment, the proximity of man and a warmer climate, rather in the manner of the common cranes. On the spacious lawns for wading birds of large zoological gardens and bird preserves this species is rarely missing, but they are seldom kept by private enthusiasts.

Housing: In zoos they are usually kept in mixed collections of wading birds; where breeding results are hoped for they are put into spacious solitary enclosures containing many bushes, and an area of short lawn and water. For the cold months the hooded cranes need a shelter; in common with other birds in preserves they often lack the space to move around freely and then suffer particularly in prolonged periods of wet-cold weather. If the weather is cold and clear the hooded cranes should be allowed the run of the outside enclosure during the day, even if snow covers the ground.

Food: See common crane.

Breeding: Most of the hooded cranes inhabiting preserves have been caught as mature birds in their wintering grounds (usually China). The necessary impulse for reproductive activity is triggered off most of the birds. For this a number of factors are responsible; the stress of the period of adaptation; the arbitrary making up of 'pairs' when even the zoological expert often does not know whether he is dealing with a male or a female, and finally the birds have to become used to being kept in a preserve. To a certain degree the cranes longevity compensates for their lack of reproductivity. The Berlin Zoo bought two hooded cranes in 1912; in the 1930s they repeatedly laid unfertilised eggs; one of the birds lived until 1937, the other until 1944. In the 1920s and 1930s hooded cranes also laid eggs in the British Bird Preserve, Scampton Hall, run by the breeder H. St. QUENTIN, but the eggs were also sterile. As far as to my knowledge, there are no breeding results with hooded cranes up to the present.

Hybridization: Does not exist.

Sandhill Crane
Grus canadensis (L.)

Comparative Size: Approximately stork-sized.

Plumage: Adults see plate 109; the four sub-species differ slightly, but not clearly, from each other in size and colour; thus the basic colour tone of the body is variable and may be light-brown, light-grey or dark-brown. Forehead and top of the head are unfeathered and red, innermost secondaries slightly elongated but not ragged. Juveniles overall more brown, head fully feathered.

NATURAL HABIT

Status: In several USA states either endangered or extinct. At present approximately 5,000 individuals of the Central American race, *G. c. tabida*, and an equal number of the Florida race, *G. c. pratensis*, spend the winters in Florida. Populations inhabiting Canada, Alaska and the USSR are supposed to be stable.

Habitat: The northern populations breed near tundra lakes, in moors and swamps,

99 ↑ Goldeneye M.
100 ↓ Bufflehead

101 ↑ Hooded Merganser M.

102 ↑ Red-breasted Merganser M. moulting into breeding plumage

103 ↓ North American Ruddy Duck

104 ↑ Purple Gallinule
105 ↗ Coot
106 ↓ Sunbittern

107 ↑ Common Crane
108 ↗ Sarus Crane
109 ↓ Sandhill Crane

110 ↑   Hooded Crane
111 ↗   Demoiselle Crane
112 ↓   Stanley Crane

113 ↑ West African Crowned Crane
114 ↗ Wattled Crane
115 ↓ East African Crowned Crane

116 ↑ African Jacana
117 ↓ Oyster Catcher

118 ↑ Lapwing in juvenile plumage
119 ↓ Crowned Plover

120 ↑ Spurwing Plover
121 ↓ Masked Plover

122 ↑ Ruff M.
123 ↗ Ruff M.
124 ↓ Ruffs on the display ground

125 ↑ Avocet
126 ↓ Black-necked Stilt

127 ↑ Black-headed Gull
128 ↓ Common Gulls and matured juvenile

those of the medium latitudes near the large prairie lakes, and the southern populations—rather like the common cranes—in boogy woods, near forest pools and in lowlands.

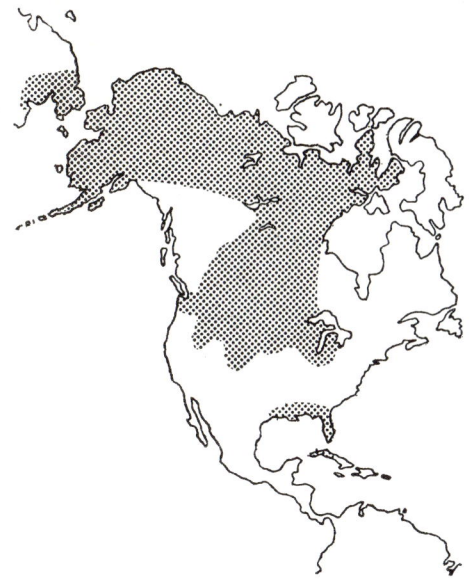

Breeding Biology: The sandhill cranes' pairing ritual also includes courtship dances and loud, blaring calls. The nest is huge and made of marsh vegetation; its site is either in the reeds of the shallow water zone, on islands or on the tundra meadows where they have but poor cover. The two eggs are ochre coloured flecked with dark-brown and they are incubated by the male and female for 29–30 days. Both parents care for their young and the family bond is not broken until the sandhill cranes have reached their winter grounds.

Migration: The sandhill cranes whose home grounds are in the North, *G. c. canadensis*, together with the prairie race, *G. c. tabida*, spend winters in the breeding grounds of the most southerly mainland race, *G. c. pratensis*—from Florida to central Mexico. The Cuban race, *G. c. nesiotes*, are year-round residents.

Yearly Cycle: Very variable and in accordance with the extensive distribution from north to south. The sandhill cranes are leaving their wintering areas between February and April. In the medium latitudes the spring migration is in March, egg-laying period between April and June, and the autumnal migration takes place in October and November.

Climate: Sandhill cranes inhabit mainly areas with rather low temperatures throughout the year. Although hot summers prevail in the breeding grounds of the prairie race, temperatures at times of migration are near freezing point. The southern races, on the other hand, inhabit areas with warm-temperate and subtropical climates.

AVICULTURE

The sandhill crane is the counterpart of the common crane on the North American continent as regards natural environment and aviculture. Sandhill cranes are very rare in many areas and, therefore, they are strictly protected; it is illegal to catch and sell them. Thus in European zoos it has not been possible to show the sandhill crane often in recent years (like some other species of cranes); it is kept and bred in zoos and private preserves of its homelands, however.

Housing: Compare with common crane. In zoological gardens they are normally accommodated on lawns together with other wading birds. Shy birds, not fully established, are able to get over fences, 1.5–2 m high, by jumping over them. Once the cranes have quietened down the railings need to be no higher than 1 m.

Food: Like that of other species of cranes.

Breeding: At the turn of the century several large import consignments of sandhill cranes reached Europe; reputedly, they have bred occasionally. Of the few pairs kept nowadays breeding results are hardly known. One of the difficulties in breeding them is the uncertainty of sex recognition (which applies to breeding of cranes in general), another is the unwillingness on the part of birds to form pairs and breed. Any breeding success which is achieved has to be evaluated largely as incidental.

Hybridization: Tendencies apparently very pronounced. As early as 1911 a hybrid grew to maturity from a sandhill crane interbreeding with a wattled crane. Hybridization is also known to have occurred with the White-necked Crane, *Grus vipio*, and the Manchurian Crane, *Grus japonensis*.

Sarus Crane
Grus antigone (L.)

Comparative Size: Considerably larger and more bulky than a white stork; the largest species of cranes.

Plumage: Adults see plate 108; all of the plumage dark grey-brown, head and upper neck unfeathered and red. Another race, *G. a. sharpii*, is lighter overall, sides of the face covered with feathery black bristles; below the red, unfeathered head and upper neck the birds have a visible band of white feathers. In juveniles head and upper neck covered with light brown feathers.

Natural Habit

Status: Neither of the two sub-species appears to be endangered so far.

Habitat: *G. a. sharpii* inhabits grass savannas, rice paddies and swamps of the open landscape. The Indo-Chinese sarus crane also breeds in forested swamps and in the woods of river plains. Outside the breeding season sarus cranes often make use of cultivated lands.

Breeding Biology: Pair formation and display are accompanied by impressive courtship dances and calls. The compact nests are placed in inaccessible areas of reedy bogs. A full clutch contains two — rarely three — white eggs often flecked slightly with ochre and lilac-grey. Incubation takes 32–33 days; the parent birds take turns in sitting on the eggs and, later, both look after the young together.

Migration: They winter in or near their breeding grounds. As two sub-species have evolved on one sub-continent, the sarus cranes' migratory urge does not appear ot be at all pronounced.

Yearly Cycle: The breeding season is between July and September. It begins at the time of the heaviest monsoon rain; nests are built, eggs are laid and breeding takes place. In the following period with little rainfall the young cranes mature and the older birds moult.

Climate: Monsoon climate with poor rainfall and year-round high temperatures (yearly average approximately 25°C).

Aviculture

The animal trade offers the large, bulky and not very attractively coloured sarus cranes for sale quite frequently; if they are bought it is almost exclusively by zoos or bird preserves. The Berlin Zoo showed the sarus crane for the first time in 1869 and *G. a. sharpii* in 1873. On the whole, the sarus cranes which are not breeding are fairly peaceable; nonetheless, if kept in too confined a space, they may stab at the other and weaker birds and kill them. The well-known director of the Leipzig Zoo, K. M. SCHNEIDER (1887 to 1955) observed how a sarus crane killed a stork standing next to it by a thrust of its bill while another stabbed a flamingo to death.

Housing: Spacious wading bird lawns or large solitary enclosures which should contain groups of bushes and an area of water. Sarus cranes should be given a frost-free shelter for the winter, but as neither sub-species is very sensitive to cold, they should be allowed runs in the open enclosure, even if the weather is frosty.

Food: Like that of other cranes; the birds are not very choosy. At the feeding throghs the sarus cranes kill birds up to pigeon-size and eat them as well as mice and small birds.

Breeding: Nowadays breeding results are achieved in numerous zoos and bird preserves throughout the world, not only with the sarus crane but also with *G. a. sharpii*. The sarus crane is probably the most frequently bred crane species in captivity and the breeding success rate is obviously no longer pure chance. Bird preserves at Rotterdam, Munich-Hellabrunn, Wuppertal and Walsrode have repeatedly reared young birds (KUSSMANN, by letter).

The Rostock Zoo imported three sarus cranes from India in 1960. Until 1963 they were kept with other species in a preserve for wading birds. In the autumn of that year a pair formation appeared likely whereupon two of the cranes were put into a solitary enclosure in the following spring; the enclosure was 110 m × 20 m, well-grown with dense bushes but lacked a larger area of water. Shortly afterwards the sarus cranes gathered twigs, sticks and blades of grasses and made a nest of them. From May 31st to July 3rd a total of eleven eggs was laid and—predominantly—incubated by the parent birds. Nine chicks were hatched, but only one of the young birds survived for more than one year. The maturing young cranes succumbed to a number of infectious, parasitic and metabolic diseases; on the other hand, they did learn quite easily how to pick up food PREUSS 1971). The Wuppertal Zoo had similar high losses initially; most of their young cranes grew to maturity only after it had been decided to remove them from the parents and hand-rear them. The disadvantage of this method is that the birds become imprinted to humans and are of no further use for breeding purposes (KUSSMANN, written communication).

Hybridization: Interbreeding is known to have occurred with the common and Australian crane.

Wattled Crane

Bugeranus carunculatus (Gmelin)

Comparative Size: Much larger than a white stork.

Plumage: Adult see plate 114; most of the body is slate-grey; neck, chest and the feathered wattles on the throat are white; eyes, unfeathered part of face and bill are vermillion red. The very much elongated innermost secondaries are deceptive as they make the wattled cranes look as though they had a long tail. Juveniles very similar to adults in coloration, but the wattles on the chin are smaller.

Natural Habit

Status: A small population inhabits a very confined area in the Ethiopian highland. A considerably larger number of breeding birds occurs on the highlying plateaux of southern and central Africa. Many wattled cranes breed in southern Katanga, Zambia and Rhodesia where they are often more common than East African crowned cranes.

Habitat: The Ethiopian wattled cranes inhabit swamps, grass and alpine bushy heathlands of the climatically inhospitable high plateaux of Abyssinia. The breeding grounds of the southern populations are found in the vleis, reed and sedge swamps lying between the mountain ranges of the South African highlands which are traversed by clear streams.

Breeding Biology: As soon as the rainy season begins, the wattled cranes return to their breeding grounds; approximately three weeks later they start building their nests. Favourite nest sites are island-like rises in water-rich swampy plains. The two eggs are ochre-brown, flecked with purple; they are laid in intervals of one or two days and incubated for 36 days. While the wattled cranes are rearing their young they lead a very withdrawn and secretive life; once the young are able to fly the family leaves the breeding area.

Migration: Wattled cranes remain within the limits of their breeding grounds throughout the year; however, they do undertake flights to areas which offer a more favourable food supply where they may be seen in troops of up to 100 individuals.

Yearly Cycle: The start of the breeding season coincides with the periods of rainfall; it is said that the breeding season in Abyssinia is from May until September and in South Africa from March until October and from December until February.

Climate: The Abyssinian highland climate is extremely inhospitable: low temperatures, rain, hail and fog are prevalent in eight months of the year. The dry-hot steppe and savanna climate with variable rainy seasons prevails in the southern breeding grounds.

Aviculture

Of all the crane species it is the wattled cranes which are the most colourful. In their African homeland they are almost as common as the Stanley crane; nonetheless, very few of them have been offered for sale in Europe and North America and, therefore, they belong to the precious rarities of zoological gardens and the collections of those enthusiasts who keep cranes not just to lend character to their parks. With proper expert treatment the birds soon quieten down and become tame, but they never attach themselves to humans as closely as do demoiselle and Stanley cranes. They are also much more inclined to use their dagger-like bill as a weapon.

Housing: Preferably in spacious solitary enclosures which should have a winter shelter that can be heated. Fencing ought to be at least two metres high; dancing

cranes jump up several metres and might well use this elasticity to break out of their preserves (applies particularly to newly acquired and not yet established birds). Well arranged crane preserves are also a pre-condition for breeding them; results are still unsatisfactory.
Food: Like that of other species of cranes.
Breeding: The best known breeding results have been achieved by the Bronx Zoo, New York. There the first young bird hatched in July 1944; it thrived splendidly, but when it was transferred to the winter shelter in November of the same year it died. Further young wattled cranes were hatched—for example, in May 1945 and mid-December 1963; the young proved to be remarkably fast growing. More recently, breeding the beautiful cranes has also been achieved by the bird preserve at Walsrode (GFR).
Hybridization: Because the wattled cranes are so aggressive they are rarely kept in mixed collections which, at the same time, prevents interbreeding. One case of interbreeding is known to have occurred in England in 1911; a female wattled crane mated with a male sandhill crane and their hybrid chick was reared to maturity; it was also the first time a wattled crane had ever bred in England.

Demoiselle Crane

Anthropoides virgo (L.)

Comparative Size: Smaller than a white stork.
Plumage: Adults birds see plate 111; no sexual dimorphism. Juvenile plumage more brownish ash-grey, feather bunches behind the eyes shorter and grey; plumes of the neck not elongated into a train.

NATURAL HABIT

Status: Populations in the steppe areas of central Asia are stable, but all southern and eastern European populations are either declining or extinct (owing to cultivation and use for agriculture of former steppes).
Habitat: Semi-deserts, steppes, high plateaux with poor vegetation and similar dry zones. Although the demoiselle cranes do not depend on areas of water, their breeding sites are rarely more than 1.5 km distant from water. They also nest in moist depressions (grown with bushes) of cultivated lands. After the breeding season they often stay on gravel banks of rivers.
Breeding Biology: After a short period of courtship display which is similar intensive like that of the common crane, pairs spread out over the extensive breeding grounds. The nest is usually on dry ground, either grown with short grasses or without any vegetation. The clutch contains two eggs, very similar in colour to those of the common crane, but much smaller. Incubation takes 27–31 days. The male does not really share the incubating, but he will sit on the nest for a short period while the female leaves it. Both parents guide the initially clumsy young; from the third or fourth day onwards the latter are able to catch insects for themselves. The young are guided by the parents for seven to eight weeks; they are sexually mature in the second year of life.
Migration: Demoiselle cranes winter south of the Himalayas and the Sahara.
Yearly Cycle: Arrival in breeding grounds between end-March (Crimean peninsula) and beginning of May (Mongolia); depending on time of arrival in the local area, eggs may be laid well into June. Autumnal migration starts in August.
Climate: Cold winters and hot, dry summers are typical for most of the breeding

grounds. Demoiselle cranes arrive in their home breeding grounds as soon as most of the snow has thawed and leave again at the end of the hot, late summer.

AVICULTURE

The small, elegant demoiselle cranes are the species most frequently kept in zoological gardens and preserves of waterfowl enthusiasts. They do little digging in the ground and therefore cause practically no damage; thus they can be kept in fairly small, landscaped gardens. The noise made by calling, dancing cranes should not be underestimated, however. SCHIEFERDECKER (1966) wrote: "I have very understanding neighbours, but when the sun is greeted with loud fanfares at daybreak on summer days—audible for 300 m—I deem it prudent to confine the birds in a hut and let them out into the open later in the morning."

Housing: Spacious enclosures suitable for ducks and fowl, fenced gardens and meadows; a bathing pool is desirable but not essential. In wet-cold weather the birds should be offered a draught-free, dry shelter which they can seek or leave as they wish.

Food: A nutritious crushed corn and grain mixture, shrimp or insect pellets and, additionally, a little raw meat from time to time; also insects, sparrows and mice, although the birds often catch these themselves. They pick insects and tiny plantlice off leaves of plants.

Breeding: To avoid unverified generalizations two breeding records are quoted below, as follows:

ENCKE (1966) reported from the Tierpark Krefeld (GFR):
"A pair purchased in 1960 bred for the first time in 1964. The nest was built under good cover, in the brushwood of a beech forest. Eggs were laid in midmay 1964 (in 1965 end-April). While the female was incubating the male defended the territory and even attacked visitors who came too near to the nest. Four young hatched weighing between 75 and 85 g each; the two heaviest grew into mature birds. They were reared in a box, 80 cm × 80 cm in size and heated to a temperature of 30 °C. A mixture of minced meat, shell-lime, moth larvae, worms, flies and boiled egg was shaped into small balls, and this food was presented to the young with unlimited patience. After two or three days they started pecking at it by themselves and, shortly

afterwards, they were taken out to a lawn when the weather was sunny. There they hunted for worms and insects indefatigably. After 24 days one of the young cranes pecked at the crushed corn without being prompted and, when two months old, it made the first attempt to fly."

STEHLIK (1970) wrote:

"The Ostrava Zoo (CSSR) bought four demoiselle cranes from the Soviet Union in 1965; one pair started building a nest and defending the territory in 1967. Egg-laying and brooding took place in 1968 and 1969. The nest was made on the shore of a pond, surrounded by aldertrees. Eggs were laid at the end of April and the beginning of May and incubation began after the first egg had been laid; initially the female alone incubated but, later, took turns with the male. Rearing of the three hatched young was left to the very anxious parent birds; unfortunately it was not successful because of poor weather conditions. After these experiences the author considers artificial rearing as the better method."

Hybridization: Cranes normally pair for life. Once the birds have formed a proper pair bond they usually stay together, even in mixed collections. On the other hand, cranes which have not yet paired may mate with birds of a different species. Interbreeding is known to have occurred with the white-necked and Stanley crane.

Stanley Crane
Anthropoides paradisea (Lichtenstein)

NATURAL HABIT

Although this large birds does not belong to the endangered species the size of the population is, nevertheless, subject to natural limitations; the area where the birds occur is very small and even within it the Stanley crane uses only selected parts (see Habitat). Pairs need very large breeding territories.

Habitat: Dry, high plateaux with a steppe or semi-desert character as well as extensive grasslands. Although Stanley cranes prefer being near water after the breeding season they do not depend on the water; they quench their thirst on the succulent leaves of desert plants.

Comparative Size: Much larger than a white stork.

Plumage: Adults see plate 112; sexes differ slightly in size and behaviour, but it is not always possible to distinguish one from the other with certainty. In juveniles, scapulars only slightly elongated, the body is darker and browner than that of adults.

Breeding Biology: Like other cranes Stanley cranes begin their breeding season with display dances and loud calls. The male chooses the nest site about one week before the female begins laying. Two eggs are laid in a shallow depression in the ground; they are ochre-brown and have dark blotches. The female does most of the incubating which takes circa 30 days.

While the parents guide their young, the males are supposedly very aggressive towards all enemies. Once the juveniles are able to fly the families leave the breeding territory.

Migration: Some of the Stanley cranes are sedentary and resident; the majority of them move to areas with a more favourable food supply.

Yearly Cycle: The egg-laying period is fairly uniform throughout the southwest African region. It is in November and December—the beginning of the rainy season. A very few eggs only are laid between October and February. Groups of non-breeding birds have been sighted in the dry winter months, between May and September.

Climate: The northern savanna breeding grounds are very hot, while the southern breeding grounds have a warm-to-temperate climate.

Aviculture

The obvious attachment Stanley cranes show for their keepers is probably one of the reasons for their great popularity in Europe and North America as well as in their African homelands. In Africa they are often kept on farms where they move around freely; single birds may even seek out the proximity of man. It should be noted, however, that the Stanley crane—despite its friendliness—may suddenly and without apparent reason strike at people's eyes with its bill; its aim is remarkably accurate.

Housing: Private owners usually keep the Stanley cranes in large, fenced gardens or parks; in zoos they are predominantly kept on the large lawns of wading birds. Breeding results cannot be expected unless the birds are put into an enclosure by themselves. They have to be kept warm during the winter.

Food: They should be given a large variety of animal and vegetarian food; the Stanley crane is neither choosy nor particularly demanding as regards food.

Breeding: In England a first breeding result was achieved by a menagerie as early as 1851 and in USA in 1917. The Stanley cranes were also bred successfully in England on a number of occasions between the First and Second World Wars—at Foxwarren, Woburn and the London Zoo.

Van Ee (1966) gave full particulars of several Stanley crane broods in a South African zoo.

The West Berlin Zoo houses each pair of Stanley cranes in a separate enclosure, approximately 10×12 m in size, containing some dense vegetation and an indoor shelter. Stanley cranes imported from South Africa in 1957 and 1958 laid for the first time in 1961, but the nine eggs were sterile. Seven fertile eggs were laid between June 1st and June 18th, 1963. Three young hatched in an incubator, each weighing 125 g. They were reared in initial temperatures of 28 to 33°C, in a box especially constructed for the purpose. As the young cranes were extremely quarrelsome they had to be separated and each one was cared for on its own. They were fed on fresh fish-eyes rolled in either hard-boiled egg or chicken starter crumbs, rice formed into small balls, together with multivitamins and minerals. The food was presented to them with forceps. At a later stage the young cranes were not only given this basic food but also—additionally—pieces of fish, ox heart, young mice, insects and chopped up green stuff (E. and G. Johst, 1966). A particularly interested breeder should look up the reports by Schmidt (1969), Müller-Langenbeck (1970) and D'Eath (1972).

Hybridization: See under demoiselle crane.

Crowned Crane
Balearica pavonina L.

Of the four sub-species of crowned cranes there are two black-necked and two grey-necked forms. The two groups are easily distinguished from each other and are often treated as two species: the West African and the East African crowned cranes. In preserves both groups need almost identical treatment and, therefore, only one comprehensive chapter on aviculture is devoted to them.

West African Crowned Crane
Balearica pavonina pavonina L.

Comparative Size: Only a little larger than a white stork.

Plumage: Adults see plate 113; upper half of unfeathered face white, lower red, no wattle-like appendages on neck. Neck an body dark slate-grey. Sexes not clearly distinguishable. Feathers of juveniles' bodies have a light-brown border at the tips; white wing coverts interspersed with grey-brown feathers, feather crown on back of head very much shorter.

Natural Habit

Status: By no means rare in their original habitats; crowned cranes also locally nest on cultivated land.

Habitat: Damp lowlands, vegetated lake shores and swamps within the otherwise dry steppes. On cultivated land nests have been found in small moist depressions of dry ground. The crowned cranes avoid forested regions; after the breeding season they like staying on gravelbanks of rivers.

Breeding Biology: Compare with East African crowned crane.

Crowned cranes enjoy 'dancing' and the dancing movements are made not only during courtship display but throughout the year. The birds jump high into the air with outstretched wings, bow down, walk with quick steps in circles and loops and end up by again jumping up, wings opened to their full span so that the rust-red secondaries and white wing coverts are displayed to their best advantage.

Migration: Resident and also partial migrant; crowned cranes undertake irregular short roaming flights, often forming into swarms—frequently in association with the northern common and demoiselle cranes.

Yearly Cycle: The breeding season is predominantly between July and November. Whilst the young are being reared the adults pass through their moult.

Climate: High temperatures throughout the year; a rapid decrease of rainfall from the Congo basin (southern limit of distribution) to the southernborder of the Sahara (northern limit of distribution).

237

East African Crowned Crane
Balearica pavonina regulorum (Bennett)

Comparative Size: Little larger than a white stork.

Plumage: Adults see plate 115; top quarter of unfeathered face is red, the rest white; lappets on throat red, neck light-grey, body slate-grey. Juveniles: compare with West African crowned crane.

Natural Habit

Status: A characteristic bird of game-rich East and South Africa. Since crowned cranes consume quantities of locusts and thus help rid the country of this pest; they have been for a long time among the group of large birds little hunted for htat reason.

Habitat: Wet depressions in the grassy ground of the savannas; favoured habitats outside the breeding season are meandering river courses with poor vegetation, gravel banks and lake shores.

Breeding Biology: Non-breeding crowned cranes roam freely without hiding and they do not shy away from man. In breeding preserves, on the other hand, they are timid and secretive. The nest is very bulky like that of other cranes and it is usually built in the vegetation on the ground, occasionally in trees. A full clutch contains two to three bluish-white eggs (sometimes flecked with a delicate brown). Incubation takes 22–25 days; both the female and the male incubate and, later, jointly guide their young.

Migration: In many areas the onset of the dry period forces the crowned cranes to migrate to regions with better conditions, particularly river plains and the lakes of the African rift valleys.

Yearly Cycle: When the rainy period begins in an area so does the crowned cranes' reproductive activity; the young are hatched towards the end of the rainy season and they are fully grown by the time the dry period sets in. Times of breeding are held to be from September until March, and, even more, the months of the southern summer: December until March.

Climate: Hot savanna climate throughout with few seasonal fluctuations in temperature.

Aviculture

Crowned cranes have been kept in European zoos for more than a century; in recent years many private owners have also cared for them. The yellow-gold feather crown and the glowing colours of the wing feathers displayed by the dancing cranes are very effective and decorative. Single cranes used to man are trusting and attached; they greet people they know by bowing and by dancing jumps. But 'badly brought-up' birds may be quite dangerous as they may use their bill to stab with lightning speed.

Housing: In zoos on the lawns where large wading birds are kept, or they may be left to run free on the grass-grown part of the gardens. People who make a hobby of caring for waterfowl keep them in fenced-in gardens or in an enclosure together with Anatidae, just like the demoiselle and Stanley cranes. Crowned cranes should not be exposed to frost in the winter, but in a dry, draught-proof indoor shelter they are well able to withstand a short period of low temperature without suffering any damage.

Food: The fact that crowned cranes are quite easy to keep does not mean that their food can be restricted to grain and mixed food, although this may form the bulk of their food intake. Fresh animal and vegetable matter—the cranes' favourite food—should always be given additionally as part of their diet.

Breeding: Compared with the number of crowned cranes kept in zoos and private preserves breeding results have been rather poor. The majority of crowned cranes is really mainly kept for show. If they do breed successfully they do so rather by chance than planning. Crowned cranes bred in the Budapest Zoo and the event has been described as follows: in 1912 three crowned cranes were imported from the former German East Africa; two of them paired in the summer of 1918. Display dances increased and the birds' calls became far more frequent; both mates occupied an eyrie, originally put up for storks above a small fish pond in the preserve; the cranes added nesting material and built the nest out to meet their own requirements. Egg-laying took place on August 10, 12 and 13 and both the male and the female incubated the eggs from the moment the last egg was laid. The parents were left to guide their young themselves and they were given additional food such as hard-boiled eggs, ant larvae, earth and meal worms. The young cranes thrived splendidly; when they were just a few days old they pecked at food morsels by themselves and, at three weeks old, they pecked at grain. The first wing quills began developing in the fifth week; shoulder and back feathers and tail quills followed shortly afterwards. Just before the young were fully feathered the feather crown on the nape of the head appeared; it was downy rather than bristly (CERVA 1931).

In South Africa a breeding success with crowned cranes was achieved in 1964; they had lived in the preserve for 14 years. Three eggs were laid in November; they were incubated for 28 days and two chicks were hatched.

Hybridization: It is known that crowned cranes have bred successfully a number of times; nonetheless the descendants are almost certainly birds derived from parents belonging to different sub-species.

Waders and Gulls

Looking after waders has never been as popular as keeping parrots and ducks. Nonetheless, enthusiastic reports in the *Avicultural Magazine* and the *Gefiederte Welt* give an indication of the numerous species of waders kept in cages. The Berlin Zoo kept 13 different species as early as from 1844 until 1888. In the 1920s HEINROTH reared 17 chicks belonging to the order of Charadriiformes from eggs collected from European wild birds. The Copenhagen and Cologne Zoos, the Waasenaar and Walsrode Bird Parks, among others, have shown numerous waders and gulls in modern spacious preserves since 1950. Private owners and bird enthusiasts have also changed their methods; they no longer keep the birds in cages but put them into large outside aviaries and enclosures instead. However, so far no definite efforts to breed the birds appear to have been made.

Maintaining waders and gulls is not particularly difficult, but it is very time-consuming.

During the period of adaptation the birds' natural feeding habits have to be changed — step by step. In their natural environment the birds catch their prey in mud and shallow water; in captivity they have to become used to accepting food from a trough. At a later stage they are fed on a moistened mixture of a nutritious prepared food (such as is given to insect eaters or is used for rearing pheasants), also minced fish and lean meat, shrimp pellets, white bread and meal-worms.

The majority of waders become tame surprisingly quickly, although they do not get imprinted to humans like cranes. Some remain timid and easily frightened; they may fly against the wire fences in an attempt to escape which may injure them (fracturing the bill). Some species show a distinct restlessness during their seasons of migration. A pool with a shallow rim allows the birds to keep themselves clean and their plumage in a healthy condition; moulting problems are rare, but the bill may grow to an abnormal length. In their natural environment waders continually dig in mud and sand to find their food. Thus the bill becomes worn down in the same measure as it re-grows. If preserve birds take all their food from a trough the bill is not subjected to its proper use and grows too long. The birds should be encouraged to dig by means of dishes with meal-worms buried underneath a thick layer of sand or peat.

The main problem is to see to it that the waders can keep their legs in a healthy condition. Cleanliness and the right kind of ground cover are essential. Sharp edges of concrete pools have to be covered either with a layer of soft bitumen or plastic. The ground of the aviary should be covered with either sea or river sand (not gravel which has sharp corners), short-growing lawn, or a layer of peat on a support of plastic which has to be kept moist. Tussocks of dry grasses are suitable as single plants. The ground must always be kept clean; food remnants and faeces soil it quickly and the sand has to be changed frequently. It is not advisable to house pigeons and finches together with the waders; the process of soiling would be that much quicker.

RADTKE (1959) summed up the habits and behaviour of the various species of waders and gulls kept in aviaries; according to his report, most of them are suited to being kept quite safely. With the help of the modern prepared foods and prophylactic medication and, provided the aviary or enclosure is really well arranged and suitable, it is possible to keep all species of waders as well as gulls and terns nowadays. They are likely to survive for many years. Anyone observing the free-living populations of waders in Europe and weighing their prospects of preservation cannot arrive at an encouraging conclusion, particularly as regards breeding stocks. Land drainage is driving away the last dunlins, golden plovers and redshanks from their natural habitats: swamps and moors. Intensive farming and soil cultivation affects lapwings and curlews so that they only rarely manage to rear their young. On all coasts the summer visitor disturbs the plovers, oyster-catchers and avocets; they now breed almost exclusively in sanctuaries. Ornithologists quite rightly demand a complete ban on the sale of all indigenous waders; naturally such a ban would restrict the numbers that may be kept in preserves.

A related group of birds, the jacanas, are wading birds inhabiting tropical waters; two of their best known representatives are the African Jacana, *Jacana* sp. (see plate 116), and the Pheasant-tailed Jacana, *Hydrophasianus chirurgus*. These lively and agile birds are now frequently kept in tropical halls, on ponds grown with water lilies.

Oyster-Catcher

Haematopus ostralegus L.

Comparative Size: A little larger than a lapwing.
Plumage: Adults in breeding plumage see plate 117; in eclipse they have a white or grey-white band around the throat, so do juveniles whose feathers on the back and inner secondaries are dark-brown—initially with red-brown borders.

NATURAL HABIT

Status: The oyster-catcher has a worldwide distribution and in many areas it is very abundant. But is has never been absolutely certain whether all the birds, even the completely black populations of America, Africa and New Zealand, are members of the same species.
Habitat: In Europe predominantly on gravelly oceanic coasts and muddy tidal stretches; some oyster-catchers breed inland. In America they nest on rocky coasts, in southern latitudes on coral reefs, and in central Asia on the gravel banks of saline lakes in the continental steppes.
Breeding Biology: Oyster-catchers are gregarious and often breed in loose colonies. A cup-shaped depression in the ground containing some shells and a few small stones at the bottom holds three to four large, dark-flecked eggs. Male and female incubate the eggs jointly for approximately 27 days; to start with they bring food to the young in the nest and later move with them to the shore region. Young oyster-catchers are excellent swimmers and divers; if danger threatens them they lie flat on the ground. They are sexually mature in the third year.

Migration: Sedentary resident, partial migrant and bird of passage. Some of the breeding birds of the North and Baltic Sea regions roam over short distances only; a few may even spend the winters in their breeding grounds; others migrate to Africa.

Yearly Cycle: The European nesting birds return to their home grounds by April and, by mid-May, they have produced a full clutch. Numerous non-breeders roam the European coasts during the summer months. Autumnal migration takes place in August and September.

Climate: If one includes the black forms, then it may be said that the oyster-catchers inhabit all the main climatic zones on earth; the most northerly breeding grounds are in areas with average July temperatures of 8–10°C.

Aviculture

Like the lapwings oyster-catchers are robust and easy to keep. Provided they are given sufficient space to move around and a pool to bathe in their black-white plumage stays clean, glossy and smooth. Oyster-catchers have a strong chisel-like bill with which they are able to open mussels and other shellfish; occasionally—when breeding—they threaten other birds in the preserve with their bill and have even killed some. But such aggressiveness is rare.

Housing: Together with other waders in large aviaries or pinioned in outside enclosures landscaped to look like the dunes of the coast. They should always have a shallow-rimmed bathing pool at their disposal. Oyster-catchers are not sensitive to cold; nevertheless in periods of frost they should be offered a shelter in which the ground should never reach freezing point; the floor of the shelter has to be strewn with sufficient dry stuff so that ice cannot develop.

Food: In addition to the food given to waders and already described, oyster-catchers also like somewhat larger pieces of fish or meat and, particularly, mussels (also freshwater mussels of which there are good supplies in many inland lakes).

Breeding: So far little has been reported about breeding results and information is very scanty. Nor do the reports clarify whether the eggs were actually laid by oyster-catchers in preserves or collected from wild birds. Nevertheless, the oyster-catcher appears to have bred more often and with less difficulty than other waders kept in preserves. SEEBOLD (written communication) reared four young oyster-catchers in a large communal aviary for waders, size 12 m × 4 m; he did not give them any additional food. Similar reports have come in from zoos. HEINROTH (1928) wrote about the species:

"Even the newly hatched oyster-catchers look solid and thick-set like the parent birds. They differ from young lapwings in their behaviour by being far more clever, tame and attached to people than the latter; unfortunately young sibling oyster-catchers quarrel a great deal among themselves."

Hybridization: Presumably they interbreed mainly with related oyster-catcher species; quite a few of these are also being imported into Europe.

Lapwing
Vanellus vanellus (L.)

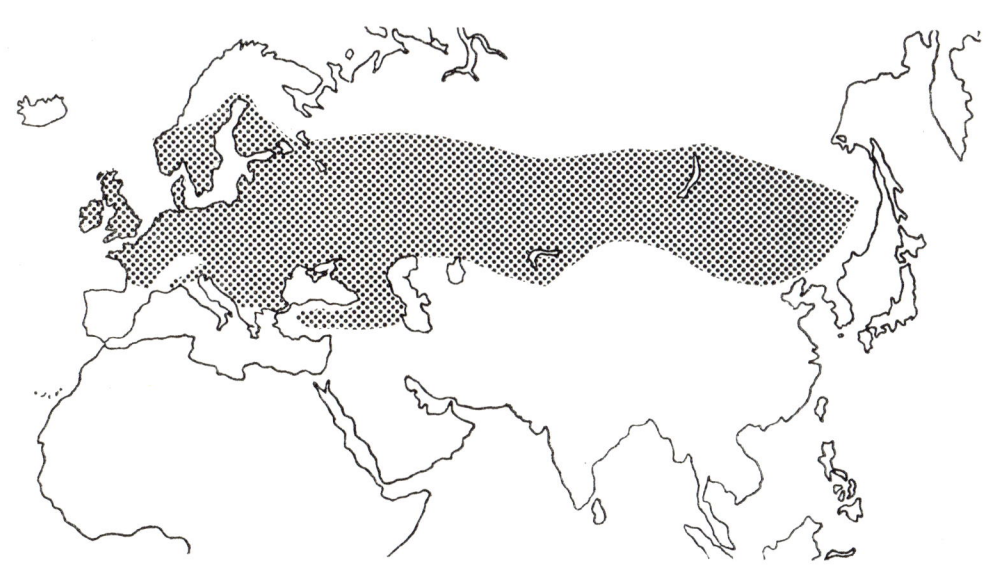

Size: Total length approximately 30 cm; weight 200–250 g; body pigeon-sized.

Plumage: Juveniles see plate 118; F. and M. resemble each other, but minor variations in size of crest, colour on head and chest and slightly differing intensity of gloss on back distinguish sexes to a certain degree. In juveniles feathers of back and shoulders have light borders and little sheen.

NATURAL HABIT

Status: Widely distributed in the area marked; lapwings are not deterred by the proximity of man and benefit from cultivated land; thus they have greater scope in the space they occupy. Local fluctuations in population size depend mainly on the amount of precipitation. In wet years many lapwings breed on tilled fields which they do not use in normal years. More recently lapwings have been threatened by a new danger; highly mechanized land cultivation often destroys their first and preplacement clutches.

Habitat: Moist soil with short vegetation such as pasture and arable land, moors and heaths. Whilst migrating they like to use mud-banks and meadows along shores as stopping places.

Breeding Biology: In spring lapwings begin the breeding season with excited calls and quivering display flights. The nest is small and scratched out of the ground on ploughed land and fields; it is lined with blades of grasses. A full clutch contains four dark-spotted ochre-yellow eggs which are incubated by both parents for 24–29 days. The newly hatched young are freckled and have the colour of earth; they are praecocial. When they are 35 days old they are able to fly and, once they are more than one year old, they are sexually mature.

Migration: Early summer migratory flights in a northerly and north-easterly direction are undertaken as soon as the first young are fledged; the flights turn into the autumn migration from July/August when the lapwings move west (Great Britain) and south-west (North Africa).

Yearly Cycle: Lapwings return to their breeding grounds from February onwards and birds of most populations have laid their first clutches by the beginning of April. Thus the first young lapwings are able to fly at the beginning of June (start of early summer migration). In November the last lapwings leave central Europe.

Climate: Although lapwings inhabit mainly temperate latitudes their breeding range extends from cool Iceland to hot central Asia. Their habit of migrating rather near winter time suggests that they are well able to tolerate different climatic conditions.

AVICULTURE

Most of the world's lapwings and their kindred are inhabitants of the steppes rather than the swamps, a fact which probably explains their hardiness and the lack of sensitivity of their legs. Although in small numbers, the following are the species most often imported over the last 100 years: Cayenne Lapwing, *Belonopterus cayennensis*, from South America; Spurwing Plover (Plate 120) and Crowned Plover (plate 119), *Hoplopterus armatus* and *Stephanibyx coronatus* from Africa; Masked Plover (plate 121), *Vanellus miles-novaehollandiae*, from Australia; Wattled Lapwing, *Lobivanellus indicus*, from India; and Banded Plover, *Zonifer tricolor*, from Australia.

Keeping the paleoarctic lapwing and most of the tropical species is not difficult; the birds soon lose their timidity, run around in their pens without appearing to be nervy (like many pheasants, for instance), and, on the whole, they are peaceable unless they are breeding or guiding young; then they may well become aggressive towards the smaller species of waders.

Housing: Preferably in large outdoor aviaries. Gravel from the bottom of rivers or sea sand can be recommended as suitable ground cover; a bathing pool is essential, even for the species normally inhabiting the steppes. They should be wintered in a warm indoor shelter.

Food: See introduction: waders and gulls (page 240). In outdoor aviaries lapwings continually hunt for insects and worms.

Breeding: The majority of lapwings kept in Europe came into the possession of bird lovers either as mature birds who had suffered accidents or as young birds deserted by their parents. The mature birds adapt quickly; rearing of the young causes some trouble but is quite possible with the aid of a heat lamp. The young are at first fed on small moving worms (tubifex, earth worms and also meal-worms which have just sloughed their skins) and, later, on ant cocoons and a prepared food such as given to other insect eaters.

Hybridization: Very little tendency if any.

Crowned Plover

Stephanibyx coronatus (Boddaert)

Comparative Size: Body smaller than that of Lapwing, *Vanellus vanellus*, but legs are longer.

Plumage: Adults see plate 119; head and upper neck are black-white, bill red with black tip, legs coral-red. M. a little larger than F. Several sub-species show colour variants. In juveniles parts of the head ochre-brown, upper wing-coverts have broad creamy borders, bill and legs rust-brown.

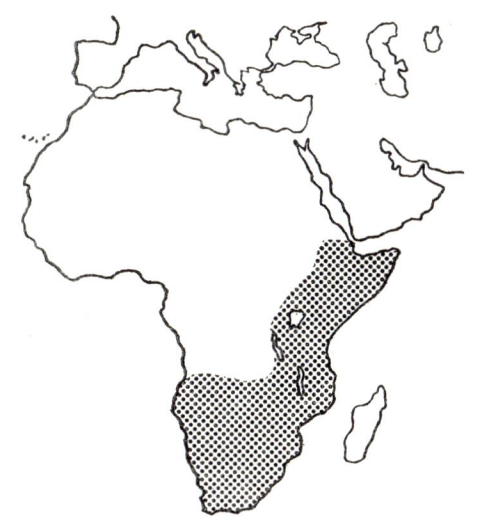

NATURAL HABIT

Status: In modern literature crowned plovers are referred to as locally abundant; no doubt 'local' means areas providing suitable habitats.

Habitat: Areas of steppe with poor vegetation and open scrubland; a few crowned plovers inhabit arable land and cattle pastures, and they may be found on lake shores as long as these are surrounded by large gravel banks.

Breeding Biology: Not significantly different from other species of lapwings and plovers. The breeding season begins with display flights and loud calls. The female scratches out the nest and lines it sparsely with some blades and pebbles. A clutch consists of three densely spotted eggs. Incubation takes approximately 26 days (from the time the last egg has been laid). Both the male and female incubate and later jointly guide their young.

Migration: Sedentary resident birds in most areas with a tendency to undertake roaming flights within particular landscapes.

Yearly Cycle: Crowned plovers breed at different times depending on a region's climate; in the southernmost third of Africa they breed predominantly between July and December.

Climate: Mainly hot, tropical savanna climate with poor rainfall throughout the year; temperatures in South Africa and on the high plateaux of Ethiopia are slightly lower.

AVICULTURE

The first crowned plovers to reach Europe were brought from South Africa in 1925; imports from Abyssinia followed a little later. At that time crowned plovers were kept singly or in pairs in aviaries or in bird houses in zoos. Difficulties in establishing and maintaining the birds did not arise (despite dense population of the places where they were kept). The crowned plovers soon became tame and their graceful movements enlivened their environment.

Housing: In modern zoos and bird preserves the southern plover species are shown in the tropical houses. Private owners keep the birds in a dry outdoor aviary and in a warm room in the winter.

Food: See introduction: waders and gulls (page 240).

Breeding: The first breeding result was achieved by the Frankfurt on Main Zoo; WIESCHKE (1929) wrote about it as follows: "The Zoo purchased the species in 1925 and incubated eggs were discovered in the aviary just a year later. By 1928 the female had laid a total of seven clutches; each one contained three eggs. The laying took place between mid-April and mid-September; the young were hatched after 25–27 days of incubation."

NEUNZIG (1935) reported on the crowned plover: A pair acquired in 1913 inhabited the inner shelter (only 3 m ×2 m in size) of their aviary and the female began laying eggs from 1933 onwards. The female always showed herself ready to breed before the male did. She scratched the nest together and lined it with dried pigeon droppings; in each case she laid a clutch of three eggs in laying intervals of one to two days. Until the clutch was completed the eggs were covered with sand. The male undertook the main share of incubation and rearing the chicks whereas the female defended nest and young from other birds coming too close to them. During the first few days the male's main preoccupation was brooding the young rather than teaching them to feed; the chicks did not run to the parent bird when they wanted to be brooded, he just sat on them wherever they happened to be. They were fed on ant cocoons and small morsels of food. Nowadays crowned plovers are successfully kept and bred in numerous zoos, bird parks and breeders' preserves; eggs are often put into incubators and the young are reared under a heat lamp. Other species of southern plovers are also found in zoos and bird preserves, for instance: the Cayenne lapwing in the Frankfurt on Main Zoo since 1966, and the Australian banded plover in the Louise Hall, Wassenaar since 1956. The birds are bred in these places.

Hybridization: None known to have occurred so far; it remains to be seen whether some interbreeding might take place in the modern tropical houses where several plover species are kept together.

Ruff

Philomachus pugnax (L.)

Comparative Size: Smaller and slimmer than a lapwing.
Plumage: Ms. in breeding plumage see plates 122–124; the large, striking erectile ruff of feathers around the neck varies in colour between white, yellow, rust-brown and steel-blue. In eclipse the M. resembles the much smaller sand-coloured F. Legs vary in colour between greenish (F.) and reddish (M.). Juvenile M. larger than F. of the same age.

NATURAL HABIT

Status: Land drainage has robbed the ruffs of most of their central and western European breeding grounds. The numerous birds passing through are at home in Scandinavia and the wide spaces of Siberia.
Habitat: Grassy swamps in the open northern birch-grove zone of the bush and moss tundra; extensive swampy river plains; coastal greens traversed by river courses; a few ruffs may be found on large meadows.
Breeding Biology: In the spring the males collect in the display grounds where they fight 'tournaments' for the position of being the dominant male of the highest rank. The females remain on the edge of the display area and, in the end, mate with one of the victorious males. The females (called 'reeves') make their nests far away from the display area and incubate the four olive-green, dark-spotted eggs in 21 days. The males do not participate either with incubating or rearing the chicks. Juveniles are able to fly when they are circa six weeks old and they are sexually mature after one year.

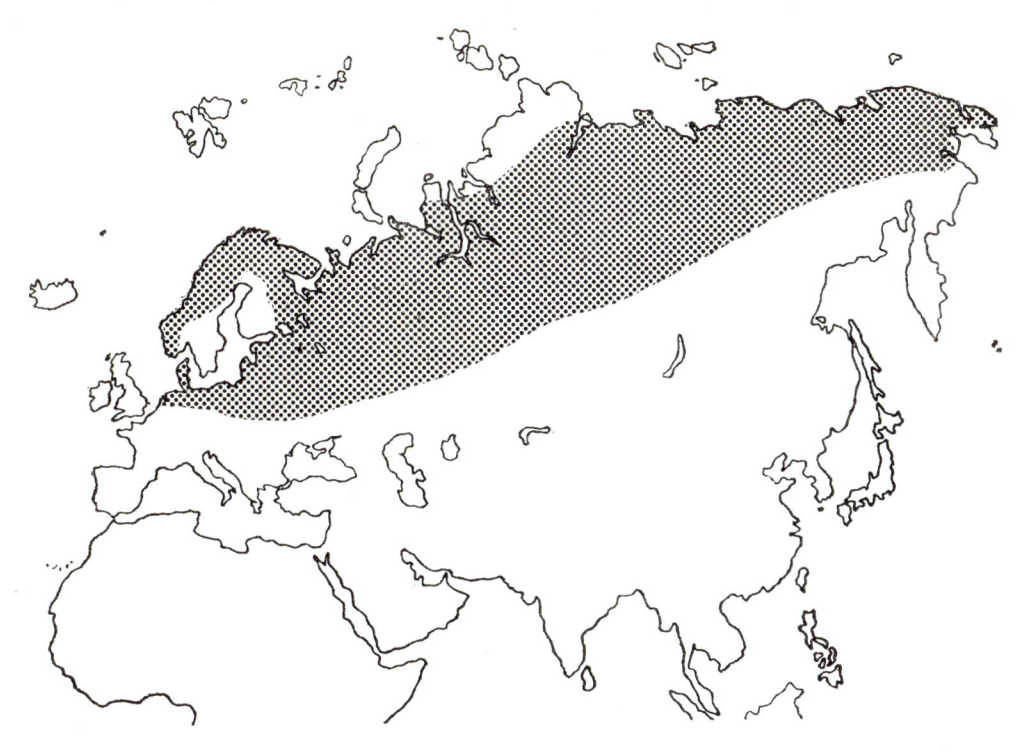

Migration: Birds of passage covering enormous distances in their migratory flights. Data obtained from ringed birds have proved that East Siberian breeding birds migrate to Africa flying over western Europe. One bird banded by myself flew from the middle course of the river Elbe to the Lena in 30 days.

Yearly Cycle: The central and western European populations arrive in their breeding grounds from March onwards. The display grounds are most densely occupied in April and May and, from May onwards, the reeves start to lay. Birds passing through central Europe or spending the summer there remain until the late summer and then begin their autumnal migration.

Climate: Breeding grounds are predominantly in the cooler regions, but the ruffs migrate to areas of Africa and Asia with very varied tropical and sub-tropical climatic conditions.

AVICULTURE

Some private owners and zoological experts wish to make up groups of ruffs in such a way that they show their full courtship display in spring and summer—something that involves a preserve owner in a great deal of expenditure. But, as far as the birds themselves are concerned, it is not nearly as difficult as was formerly assumed. Ruffs soon adapt to a new environment, even the males' moult of the thick ruff of feathers around the neck proceeds quite smoothly. FRISCH (1960) reported that his ruffs showed little migratory restlessness and that they spent the winter in an outdoor aviary in temperatures as low as −20°C. Three males and one reeve together with approximately 30 other waders were kept in a large aviary and between April and June the males displayed with great intensity.

Housing: In zoos and bird preserves single ruffs are shown with groups of waders. Breeding and display enclosures, on the other hand, have to be large enough to allow the ruffs wishing to mate occupation of an area several square metres in size, where they can be apart from the other waders and display in courtship. A short sward is a suitable ground cover for the enclosure.

Food: Apart from the food for waders described previously ruffs also eat grain (a mixture of goldfinch and siskin food).

Breeding: Probably very few ruffs only have been bred in captivity so far. On the whole, breeders and zoological experts have shown a limited interest in breeding this 'simple' species whose reproductive activity is quite well developed. FRISCH (1960) caught two males and one female in 1957. He kept them in the aviary mentioned above and although he kept them together with 30 other waders the reeve laid four eggs in June 1959 and incubated them. The chicks did not hatch because the weather was poor. SEEBOLD (written communication) also had a reeve who laid four eggs in a densely populated communal enclosure. The four chicks were hatched after 21 days but, by the next morning they had disappeared without leaving a trace.

The examples above illustrate that ruffs engage in reproductive activity after a short period of adaptation, even in crowded enclosures; rearing of the chicks, however, needs a great deal of extra care and vigilance.

Hybridization: According to RUTGERS (1966) ruffs have interbred in preserves with the Spotted Redshank, *Tringa erythropus*, the Wood Sandpiper, *Tringa glareola* and the Crowned Plover, *Stephanibyx coronatus*; hybrid young hatched as a result of the interbreeding.

Avocet

Recurvirostra avosetta L.

Comparative Size: Considerably larger than lapwing.

Plumage: Adults see plate 125; sexes resemble each other and cannot always be distinguished; F. often has minor colour variants; e. g. some white feathers may be scattered in black parts of forehead, irides may be nut-brown rather than red-brown. In juveniles the dark parts of the plumage are brownish.

NATURAL HABIT

The avocets' food requirements are highly specialised; thus they are confined to particular ecological areas and, therefore' very easily affected by changes in the environment. On the western European coasts avocets breed almost solely in protected areas where they experience a general—although minor—increase in population size. In America and Australia avocets are represented by closely related species.

Habitat: Shallow, sandy and muddy shores along the coasts and coastal lagoons, also brackish and salty lakes in the steppes.

Breeding Biology: After a short period of display which takes place on the shore zone, nest sites are occupied in dunes, on stretches of gravel and dry silt. The nest has no cover and is scratched out by the female; she lines it with grasses and sea shells. A full clutch consists of four ochre-brown, black spotted eggs which both the male and female incubate for 24–25 days. The chicks are taken to the shore zone; they are clever swimmers and divers and it does not take long before they sieve animal and vegetable matter from the water, following their parents' example. After one year they are sexually mature.

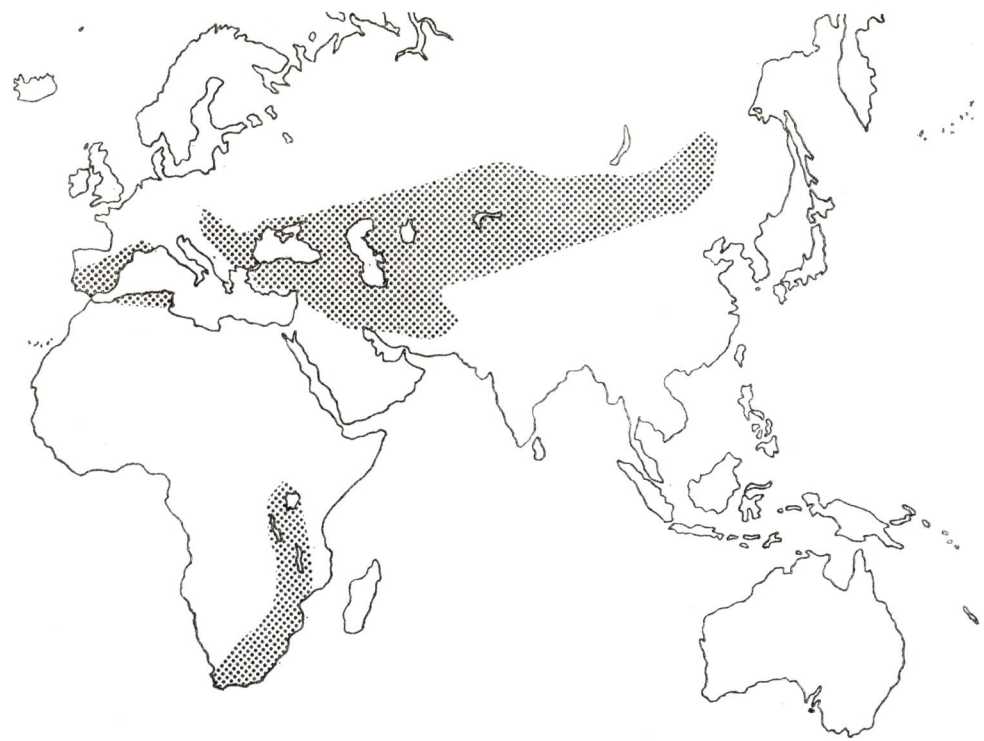

Migration: The north-western European avocets winter on the Atlantic coasts of France, Portugal and Spain; others winter on the coast of the Mediterranean, in Africa and India.

Yearly Cycle: Avocets move to their breeding grounds on the shores of the North Sea and the Baltic between February and May; main breeding months are May and June. Large swarms aggregate on some moulting sites in August; autumn migration lasts until October.

Climate: With the exception of the fairly small North and Baltic Sea population which is quite able to withstand periods of bad weather, the majority of avocets inhabit dry-hot continental and Mediterranean regions.

AVICULTURE

Avocets are among the most attractive and interesting waders, but they also belong to the species most difficult to maintain. The two main problems are abnormal growth of the bill (see page 240) and foot ailments. It is absolutely essential to keep the ground spotlessly clean and cover it with a material which does not irritate the skin of the feet. The tiny pebbles, washed round and smoothed by water and found in river and sea sand, have proved to be the best ground cover. Droppings and food remnants have to be removed daily or they have to be covered with sand. The water basin (1–2 m^2) has to have shallow surrounds and, according to RUEMPLER (1971) it should not be more than 8 cm in depth. BENKE (by letter), on the other hand, writes:

"My avocets like the water and swim out for quite a distance; they are playful whilst they are bathing and, like the dabbling ducks, they often upend with the aid of their wings and also swim below the water. My birds do not have diseased feet because they spend most of their time in shallow water, 3–5 cm deep, and even sleep there in the night. Rims of their ponds are all covered over with sand."

Based on my own experiences with oil-polluted sea ducks which tend to have similar foot ailments during the period of becoming established, I can confirm that lacking opportunity for staying on water is the main cause for diseased feet. The skin covering the feet dries out and cracks; micro-organisms penetrate and cause inflammation, particularly on those underparts of the feet on which the birds walk. Rubbing the skin with vitamin A oil not only furthers the healing process but also keeps the skin smooth.

Housing: Spacious aviaries with not too many occupants or outdoor enclosures; avocets should be wintered in approximately 10°C of warmth. RUEMPLER (1971) pointed out that long-billed waders are always exposed to the danger of bill fractures; it happens rather frequently if they fly against wire fencing, and he recommends that avocets should be pinioned. If their wings are clipped then they can be maintained in large enclusores in the open air.

Food: See introduction: waders and gulls (page 240). Additionally, avocets are given a dry mixed food and shrimp meal which is dropped on the water for them; they pick this up with a side to side sweep of the bill, a movement typical of avocets.

Breeding: Avocets have bred successfully and repeatedly in aviaries. RUEMPLER (1971) has given a detailed account of avocet breeding:

"In the Tierpark Rheime (GFR) several avocet chicks were hatched and subsequently reared; seven of these birds were put into an aviary, 4 m × 11 m in size. By 1972 three pairs had formed; each pair produced a clutch before mid-June and started to incubate. A few days later the eggs were removed and put into an inucbator with a temperature of 37.5°C and maximum air humidity of 55%. After an incubation which lasted for 24–27 days, eleven chicks were hatched; they were reared without losses. During the first few days the chicks were fed on mixed food for warblers which was dropped on the water for them, and they were also given small earth worms. Eye inflammations occurred a number of times; they were treated with Chloramphenicol eye drops."

It may well be advantageous to give maturing (and adult) avocets saltwater (up to 0.5% salt content). Sea birds absorb excessive salt; at the same time the salts ward off germs and, particularly, fungus spores; they also provide the birds with a better resistance against disease.

Hybridization: Not known to have occurred so far.

Black-headed Gull

Larus ridibundus L.

Comparative Size: Approximately like a lapwing, but with longer wings.

Plumage: Adults in breeding plumage see plate 127; in eclipse plumage completely white with a black-brown patch near the ear. Juveniles' plumage a dirty white containing some dark parts, the tail ending in a black band (a general characteristic of juvenile gulls).

NATURAL HABIT

Status: A typical gull of the interior but by no means absent on the coasts. Black-headed gulls breed in large colonies on numerous lakes; many populations have specialised on agricultural pests for food. In the last century the area of their distribution spread to north and north-west Europe.

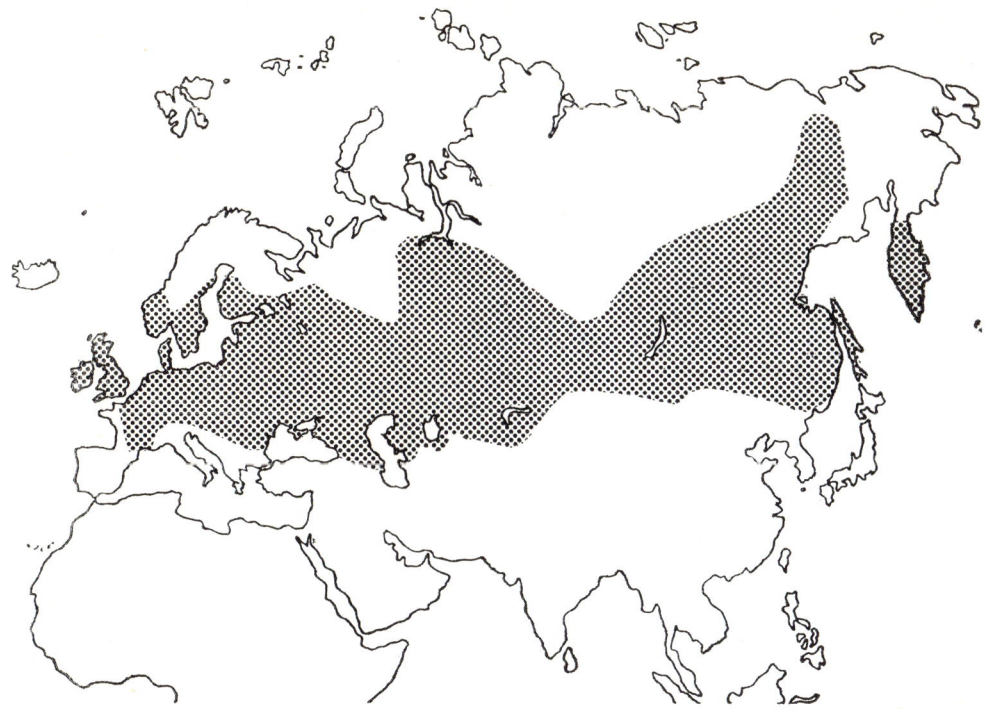

Habitat: Inland they nest on eutrophic lakes and ponds with wide sedge and reed zones. On the coasts they breed on marshland and grass-grown islands. Outside the breeding season they are found along river courses, in fishing harbours (especially in winter) and on urban waters.

Breeding Biology: The nests are packed close to each other, placed either on broken rushes or sedge stands—usually in the zone of shallow water. A full clutch contains two to three brownish, dark blotched eggs which are incubated by the male and female for 22–24 days. Although young black-headed gulls are praecocial they remain in the nest for several days before they start wandering around in the colony. At six weeks they are able to fly, and after one or two years they are sexually mature.

Migration: Only some black-headed gulls are sedentary, most of them are partial migrants or birds of passage. Quite a few migrate to North Africa, and many spend the winters on urban waters as long as these are not frozen.

Yearly Cycle: If the weather is favourable spring migration begins in early February, and by March many black-headed gulls are seen on their breeding waters. Eggs are laid in April and May. As soon as the juveniles are able to fly they leave the breeding colony together with the adults. Autumn migration takes place from October until November.

Climate: Black-headed gulls remain in central and western Europe until the water freezes. In Asia their distribution ranges from the cool northern coniferous region to the hot central Asiatic steppes.

AVICULTURE

As their calls are noisy, their metabolism very active and their peaceableness rather questionable gulls are generally not kept in any numbers by private preserves. On the other hand, zoos and bird parks show all sorts of species of gulls. Although the characteristics of black-headed gulls are like those of other gulls their small size (in contrast to the buzzard-sized herring gull) is in their favour; waterfowl enthusiasts who wish to do so can care for the birds quite easily in their preserves. If black-headed gulls are provided with adequate bathing facilities their plumage is always clean and smooth; they are delightful to watch, particularly as they are very active and agile.

Housing: In aviaries black-headed gulls may be kept together with rails and waders; zoos often keep them in company with herons, and some breeders specialised for Anatidae put them on their duck ponds with clipped wings. Black-headed gulls like the companionship of their own species throughout the year; therefore they should be maintained in small groups always. They should be wintered on sheltered ponds free of ice.

Food: The bulk of the food given to black-headed gulls is white bread and shrimps thrown on the water for them as well as a moistened mixed food; additionally they are fed some fish, pieces of meat, mice, raw eggs, worms and insects.

Breeding: Whereas herring gulls breed in most zoological gardens and rear their own young without losses even in overpopulated aviaries, black-headed gulls, in contrast, rarely breed in preserves. Duck breeders have written and informed me that they have kept black-headed gulls on their ponds for many years but that the gulls have never laid an egg. A report from HUNGER (1973) is therefore all the more remarkable; he obtained two mature birds in 1971 (by chance a male and a female) and put them into an aviary. The birds were not at all timid, fought each other for a time, but started displaying in the following spring and, in May 1973 they made a nest and the female laid eggs. The clutch of three eggs was incubated for 23 days, all three chicks were hatched and the parent birds reared them jointly.

HUNGER writes:

"Gull chicks are hardy birds, they soon learn to open their strong bill begging for food. For the first days the parent birds regurgitated the food for them and the young took it. Within a short period of time they were sufficiently independent to pick up their food from the feeding trough. They were reared on a mixture of soft food (such as given to thrushes) and food used for pheasant rearing, also meal-worms, hard-boiled egg and some shrimps."

Hybridization: Not known to have occurred so far and, in any case, unlikely with the larger species.

Common Gull
Larus canus L.

Comparative Size: Medium-sized species of gull.

Plumage: Adults and fully grown juveniles see plate 128; M. and F. white throughout the year, back shaded pale-grey. Upperside of juveniles mottled dark grey-brown, underparts lighter, tail grey-white ending in a black band.

NATURAL HABIT

Status: The distribution of common gulls is world-wide and they occur in huge populations. In comparatively recent times their area of distribution spread to northwest Europe and the interior of central Europe. In some sea-bird sanctuaries their numbers had to be reduced because the presence of so many common gulls drove other sea-birds out of the breeding reserves.

Habitat: They breed in large colonies on coastal offshore islands and—inland—on fairly large lakes, in gravel pits and along river courses.

Breeding Biology: Within the breeding colonies, where sometimes thousands of common gulls nest, every available nest site is occupied. The rather carelessly constructed nests may be on the grass, between stones and brushwood, on roofs of houses and even on stored goods. Incubation of the three ochre-brown or olive-grey, dark spotted eggs takes 23–25 days. The young are nidifugous and strong on their feet; at 35 days they are able to fly. They are sexually mature from the second or third year of life.

Migration: Once the breeding season is finished common gulls stay on the coasts, in particularly large numbers in fishing harbours; for the winter months they migrate to west and south-west Europe. At that time common gulls coming from further east settle on the central European waters.

Yearly Cycle: Common gulls occupy their breeding colonies from end-March and begin laying eggs one month later. Summer and autumn migration of the non-breeders begins in June, the juveniles follow in July and the adults at the onset of winter.

Climate: On the whole, breeding and wintering grounds are restricted to the cool, temperate latitudes; in a few regions only do the common gulls range as far as the tundra zone and the continental steppes.

AVICULTURE

The common gull is the smallest representative of the seagulls and therefore it is the one most suited to being kept in preserves. Although the habit of robbing other birds' nests of eggs and young is not nearly as pronounced in the common gull as it is in the large herring and lesser black-backed gull, caution is nonetheless advisable. Furthermore, all gulls attack birds weaker than themselves and may therefore endanger, for instance, the small species of ducks and rails. On the whole, seagulls thrive in preserves; their requirements are few, they are robust, hardy in the winter and they live for a long time. They need neither sea nor saltwater.

Housing: Either in large aviaries or, pinioned, in outdoor enclosures. Gulls with impeded flight ability adapt themselves completely to life on the ground and produce young just as easily as the birds which are able to fly.

Food: Gulls are omnivorous; they are neither choosy nor demanding. Their basic food is plant matter, but it should be enriched with animal matter such as pieces of fish and meat, mice and offal.

Breeding: Breeding seagulls are a common sight in zoos. Whether kept in pairs or small breeding groups, the gulls make a carelessly constructed nest on the ground, preferably behind stones; they use broken blades of grass, twigs and feathers as nesting materials. They lay their eggs and incubate without taking the slightest notice of the other birds in their surroundings. The young gulls mature without the need of any special rearing food. As colony breeders the adult gulls defend their own, very limited nest territory only; the presence of other birds does not disturb them.

Rearing gull chicks without parents is also quite easy. During the first few days they are fed on a finely minced food mixture, held out to them in tweezers near ground level; the young peck at the food and, two to four days later, they find it for themselves in their feeding trough. Care has to be taken that each chick is given enough food; the stronger birds push the weaker ones aside, the latter are then under-nourished, their development is impeded and they may die eventually.

Hybridization: Interbreeding particularly pronounced between Herring and Lesser Black-backed Gulls (*Larus argentatus* and *L. fuscus*), but the common gull also hybridizes—namely with the larger species.

Bibliography

Standard works

Delacour, J. (1954–64): The Waterfowl of the World. London
Frith, H. J. (1967): Waterfowl in Australia. Sydney, London, Melbourne
Glutz von Blotzheim, U. N., K. M. Bauer and E. Bezzel (1966–73): Handbuch der Vögel Mitteleuropas. Vol. 1–5. Frankfort-on the-Main
Gray, A. P. (1958): Bird Hybrids. A Check-List with Bibliography. Farnham Royal, Bucks
Grzimek, B. (1968–69): Grzimeks Tierleben. Vol. 7 and 8. Zurich
Heinroth, O., and M. Heinroth (1924–31): Die Vögel Mitteleuropas. Vol. 1–4. Berlin-Lichterfelde
International Zoo Yearbook. Vol. 1–14. 1959 to 1974. London
Kolbe, H. (1972): Die Entenvögel der Welt. Melsungen, Basle, Vienna
Rutgers, A. (1966): Enzyklopädie für den Vogelliebhaber, Vol. 1. Grossel
Schlawe, L. (1969): Die für die Zeit vom 1. August 1844 bis 31. Mai 1888 nachweisbaren Thiere im zoologischen Garten zu Berlin. Berlin
The Wildfowl Trust. Annual Reports up to Vol. 23 (1972); later Wildfowl up to Vol. 25 (1974)

Periodicals

Bartlett, A. D. (1866): Notes on the breeding of several species of birds in the Society's Gardens during the year 1865. Proc. Zool. Soc. London, 76–79
Bolen, E. G. (1973): Breeding whistling ducks *Dendrocygna* spp. in captivity. Inter. Zoo Yearbook **13**, 32–37
Cerva, F. A. (1931): Brütende Kronenkraniche (*Balearica gibbericeps* Rchw.) im Budapester Zoo. Der Zool. Garten NF **4**, 9–13
Cordier, Ch. (1968): Flamingos in Bolivien. Freunde d. Kölner Zoo **11**, 13–16
D'Eath, J. O. (1972): Some notes on breeding the Stanley crane. Avic. Mag. **78**, 165–169
Ee, C. A. van (1966): Notes on the breeding behaviour of the Blue Crane *Tetrapteryx paradisea* Ostrich **37**, 23–29
Encke, B. (1966): Aufzucht von Jungfernkranichen im Krefelder Tierpark. Gef. Welt **90**, 163–164
Frisch, O. v. (1960): Gefangenschaftsbeobachtungen am Kampfläufer (*Philomachus pugnax*). Anz. Ornith. Gesell. Bayern **5**, 507–509
Gorgas, M. (1969): Flamingos – stelzbeinige Wasservögel von vier Kontinenten. Freunde d. Kölner Zoo **12**, 15–19
Griswold, J. A. (1973): The coscoroba, *Coscoroba coscoroba*. Inter. Zoo Yearbook **13**, 38–40
Harrison, C. J. O. (1970): Helpers at the nest in the Purple Gallinule (*Porphyrio porphyrio*). Avic. Mag. **76**, 2–4
Heinroth, O. (1910): Beitr. zur Biologie, namentlich Ethologie und Physiologie der Anatiden. Verh. d. 5. Intern. Ornith. Kongreß in Berlin 1909. Berlin
– (1921): 19. Purpurhühner und ihre Küchlein. Alfred Brehm, Kleine Schriften. Leipzig
Holyoak, D. T. (1970): The behaviour of captive Purple Gallinules (*Porphyrio porphyrio*). Avic. Mag. **76**, 98–109

HUNGER, D. (1973): Die Zucht einer Lachmöwe in der Voliere. Gef. Welt 97, 217–218

IMMELMANN, K. (1969): Nakuru – See der Flamingos. Vogelkosmos 6, 96–99

JOHNSTONE, S. T. (1970): Waterfowl eggs. Avic. Mag. 76, 52–55

JOHST, E., and G. JOHST (1966): Die Kranichzucht hat viele Tücken. Im Berliner Zoo wurden Paradieskraniche gezüchtet. Vogelkosmos 3, 148–150

KEAR, J., and N. DUPLAIX-HALL (1975): Flamingos. Flamingo-Symposium by The Wildfowl Trust 1973. Berghamsted

KLIKA, I. (1970): Ein Beitrag zur Biologie des Saruskranichs (*Grus antigone*). Sarus. Bratislava, 231–239

LAMPSON, B. L. (1973): First breeding of the Long-tailed duck, *Clangula hyemalis*, in captivity. Inter. Zoo Yearbook 13, 70–71

MEISE, W. (1934): Zur Biologie der Brasilien-Zwergralle. Journ. f. Ornith. 82, 257–268

MÜLLER-LANGENBECK, G. (1970): Einige Bemerkungen zur Aufzucht eines Paradieskranichs (*Anthropoides paradisea*). Gef. Welt 94, 15–16

NEUNZIG, R. (1931): Afrikanische Kiebitze als Stubenvögel. Kronenkiebitz. Gef. Welt 60, 363–364

– (1935): Züchtung des Kronenkiebitzes (Stephanibyx coronatus). Gef. Welt 64, 463–464

OLIVER, W. R. B. (1930): New Zealand Birds. Wellington

POLEY, D. (1971): Flamingos. Gef. Welt 95, 92–95

– (1972): Sonnenrallen. Gef. Welt 96, 11–12

PREUSS, B. (1971): Haltung und Zucht von Saruskranichen, *Grus antigone* (L. 1758), im Zoologischen Garten Rostock. Der Zool. Garten NF 40, 193–199

RADTKE, G. A. (1959): Zur Haltung von Limikolen. Gef. Welt 83, 201–204

RAETHEL, H. S. (1968): Afrikas größter Kranich stellt sich vor. Klunkerkraniche im Berliner Zoo. Vogelkosmos 11, 369–373

REICHHOLF, J. (1975): Biogeographie und Ökologie der Wasservögel im subtropisch-tropischen Südamerika. Anz. Orn. Ges. Bayern 14, 1–69

RIPLEY, S. D. (1951): Remarks on the Philippine Mallard. Wilson Bulletin 63, 189–191

ROHR, W. (1964): Beobachtungen bei der Erstzucht eines Rosaflamingos in Deutschland im Zoo Berlin. Gef. Welt 88, 46–49

RUEMPLER, CH., and G. RUEMPLER (1973): Zur künstlichen Erbrütung und Handaufzucht von Säbelschnäblern (*Recurvirostra avosetta*). Zeitschr. d. Kölner Zoo 16, 31–33

RUEMPLER, G. (1971): Erfahrungen in der Haltung von Säbelschnäblern (*Recurvirostra avosetta*). Zeitschr. d. Kölner Zoo 14, 111–113

SCHIEFERDECKER, R. (1966): Schöne Vögel im kleinen Garten. Gef. Welt 90, 43–45.

SCHMIDT, C. R. (1969): Notizen zur Zucht des Paradieskranichs (*Anthropoides paradisea*). Der Zool. Garten NF 36, 186–190

SCHNEIDER, K. M. (1952): Vom Kropfstorch (*Leptoptilos Lesson*) in Gefangenschaft. Beitr. z. Vogelkunde 2, 196–286

SCHUMACHER, E. (1969): Bei den tanzenden Kranichen im Akan-Nationalpark. Vogelkosmos 11, 364–366

SCOTT, P. (1953): South America–1953. Wildfowl Trust, 5th Ann. Rep., 20–26

STEHLIK, J. (1970): Beitrag zur Biologie der Jungfernkraniche (*Anthropoides vitgo*). Freunde d. Kölner Zoo 13, 115–119

STRUDER-THIERSCH, A. (1967): Beiträge zur Biologie der Flamingos (Gattung Phoenicopterus.) Der Zool. Garten NF 34, 159–229

WACKERNAGEL, H. (1959): Ein Bruterfolg beim Chilenischen Flamingo im Zoologischen Garten Basel. Ornith. Beobachter 56, 33–40

WELLER, M. W. (1969): Comments on waterfowl habitat and management problems in Argentina. Wildfowl 20, 126–130

– (1972): Ecological studies of Falkland Islands' waterfowl. Wildfowl 23, 25–44

WIENANDS, J. (1974): Gelungene Zucht des Kappensägers (*Mergus cucullatus* L.). Gef. Welt 98, 81–82

WIESCHKE, R. (1929): Über das Brutgeschäft des Kronenkiebitzes (*Stephanibyx coronatus* Bodd.) im Frankfurter Zoologischen Garten. Der Zool. Garten NF 1, 305–307

WILLIAMS, J. G. (1973): Die Vögel Ost- und Zentralafrikas. Hamburg and Berlin (West)

WILLIAMS, W. M. H. (1971): Some notes on the rearing of Bufflehead and Hooded Merganser (*Bucephala albeola* and *Mergus cucullatus*). Avic. Mag. 77, 58–65

Index

African Pygmy Goose 173
Aix galericulata 176
Aix sponsa 186
Ajaja ajaja 27
Alopochen aegyptiacus 112
Amazonetta brasiliensis 187
American Wigeon 116
Anas acuta 133
Anas americana 116
Anas angustirostris 150
Anas bahamensis 134
Anas capensis 148
Anas castanea 128
Anas clypeata 156
Anas crecca 129
Anas cyanoptera 155
Anas discors 153
Anas erythrorhyncha 136
Anas falcata 118
Anas flavirostris 131
Anas formosa 120
Anas luzonica 127
Anas penelope 114
Anas platyrhynchos 122
Anas poecilorhyncha 125
Anas punctata 147
Anas querquedula 151
Anas sibilatrix 117
Anas superciliosa 124
Anas versicolor 145
Andean Goose 87
Anser anser 68
Anser brachyrhynchus 72
Anser caerulescens 75
Anser canagicus 77
Anser erythropus 70
Anser indicus 74
Anthropoides paradisea 235
Anthropoides virgo 233
Ardea cinerea 11
Ardeola ibis 15
Ardeola ralloides 15
Ashy-headed Goose 90
Australian Shelduck 111

Avocet 246
Aythya affinis 172
Aythya americana 164
Aythya collaris 170
Aythya ferina 163
Aythya fuligula 168
Aythya nyroca 166
Aythya valisneria 165

Bahama Pintail 134
Baikal Teal 120
Balearica pavonina 237
Balearica pavonina pavonina 237
Balearica pavonina regulorum 238
Bar-headed Goose 74
Barnacle Goose 82
Black-headed Gull 248
Black-necked Swan 56
Black Stork 20
Black Swan 65
Blue-winged Teal 153
Branta bernicla 79
Branta canadensis 81
Branta leucopsis 82
Branta ruficollis 84
Branta sandvicensis 85
Brazilian Teal 187
Brent Goose 79
Bucephala albeola 217
Bucephala clangula 194
Bufflehead 217
Bugeranus carunculatus 231

Cairina hartlaubi 182
Calonetta leucophrys 189
Canada Goose 81
Canvasback 165
Cape Shelduck 108
Cape Teal 148
Caribbean Flamingo 31
Cereopsis 93
Cereopsis novaehollandiae 93

Chenonetta jubata 174
Chestnut Teal 128
Chilean Flamingo 41
Chilean Teal 131
Chiloe Wigeon 117
Chloephaga melanoptera 87
Chloephaga picta 89
Chloephaga poliocephala 90
Chloephaga rubidiceps 92
Ciconia ciconia 19
Ciconia nigra 20
Cinnamon Teal 155
Clangula hyemalis 192
Common Crane 213
Common Gull 250
Common Shelduck 95
Common Shoveler 156
Common White-eye 166
Coot 207
Coscoroba coscoroba 54
Coscoroba Swan 54
Cranes 212
Crowned Crane 237
Crowned Plover 245
Cuban Whistling Duck 46
Cygnus atratus 65
Cygnus melanocoryphus 56
Cygnus olor 67

Demoiselle Crane 233
Dendrocygna arborea 46
Dendrocygna autumnalis 48
Dendrocygna bicolor 49
Dendrocygna eytoni 51
Dendrocygna viduata 52
Ducks 45

East African Crowned Crane 238
Egretta garzetta 13
Egretta thula 13
Egyptian Goose 112
Emperor Goose 77
Eudocimus ruber 25

257

European Eider 158
European Pochard 163
European Wigeon 114
Eurypyga helias 210

Falcated Duck 118
Flamingos 29
Fulica atra 207
Fulvous Whistling Duck 49

Gallinula chloropus 204
Garganey 151
Geese 45
Glossy Ibis 24
Goldeneye 194
Greater Flamingo 29
Green-winged Teal 129
Grey Duck 124
Grey Heron 11
Greylag Goose 68
Grus antigone 230
Grus canadensis 216
Grus grus 213
Grus monacha 215
Gulls 240

Haematopus ostralegus 241
Hartlaub's Duck 182
Hawaiian Goose 85
Hooded Crane 215
Hooded Merganser 196
Hoplopterus armatus 244
Hottentot Teal 147

Jacana 241

Lapwing 243
Larus canus 250
Larus ridibundus 248
Laterallus leucopyrrhus 202
Laysan Teal 137
Leptoptilos crumeniferus 22
Lesser Flamingo 43
Lesser Scaup 172
Lesser Snow Goose 38
Lesser White-fronted Goose 70
Little Egret 13
Long-legged Wading Birds 11
Long-tailed Duck 192

Magellan Goose 89
Mallard 122
Mandarin Duck 176
Maned Goose 174
Marabou Stork 22
Marbled Teal 150
Masked Plover 244
Melanitta fusca 190
Mergus cucullatus 196

Mergus serrator 197
Moorhen 204
Mute Swan 67

Netta peposaca 160
Netta rufina 161
Nettapus auritus 173
New Zealand Shelduck 109
Night Heron 17
North American Ruddy Duck 199
North American Wood Duck 186
Nycticorax nycticorax 17

Oxyura jamaicensis 199
Oyster-Catcher 241

Philippine Duck 127
Philomachus pugnax 246
Phoeniconaias minor 43
Phoenicopterus chilensis 41
Phoenicopterus ruber roseus 29
Phoenicopterus ruber ruber 31
Pink-footed Goose 72
Pintail 133
Plegadis falcinellus 24
Plumed Whistling Duck 51
Porphyrio porphyrio 206
Purple Gallinule 206

Radjah Shelduck 96
Rails and their Relatives 202
Recurvirostra avosetta 248
Red and white Crake 202
Red-billed Pintail 136
Red-billed Whistling Duck 48
Red-breasted Goose 84
Red-breasted Merganser 197
Red-crested Pochard 161
Ring-necked Duck 170
Ringed Teal 189
Roseate Spoonbill 27
Rosybill 160
Ruddy-headed Goose 92
Ruddy Shelduck 106
Ruff 246

Sacred Ibis 26
Sandhill Crane 216
Sarus Crane 230
Scarlet Ibis 25
Snow Goose 75
Snowy Egret 13
Somateria mollissima 158
Spotbill 125
Spurwing Plover 244
Squacco Heron 15
Stanley Crane 235

Stephanibyx coronatus 245
Sunbittern 210
Swans 45

Tadorna cana 108
Tadorna ferruginea 106
Tadorna radjah 96
Tadorna tadorna 95
Tadorna tadornoides 111
Tadorna variegata 109
Threskiornis aethiopica 26
Tufted Duck 168

Vanellus milesnovaehollandiae 244
Vanellus vanellus 243
Velvet Scoter 190
Versicolor Teal 145

Waders 240
Wattled Crane 231
West African Crowned Crane 237
White-faced Whistling Duck 52
White Stork 19